Bob Vivona

W9-AMW-195

ALGORITHMIC STUDIES IN MASS STORAGE SYSTEMS

OTHER BOOKS OF INTEREST

Wayne Amsbury
Structured Basic and Beyond

Jean-Loup Baer
Computer Systems Architecture

Randal Bryant, editor
Proceedings of the Third Caltech Conference on VLSI

Peter Calingaert
Assemblers, Compliers and Program Translation

M. Carberry, H. Khalil, J. Leathrum, and L. Levy
Foundations of Computer Science

Shimon Even
Graph Algorithms

William Findlay and David Watt
Pascal: An Introduction to Methodical Programming, Second Edition

Owen Hanson
Design of Computer Data Files

Ellis Horowitz
Fundamentals of Programming Languages

Ellis Horowitz, editor
Programming Languages: A Grand Tour

Ellis Horowitz and Sartaj Sahni
Fundamentals of Computer Algorithms

Ellis Horowitz and Sartaj Sahni
Fundamentals of Data Structures

Yahiko Kambayashi
Database: A Bibliography

H. T. Kung, Guy Steele, and Robert Sproull, editors
VLSI Systems and Computations

Thomas Logsdon
Computers and Social Controversy

James J. McGregor and Alan H. Watt
Simple Pascal

Theo Pavlidis
Algorithms for Graphics and Image Processing

Gerald N. Pitts and Barry L. Bateman
Essentials of COBOL Programming

Ira Pohl and Alan Shaw
The Nature of Computation: An Introduction to Computer Science

Arto Salomaa
Jewels of Formal Language Theory

Donald D. Spencer
Computers in Number Theory

Jeffrey D. Ullman
Principles of Database Systems, Second Edition

ALGORITHMIC STUDIES IN MASS STORAGE SYSTEMS

C.K. WONG

IBM
Thomas J. Watson Research Center

COMPUTER SCIENCE PRESS

Copyright © 1983 Computer Science Press, Inc.

Printed in the United States of America.

All rights reserved. No part of this book may be reproduced in any form, including photostat, microfilm, and xerography, and not in information storage and retrieval systems, without permission in writing from the publisher, except by a reviewer who may quote brief passages in a review or as provided in the Copyright Act of 1976.

Computer Science Press
11 Taft Court
Rockville, Maryland 20850

1   2   3   4   5   6   Printing   Year 88   87   86   85   84   83

Library of Congress Cataloging in Publication Data

Wong, C. K. (Chak-Kuen)
  Algorithmic studies in mass storage systems.

  Bibliography: p.
  Includes index.
  1. Computer storage devices. 2. Algorithms.
I. Title.
TK7895.M4W66   1983   621.3819′5833′015118   82-22207
ISBN 0-914894-91-9

To Catherine, Henry and Andrew

CONTENTS

3. Magnetic Bubble Memory

PREFACE

A major technological trend for large database systems has been the introduction of ever-larger mass storage systems. This allows computing centers and business data processing installations to maintain on line their program libraries, less frequently used data files, transaction logs and backup copies under unified system control.

Tapes, disks and drums are classical examples of mass storage media. The more recent IBM 3851 Mass Storage Facility, part of the IBM 3850 Mass Storage System, represents a new direction in mass storage development, namely, it is two-dimensional. With the maturity of magnetic bubble technology, more sophisticated, massive, multi-trillion-bit storage systems are not far in the future.

While large in capacity, mass storage systems have in general relatively long access times. Since record access probabilities are usually not uniform, various algorithms have been devised to position the records to decrease the average access time. *The first two chapters of this book are devoted mainly to such algorithmic studies in linear and two-dimensional mass storage systems. In the third chapter, we view the bubble memory as more than a storage medium. In fact, we discuss different structures where routine operations, such as data rearrangement, sorting, searching, etc., can be done in the memory itself, freeing the CPU for more complicated tasks.*

The problems discussed in this book are combinatorial in nature. However, to solve them a wide variety of methods and techniques are employed. They include not only the discrete, combinatorial and probabilistic methods but also some unusual mathematical techniques, such as variational calculus, vector majorization and discrete dynamic programming.

ACKNOWLEDGMENTS

There are many people whose help and guidance were instrumental in the preparation of this book, especially, J.R. Bitner, G. Bongiovanni, A. K. Chandra, H. Chang, K. C. Chu, K. M. Chung, D. Coppersmith, W. D. Frazer, U. I. Gupta, R. M. Karp, D. T. Lee, J. Y.-T. Leung, F. Luccio, A. C. McKellar, D. S. Parker, F. P. Preparata, J. W. Pruitt and P. C. Yue.

Part of this material was taught at Columbia University during the academic year 1978-1979 when the author was a visiting professor in the Department of Electrical Engineering and Computer Science. The author is especially grateful to the faculty members, including H. Hunt, J. Kam, M. Schwartz, R. J. Schwarz, T. E. Stern, S. H. Unger and O. Wing, for constant inspiration, guidance and support.

Very special thanks are due E. G. Coffman, for pointing out the possibility of such a book, and finally G. Fan, H. Kobayashi and D. T. Tang of IBM Research, for their continuing support and guidance.

The author is grateful to Marcia B. Bollard for her expert typing and formatting of this text for printing on the IBM Experimental Printer.

1. LINEAR STORAGE

1.1. Introduction

One major factor determining the overall performance of a system is the access time to auxiliary storage. This access time depends not only on the physical device characteristics but also on the procedures by which requests for records are sequenced and on the arrangement of records.

In general, the access time has two principal components: 1) seek time and 2) transfer time. By seek time we mean the time for the read/write head to travel to the requested position. Transfer time is the read/write time itself. Depending on the storage medium, we can further subdivide the seek time into various parts. For example, in a disk the seek time consists of 1) head travel time to the requested cylinder and 2) rotational delay, while in a two-dimensional storage system such as the IBM 3851 Mass Storage Facility, the seek time includes 1) head travel time to the requested compartment and 2) time to mount the cartridge. However, the first component is in general the dominating factor. Since transfer time depends largely on the physical characteristics of the hardware and the data structures used, no optimization is attempted here. Instead, we will concentrate on improving the head travel time only.

This chapter deals mainly with linear storage media (or one-dimensional storage media). Tape is the prototypical linear storage medium, but when minimization of head travel in a disk is of interest, it is useful to view the cylinders as forming a linear storage [5]. In the case of linear storage, head travel is measured by the Euclidean metric. In the following sections, we will make various assumptions about the request sequences and the record access probabilities and then we will try to allocate the records and schedule the head so that the expected head travel is minimized.

1.2.   Record arrangement to minimize head travel

We shall represent a linear storage by the real line, and records will be allocated on integral points $0, \pm 1, \pm 2, \ldots$ only. Further, we assume that a queue of requests is serviced in a first-in-first-out (FIFO) fashion and that the head stops at the position of the record last accessed. Finally, we assume that the records have independent access probabilities (or relative access frequencies). Thus, the head moves from location to location to service the requests, which are independently generated from the known probability.

Consider a set of records $R_1, \ldots, R_n$, with access probabilities $p_1, \ldots, p_n$ ($\sum_{i=1}^{n} p_i = 1$). Our basic objective function to be minimized is the *expected distance* traveled by the head from one requested record to another:

$$D(\pi) = \sum_{i,j} p_i p_j d^{(\pi)}(i,j), \qquad (1.2.1)$$

where $d^{(\pi)}(i,j)$ denotes the distance between records R_i and R_j and depends on the arrangement π of records as well as on the metric.

In the present case, if records R_i, R_j are situated at points ξ, η, then

$$d^{(\pi)}(i,j) = d_2(\xi,\eta) = |\xi - \eta|,$$

where d_2 signifies the use of the Euclidean metric.

Thus, given records and their access probabilities and for a fixed metric, our goal is to find an arrangement of the records so that $D(\pi)$ is minimized.   This problem was first solved in a classical mathematical work by Hardy, Littlewood and Pólya [9, 13, 18].   The solution can be stated in the following theorem:

Theorem 1.2.1 Place the largest p_i (i.e., the record with the largest p_i) at any point.   Then repetitively place the next largest p_i, alternating between the position immediately to the left (right) of those already placed and the position immediately to the right (left).   The expected distance traveled by the head, $D(\pi)$, will be minimized.

Example If $p_1 \geq p_2 \geq ... \geq p_n$, then an optimal placement is as depicted in Figure 1.2.1.

The two optimal arrangements of records in Theorem 1.2.1 (one being the mirror image of the other) are often referred to as the organ-pipe arrangements.   For simplicity, we shall hereafter speak of optimal arrangement of probabilities rather than arrangement of

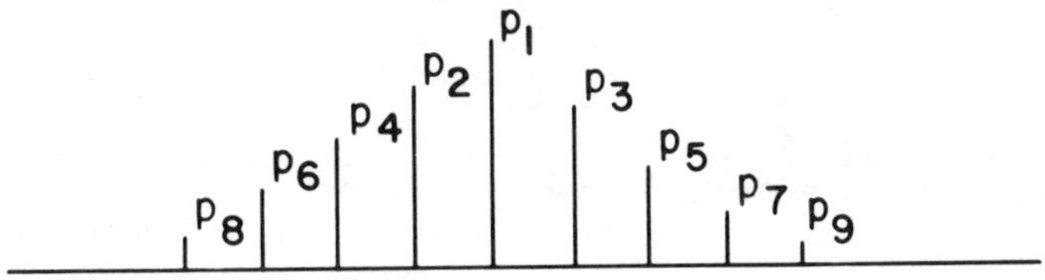

Figure 1.2.1

records. We present a simple proof here. First we need the following necessary condition:

Lemma 1.2.1 Let π be an optimal arrangement of the probabilities. Let L be any vertical line through any point of the form $y/2$, $y = 0, \pm 1, \pm 2, \ldots$. Then the probabilities arranged by π on one side of L are respectively larger than or equal to the corresponding ones on the other side.

In Figure 1.2.2, the probabilities are in the organ-pipe arrangement. Two lines are drawn to show that the necessary condition is indeed satisfied. Note that a point without any probability is regarded as having probability zero.

Proof Assume the assertion is not true; then there exists a line L such that

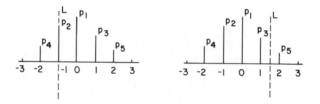

Figure 1.2.2

1) points on the left of L can be divided into two groups A and C

2) points on the right of L can be divided into two groups B and D

3) the points in A(C) are symmetric to those in B(D) with respect to L and

4) probabilities in A are larger than their symmetric counterparts in B, while those in C are less than or equal to their symmetric counterparts in D.

We shall show that exchanging all probabilities in A with their symmetric counterparts in B will result in a new arrangement with smaller expected head travel $D(\pi)$, thus violating the optimality assumption.

Note that terms in $D(\pi)$ which involve only probabilities in A,B are not affected by this exchange. Neither are those in C,D. To calculate the change in $D(\pi)$, let p_1, p_2 be any probabilities in A,C

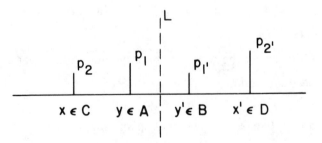

Figure 1.2.3

respectively and $p_{1'}$, $p_{2'}$, their symmetric counterparts in B,D.   (See Figure 1.2.3.)

We display the corresponding terms in $D(\pi)$ in the following table:

Table 1.2.1

Changes in $D(\pi)$

Prob. in	Before exchange	After exchange
C,A	$p_2 p_1 d_{21}$	$p_2 p_{1'} d_{21}$
C,B	$p_2 p_{1'} d_{21'}$	$p_2 p_1 d_{21'}$
D,A	$p_{2'} p_1 d_{2'1}$	$p_{2'} p_{1'} d_{2'1}$
D,B	$p_{2'} p_{1'} d_{2'1'}$	$p_{2'} p_1 d_{2'1'}$

where $d_{21} = d_2(x,y)$, $d_{21'} = d_2(x,y')$, $d_{2'1} = d_2(x',y)$ and $d_{2'1'} = d_2(x',y')$.

Summing up the terms in the table and noting that $d_{21} = d_{2'1'}$ and $d_{21'} = d_{2'1}$, we have

Sum before exchange $= (p_2 p_1 + p_{2'} p_{1'})d_{21} + (p_2 p_{1'} + p_{2'} p_1)d_{21'}$

Sum after exchange $= (p_2 p_{1'} + p_{2'} p_1)d_{21} + (p_2 p_1 + p_{2'} p_{1'})d_{21'}$

Thus,

(Sum before exchange) $-$ (sum after exchange)

$$= d_{21}\{p_2(p_1 - p_{1'}) + p_{2'}(p_{1'} - p_1)\}$$
$$+ d_{21'}\{p_2(p_{1'} - p_1) + p_{2'}(p_1 - p_{1'})\}$$
$$= d_{21}(p_1 - p_{1'})(p_2 - p_{2'})$$
$$+ d_{21'}(p_1 - p_{1'})(p_{2'} - p_2)$$
$$= (p_1 - p_{1'})(p_{2'} - p_2)(d_{21'} - d_{21}) > 0$$

since $p_1 - p_{1'} > 0$, $p_{2'} - p_2 \geq 0$ and $d_{21'} - d_{21} > 0$.

This inequality holds for any p_1, p_2 in A,C. It follows that exchanging probabilities in A and in B will result in a smaller $D(\pi)$.

□

Proof of Theorem 1.2.1 Assume without loss of generality that $p_1 \geq p_2 \geq p_3 \geq ... \geq p_n$. First place p_1 at any point, say, 0. Then an optimal solution must place p_2 at point 1 or -1. Otherwise, we can always find a suitable line L such that Lemma 1.2.1 is violated. It suffices to illustrate this by an example. (See Figure 1.2.4.)

If p_2 is, say, at point 2, then we can draw L through $1\frac{1}{2}$. Consequently, p_2 is larger than the probability at point 1, which is zero, while p_1 is larger than the probability at point 3, which is also zero. This contradicts Lemma 1.2.1. Now suppose p_2 is at point 1; by the same argument, an optimal solution must place p_3 at point -1. On the other hand, if p_2 is at point -1, p_3 must be at point 1. Continuing this argument produces the result that an optimal placement must be the organ-pipe arrangement.

□

1.3.   Record partition and page arrangement to minimize head travel

In Section 1.2, we assumed that each point of the linear storage contained one record. In the case of a disk, a point corresponds to a cylinder and a cylinder may contain more than one record. Suppose each point of the linear storage can contain a page of k records and to access a record, one has to access first the page containing it. The time needed to go to the record within the page is assumed negligible.

Consider a set of records $\{R_i, i = 1,2,...,mk\}$ with independent access probabilities $\{p_i, i = 1,2,...,mk\}$, $\sum_{i=1}^{mk} p_i = 1$. The objective is to

a) partition the mk records into m pages of k records each and

b) place the m pages in a linear storage to minimize the head travel.

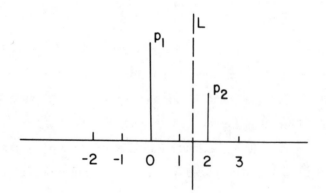

Figure 1.2.4

More specifically, suppose we put records $R_{(1)}, R_{(2)}, ..., R_{(k)}$ in a page. Then it has a (page) request probability $q = \sum_{i=1}^{k} p_{(i)}$. Thus the partitioning of the mk records into m pages results in page access probabilities $\{q_j, j = 1,...,m\}$, $\sum_{j=1}^{m} q_j = \sum_{i=1}^{mk} p_i = 1$, where q_j is the access probability for page j. The cost function to be minimized is then

$$D(\pi; q_1,...,q_m) = \sum_{i,j} q_i q_j d^{(\pi)}(i,j),$$

where $d^{(\pi)}(i,j)$ is the distance between q_i and q_j now.

However, once $\{q_j\}$ is fixed, the problem of placing the m pages in a linear storage reduces to the one studied in Section 1.2, i.e., the organ-pipe arrangement of pages according to $\{q_j\}$ will minimize $D(\pi; q_1,...,q_m)$.

Thus, the original problem can now be rephrased as follows: how to partition the mk probabilities into $\{q_1,...,q_m\}$ so that $D(\pi^*; q_1,...,q_m)$ is minimized, where π^* is the organ-pipe arrangement of $\{q_j\}$.

Let $\mathbf{q} = (q_1,...,q_m)$. We shall drop the symbol π^* and write $D(\mathbf{q})$ for $D(\pi^*; q_1,...,q_m)$. Then

$$D(\mathbf{q}) = \sum_{i,j} q_i q_j d(i,j), \qquad (1.3.1)$$

where $d(i,j)$ is the distance between q_i and q_j in the organ-pipe arrangement. If we assume $q_1 \geq q_2 \geq ... \geq q_m$ (see Figure 1.3.1), then

$$d(i,j) = \begin{cases} \dfrac{|j-i|}{2} & \text{for i,j both odd or both even ;} \\[2ex] \dfrac{j+i-1}{2} & \text{otherwise .} \end{cases} \qquad (1.3.2)$$

It is intuitively clear that the more "skewed" $\mathbf{q}$ is, the smaller $D(\mathbf{q})$ is. $\mathbf{q}$ being skewed means that a few pages have very high access probabilities, and since the organ-pipe arrangement automatically groups them together, $D(\mathbf{q})$ should be small. We have the following intuitively appealing algorithm, called the Greedy Partition Algorithm:

1) Assume without loss of generality that $p_1 \geq p_2 \geq \cdots \geq p_{mk}$.

2) Assign records $R_1,\ldots,R_k$ to page 1, records $R_{k+1},\ldots,R_{2k}$ to page 2, records $R_{2k+1},\ldots,R_{3k}$ to page 3, and so on. In other words, we sequentially assign the records to pages. Thus, the access

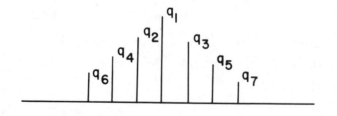

Figure 1.3.1

probability for page i is

$$q_i = \sum_{j=(i-1)k+1}^{ik} p_j.$$

3) Place the pages in the organ-pipe arrangement.

We shall prove the following result:

Theorem 1.3.1 The Greedy Partition Algorithm is optimal.

Before proving the theorem, we need some preliminary definitions and results which are quoted from [9, 15, 17, 20].

Definition 1.3.1   Let $v = (v_1,...,v_m)$, $u = (u_1,...,u_m)$, $v_1 \geq ... \geq v_m$, $u_1 \geq ... \geq u_m$. We say v majorizes u if

1) $\sum_{i=1}^{k} v_i \geq \sum_{i=1}^{k} u_i$ for $k = 1,2,...,m - 1$ and

2) $\sum_{i=1}^{m} v_i = \sum_{i=1}^{m} u_i.$

Theorem 1.3.2 [9] If $\phi(x)$ is convex (i.e., $\phi''(x) \geq 0$) and v majorizes u, then $\sum_{i=1}^{m} \phi(v_i) \geq \sum_{i=1}^{m} \phi(u_i)$.

The following generalization of the theorem will enable us to prove Theorem 1.3.1.

Definition 1.3.2 Given a function $\phi = \phi(x_1,...,x_m)$, defined for $x_1 \geq x_2 \geq ... \geq x_m$, ϕ is called a Schur function if

$$(x_i - x_j)\left(\frac{\partial \phi}{\partial x_i} - \frac{\partial \phi}{\partial x_j} \right) \geq 0 \text{ for } i \neq j.$$

Theorem 1.3.3 [15, 17, 20] If $\phi(x_1,...,x_m)$ is a Schur function and v majorizes u, then $\phi(v_1,...,v_m) \geq \phi(u_1,..,u_m)$.

Proof of Theorem 1.3.1 Let $q^* = (q_1^*,...,q_m^*)$ be the resulting page request probabilities from the Greedy Partition Algorithm. We shall show that it minimizes $D(q)$ in (1.3.1).

First note that $q_1^* \geq q_2^* \geq ... \geq q_m^*$. Let $q = (q_1,...,q_m)$ be the page request probabilities resulting from any other partition. Without loss of generality, we can assume that $q_1 \geq q_2 \geq ... \geq q_m$.

By construction, it is easy to see that q^* majorizes q.

If we can show that $-D(q)$ is a Schur function, then $-D(q^*) \geq -D(q)$ or $D(q)^* \leq D(q)$, and the proof will be complete.

It suffices to show

$$\frac{\partial D}{\partial q_j} - \frac{\partial D}{\partial q_i} \geq 0 \quad \text{for } q_i \geq q_j$$

or to show for $i = 1,2,...,m-1$,

$$q_i \geq q_{i+1} \text{ implies } \frac{\partial D}{\partial q_{i+1}} - \frac{\partial D}{\partial q_i} \geq 0.$$

Now $D(q) = \sum_{i,j} q_i q_j d(i,j)$

$$= \sum_{i \neq j} q_i q_j d(i,j).$$

$$\frac{\partial D}{\partial q_k} = \sum_{i \neq k}^{m} q_i d(i,k) + \sum_{j \neq k}^{m} q_j d(k,j)$$

$$= 2 \sum_{\ell=1}^{m} q_\ell d(k,\ell).$$

$$\frac{1}{2}\left(\frac{\partial D}{\partial q_i} - \frac{\partial D}{\partial q_{i+1}}\right) = \{d(i,1)q_1 + d(i,2)q_2 + \ldots + d(i,m)q_m\}$$

$$-\{d(i+1,1)q_1 + d(i+1,2)q_2 + \ldots + d(i+1,m)q_m\},$$

or in matrix notations

$$\frac{1}{2}\begin{bmatrix} \dfrac{\partial D}{\partial q_1} \\ \cdot \\ \dfrac{\partial D}{\partial q_m} \end{bmatrix} = [d(i,j)] \begin{bmatrix} q_1 \\ \cdot \\ \cdot \\ q_m \end{bmatrix},$$

where $d(i,j)$ was defined in (1.3.2). The matrix $[d(i,j)]$ is of a very special form. For example, when $m=5$,

$$[d(i,j)] = \begin{bmatrix} 0 & 1 & 1 & 2 & 2 \\ 1 & 0 & 2 & 1 & 3 \\ 1 & 2 & 0 & 3 & 1 \\ 2 & 1 & 3 & 0 & 4 \\ 2 & 3 & 1 & 4 & 0 \end{bmatrix}.$$

Assume m is odd and consider two consecutive rows i, i+1.

Case 1. i is odd.

For example, take rows 1 and 2 in the above matrix:

0	1	1	2	2
1	0	2	1	3.

Then

$d(1,1)=d(2,2)$, $d(1,2)=d(2,1)$, $d(1,1)\leq d(1,2)$;

$d(1,3)=d(2,4)$, $d(1,4)=d(2,3)$, $d(1,3)\leq d(1,4)$;

$d(1,5)\leq d(2,5)$.

In general,

$$d(i,1)=d(i+1,2), \; d(i,2)=d(i+1,1), \; d(i,1)\leq d(i,2); \qquad (1.3.3)$$

$$d(i,3)=d(i+1,4), \; d(i,4)=d(i+1,3), \; d(i,3)\leq d(i,4);$$

.

.

.

$$d(i,m-2)=d(i+1,m-1), \; d(i,m-1)=d(i+1,m-2),$$
$$d(i,m-2)\leq d(i,m-1);$$
$$d(i,m)\leq d(i+1,m).$$

$$(1.3.4)$$

We can regroup the terms in $\dfrac{1}{2}\left(\dfrac{\partial D}{\partial q_i}-\dfrac{\partial D}{\partial q_{i+1}}\right)$ to match the above equalities and inequalities:

$$\frac{1}{2}\left(\frac{\partial D}{\partial q_i}-\frac{\partial D}{\partial q_{i+1}}\right) =$$

$$\{d(i,1)q_1 + d(i,2)q_2 - d(i + 1,1)q_1 - d(i + 1,2)q_2\}$$

$$+ \; \{d(i,3)q_3 + d(i,4)q_4 - d(i + 1,3)q_3 - d(i + 1,4)q_4\}$$

.

.

.

$$+ \; \{d(i,m - 2)q_{m-2} + d(i,m - 1)q_{m-1} -$$

$$d(i + 1,m - 2)q_{m-2} - d(i + 1,m - 1)q_{m-1}\}$$

$$+ \; d(i,m)q_m - d(i + 1,m)q_m.$$

By (1.3.3), we can rewrite the first term as follows:

$$\{d(i,1)q_1 + d(i,2)q_2 - d(i+1,1)q_1 - d(i+1,2)q_2\}$$

$$= d(i,1)(q_1 - q_2) + d(i,2)(q_2 - q_1)$$

$$= \{d(i,1) - d(i,2)\}(q_1 - q_2)$$

$$\leq 0$$

since the first term is ≤ 0 by (1.3.3) and the second term is ≥ 0 by assumption. By the same argument, all other terms except the last are ≤ 0. For the last term,

$$d(i,m)q_m - d(i+1,m)q_m \leq 0$$

follows directly from (1.3.4). Thus, we conclude that

$$\frac{1}{2}\left(\frac{\partial D}{\partial q_i} - \frac{\partial D}{\partial q_{i+1}} \right) \leq 0 \text{ for i odd }.$$

Case 2. i is even.

Take rows 2 and 3 in the case of m=5:

1	0	2	1	3
1	2	0	3	1.

Thus,

$$d(1,1)=d(2,1);$$
$$d(1,2)=d(2,3), \ d(1,3)=d(2,2), \ d(1,2)\leq d(1,3);$$
$$d(1,4)=d(2,5), \ d(1,5)=d(2,4), \ d(1,4)\leq d(1,5).$$

In general,

$$d(i,1)=d(i+1,1);$$

$$d(i,2)=d(i+1,3),\ d(i,3)=d(i+1,2),\ d(i,2)\leq d(i,3);$$

$$d(i,4)=d(i+1,5),\ d(i,5)=d(i+1,4),\ d(i,4)\leq d(i,5);$$

.

.

.

$$d(i,m-1)=d(i+1,m),\ d(i,m)=d(i+1,m-1),\ d(i,m-1)\leq d(i,m).$$

By the same method as in Case 1, we can prove that

$$\frac{1}{2}\left(\frac{\partial D}{\partial q_i}-\frac{\partial D}{\partial q_{i+1}}\right)\leq 0 \text{ for i even }.$$

Combining both cases, we have

$$\frac{1}{2}\left(\frac{\partial D}{\partial q_i}-\frac{\partial D}{\partial q_{i+1}}\right)\leq 0$$

for m odd. By the same approach, we can prove that the same inequality holds also for m even. Therefore, $-D(\mathbf{q})$ is a Schur function.

□

The method of vector majorization and Schur function is very useful in proving optimality in many cases. In Appendix 1.1 we show another application of this technique to a problem concerning locality in reference strings.

1.4.   Dynamic allocation of records to minimize head travel

1.4.1.   Introduction   In the previous two sections, we assumed the record access probabilities were known. On the basis of these probabilities, we devised an optimal placement for the records to minimize the expected head travel. In this section, we assume the access probabilities are not known before the placement. We have to place the records one by one as they come in. Once placed, a record remains in its location all the time. At the end, all n locations are occupied. The objective is still to find a record placement such that the expected head travel is minimized. This problem is motivated by the space allocation problem for the minidisks of users of VM/370 [11]. As each user logs on, space for his minidisk, typically 5 to 15 cylinders, must be obtained on the online disks. For each user, it is possible to estimate his activity based on accounting information from past usage of the system. But since it is in general not possible to know exactly who will be logged on at a given time, relative frequency of access is not known prior to the allocation of individual disks.

In this section, we formulate a simple idealized model for this problem, suggest a simple heuristic to handle the space allocation and show that it is asymptotically optimal in a satisfying sense. We must deal with a set of n users who arrive at n distinct points in time and who are allocated space in a linear store with n locations. To minimize confusion, we will use subscripts r, s, t when indexing on arrival time and subscripts i, j, k when indexing on space allocation. We will use the symbol $\approx$ to mean that asymptotically the ratio of the two quantities is 1, and the symbol $\doteq$ to mean approximate equality.

1.4.2. Formulation of the problem A sequence of users $\{u_t\}$, $1 \leq t \leq n$, arrive at the system at distinct points in time. Associated with each user u_t is a frequency of storage access f_t. The f_t's are assumed to be independent, identically distributed random variables. We assume that f_t is uniformly distributed on the interval $(0,1)$. Our placement heuristic extends in an obvious manner to handle other distributions. However, except in the case of random placement, our analysis does not cover other distributions.

Each user on arrival is allocated a vacant space i in a linear store where, for later convenience, locations have been numbered to correspond to the optimal static placement strategy, as shown in Figure 1.4.1. We will write f_i, f_j, etc., to denote the frequency of use for the user allocated to space i,j, etc., and f_s, f_t to denote the frequency of use associated with the user who arrived at times s, t. We have chosen to ignore the variable length nature of the storage units to be allocated.

When n users have arrived at the system, thus filling the store, they generate a sequence of references $\{r_t\}$, $1 \leq t \leq \infty$, where the r_t's are independent, identically distributed random variables and where p_j, the probability that the t-th reference is by the user occupying location j, is given by

$$p_j = f_j / \sum_{j=1}^{n} f_j. \qquad (1.4.1)$$

We are interested in the effect of different placement strategies on the

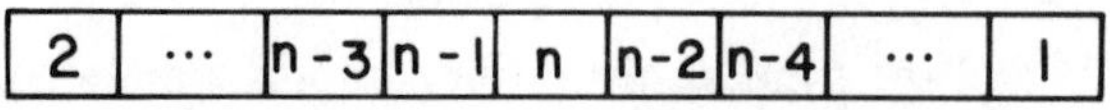

| 2 | ⋯ | n−3 | n−1 | n | n−2 | n−4 | ⋯ | 1 |

Figure 1.4.1

expected distance $E(D)$ between consecutive requests, where

$$E(D) = \sum_{i=1}^{n} \sum_{j=1}^{n} p_i p_j d(i,j) \qquad (1.4.2)$$

and

$$d(i,j) = \begin{cases} |j-i|/2 & \text{for } i,j \text{ both odd or both even ;} \\ n-(j+i-1)/2 & \text{otherwise.} \end{cases}$$

$$(1.4.3)$$

This distance is just the Euclidean distance between locations i and j when positions are numbered as shown in Figure 1.4.1. Later we will comment on the effect other measures of distance have on the results.

In Section 1.2, it was proved that the optimal static placement is one that satisfies $p_1 \leq p_2 \leq ... \leq p_n$, where the probabilities are indexed on location. This would require waiting for all n arrivals before allocation. The heuristic placement strategy we consider attempts to approximate this optimal placement by means of the following strategy. The user who arrives at time 1, u_1, is placed in position i if and only if $(i-1)/n < f_1 \leq i/n$. For the user who arrives at time t, u_t, there are $n-t+1$ vacant positions arranged according to their original ordering. Of these $n-t+1$ remaining positions, the i-th is allocated to u_t if and only if $(i-1)/(n-t+1) < f_t \leq i/(n-t+1)$. If, instead of being uniformly distributed on the interval $(0,1]$, f_t is governed by some other bounded probability distribution, we would partition the range of f_t into $n-t+1$ equally probable intervals and proceed as above, the idea being to form a simple estimate for relative frequency of each arriving user as compared to the users who have not yet arrived. To provide a basis for comparison, random placement is also considered in our analysis.

1.4.3. A basic lemma We are interested in computing

$$E(D) = E\left[\sum_{i=1}^{n}\sum_{j=1}^{n}\frac{f_i f_j d(i,j)}{\left(\sum_{k=1}^{n} f_k\right)^2}\right],\tag{1.4.4}$$

where E denotes expectation and the probability distribution for f_i and f_j is affected by the placement strategy. We shall present the results from the viewpoint of asymptotic accuracy. We need the following lemma.

Lemma 1.4.1 Let $g(n)$ satisfy

$$\lim_{n\to\infty}(g(n)/\sqrt{n}) = \infty \text{ and } \lim_{n\to\infty}(g(n)/n) = 0.$$

Then, for large n,

$$\frac{E(\sum\sum f_i f_j d(i,j))}{(n/2 + g(n))^2} - \left(\frac{n}{2\pi}\right)^{1/2}\frac{e^{-72g^2(n)/n}}{12g(n)} \le E(D)$$

$$\le \frac{E(\sum\sum f_i f_j d(i,j))}{(n/2 - g(n))^2} + \left(\frac{n}{2\pi}\right)^{1/2}\frac{e^{-72g^2(n)/n}}{12g(n)}.\tag{1.4.5}$$

Thus, asymptotically,

$$E(D) \approx (4/n^2)E[\sum\sum f_i f_j d(i,j)].\tag{1.4.6}$$

Proof The central limit theorem tells us that the quantity $\sum_{1}^{n} f_k$ appearing in the denominator of E(D) is, for large n, normally distributed around its mean, $n/2$. To exploit this fact, we expand

$E(D)$ conditioned on the magnitude of Σf_k.

$$E(D) = \Pr\left(\sum f_k \geq \frac{n}{2} - g(n) \right) E\left(\frac{\sum \sum f_i f_j d(i,j)}{\left(\sum f_k \right)^2} \mid \sum f_k \geq \frac{n}{2} - g(n) \right)$$

$$+ \Pr\left(\sum f_k < \frac{n}{2} - g(n) \right) E\left(\frac{\sum \sum f_i f_j d(i,j)}{\left(\sum f_k \right)^2} \mid \sum f_k < \frac{n}{2} - g(n) \right)$$

$$(1.4.7)$$

If we use $d(i,j) < n$ and $\left(\Sigma f_k \right)^2 = \Sigma \Sigma f_i f_j$, (1.4.7) simplifies to

$$E(D) \leq \Pr\left(\sum f_k \geq \frac{n}{2} - g(n) \right) E\left(\frac{\sum \sum f_i f_j d(i,j)}{(n/2 - g(n))^2} \mid \sum f_k \geq \frac{n}{2} - g(n) \right)$$

$$+ \Pr\left(\sum f_k < \frac{n}{2} - g(n) \right) n E\left(1 \mid \sum f_k < \frac{n}{2} - g(n) \right). \qquad (1.4.8)$$

To obtain a bound on the first term in (1.4.8), we use the following identity:

$$E\left(\frac{\sum \sum f_i f_j d(i,j)}{(n/2 - g(n))^2} \right) =$$

$$\Pr\left(\sum f_k \geq \frac{n}{2} - g(n) \right) E\left(\frac{\sum \sum f_i f_j d(i,j)}{(n/2 - g(n))^2} \mid \sum f_k \geq \frac{n}{2} - g(n) \right)$$

$$+ \Pr\left(\sum f_k < \frac{n}{2} - g(n) \right) E\left(\frac{\sum \sum f_i f_j d(i,j)}{(n/2 - g(n))^2} \mid \sum f_k < \frac{n}{2} - g(n) \right). \quad (1.4.9)$$

Solving (1.4.9) for the first term and substituting into (1.4.8), we have

$$E(D) \leq \frac{E(\sum \sum f_i f_j d(i,j))}{(n/2 - g(n))^2} + nPr\left(\sum f_k < \frac{n}{2} - g(n)\right)$$

$$-Pr\left(\sum f_k < \frac{n}{2} - g(n)\right) E\left(\frac{\sum \sum f_i f_j d(i,j)}{(n/2 - g(n))^2} \mid \sum f_k < \frac{n}{2} - g(n)\right). \quad (1.4.10)$$

Using the central limit theorem to estimate $Pr(\sum f_k < n/2 - g(n))$ and ignoring the third term yields the upper bound in the lemma. The lower bound is readily obtained in a completely analogous fashion.

The final statement of the lemma follows immediately by choosing, for example,

$$g(n) = \sqrt{n} \lg n, \tag{1.4.11}$$

and using standard asymptotic estimates for the normal density function. (Throughout this book $\lg x$ means $\lg_2 x$).

□

Since

$$E((\sum f_k)^2) = n^2/4 + n/12, \tag{1.4.12}$$

we will use the approximation

$$E(D) \approx (12/(n(3n + 1))) E[\sum \sum f_i f_j d(i,j)]. \tag{1.4.13}$$

For later calculations, we need the following sums, which can be verified directly. For simplicity, we always assume n odd.

$$\sum_{i=1}^{n} \sum_{j=1}^{n} d(i,j) = (n/3)(n^2 - 1), \tag{1.4.14}$$

$$\sum_{i=1}^{n} \sum_{j=1}^{n} (i + j)d(i,j) = \frac{1}{24}(n^2 - 1)(7n^2 + 8n + 3), \quad (1.4.15)$$

$$\sum_{i=1}^{n} \sum_{j=1}^{n} ijd(i,j) = \frac{1}{240}(n^2 - 1)(14n^3 + 35n^2 + 24n + 15),$$

$$(1.4.16)$$

$$\sum \sum_{i<j} id(i,j) = \frac{1}{24}(n - 1)n(n + 1)(n + 2), \quad (1.4.17)$$

$$\sum \sum_{i>j} id(i,j) = \frac{1}{48}(n^2 - 1)(5n^2 + 4n + 3). \quad (1.4.18)$$

For n even, the sums are not sufficiently different to affect our results.

1.4.4.   Random placement For a sequence $\{f_t\}$ of independent, identically distributed arrivals, random placement can be achieved in a variety of ways. We will assume that the arrival at time t, $1 \le t \le n$, is placed in location i=t. Under the stated assumptions, it is equivalent to assume that the arrival at time t is placed in any of the remaining vacant locations, at random.

Theorem 1.4.1 Let D_r denote the average distance under random placement; then

$$E(D_r) \approx (n^2 - 1)/(3n + 1). \quad (1.4.19)$$

Proof By the version of the lemma stated in (1.4.13),

$$E(D_r) \approx (12/(n(3n + 1))) \sum \sum E(f_i f_j d(i,j)). \qquad (1.4.20)$$

Because f_i and f_j are independent (when $i=j$, $d(i,j)=0$), with mean value of $\frac{1}{2}$, we have

$$E(D_r) \approx (12/(n(3n + 1))) \frac{1}{4} \sum \sum d(i,j). \qquad (1.4.21)$$

Substituting from (1.4.14) yields

$$E(D_r) \approx (n^2 - 1)/(3n + 1), \qquad (1.4.22)$$

as required.

$\square$

1.4.5. Optimal static placement For a given sequence $\{f_t\}$, optimal static placement requires positioning the i-th smallest of $\{f_t\}$ in location i. Thus an implementation of this strategy would require waiting for all n arrivals before any allocation is made.

Theorem 1.4.2 Let D_0 denote the average distance under optimal static placement. Then

$$E(D_0) \approx (14n^4 + 41n^3 + 9n^2 - 49n - 15)/(60n^3 + 140n^2 + 40)$$

$$(1.4.23)$$

$$\doteq 7n/30 + \frac{5}{36}. \qquad (1.4.24)$$

Proof From Lemma 1.4.1, we have

$$E(D_0) \approx 12 \sum_{i=1}^{n} \sum_{j=1}^{n} d(i,j)E(f_i f_j)/(n(3n+1)). \qquad (1.4.25)$$

We shall compute $E(f_i f_j)$ directly.

Note that by assumption of uniform distribution, for $0 \leq x_1 \leq x_2 \leq ... \leq x_n \leq 1$,

$$Pr\{x_1 \leq f_1 \leq x_1 + dx_1, x_2 \leq f_2 \leq x_2 + dx_2,...,$$

$$x_n \leq f_n \leq x_n + dx_n\} = n! dx_1 ... dx_n \qquad (1.4.26)$$

since $Pr(x_k = x_{k+1}) = 0$. Thus,

$$E(f_i f_j) = \int ... \int x_i x_j n! dx_1 ... dx_n, \qquad (1.4.27)$$

where integration is taken over the region $0 \leq x_1 \leq x_2 \leq ... \leq x_n \leq 1$.

Let $y_1 = x_1$, $y_i = x_i - x_{i-1}$, for $2 \leq i \leq n$. Then $x_i = \sum_{m=1}^{i} y_m$

and

$$E(f_i f_j) = \int ... \int \left(\sum_{m=1}^{i} y_m \right) \left(\sum_{p=1}^{j} y_p \right) n! dy_1 ... dy_n, \qquad (1.4.28)$$

where integration is taken over the region

$$y_1 \geq 0,...,y_n \geq 0, \sum_{k=1}^{n} y_k \leq 1.$$

This is the well-known Dirichlet integral [25, p. 258] for which

$$\int ... \int_{y_1 \geq 0,...,y_n \geq 0} y_m y_p dy_1 ... dy_n = \begin{cases} 1/(n+2)! & \text{for } m \neq p, \\ 2/(n+2)! & \text{for } m = p, \end{cases} \qquad (1.4.29)$$

$$\sum_{k=1}^{n} y_k \leq 1.$$

Assuming $i < j$, we have

$$E(f_i f_j) = n![2i/(n + 2)! + (ij - i)/(n + 2)!]$$

$$= i(j + 1)/((n + 1)(n + 2)). \tag{1.4.30}$$

Finally,

$$E(D_0) \approx 2 \sum_i \sum_{j>1} \frac{12(ij + i)d(i,j)}{(3n + 1)n(n + 1)(n + 2)}. \tag{1.4.31}$$

Substituting from (1.4.16) and (1.4.17) and simplifying yields (1.4.23). Expansion in a Laurent series gives the final statement of the theorem.

$$\square$$

1.4.6. Heuristic placement For heuristic placement, the expected frequency for the user placed in location i depends on the arrival time and on the rank of location i relative to the remaining vacant locations at the time when location i is filled. As a consequence, the analysis becomes much more tedious.

Theorem 1.4.3 Let D_h denote the average distance after placement by our heuristic. Then

$$E(D_h) \approx \frac{(n + 1)(14n^4 - 70n^3 + 194n^2 - 160n + 90)}{20n(3n + 1)(n - 2)(n - 3)}$$

$$+ \frac{(n+1)H_n(7n^3-10n^2+7n+30)}{20n^2(3n+1)(n-2)}$$

$$- \frac{(n+1)(H_n^2-H_n^{(2)})(23n^2+20n+33)}{20n(3n+1)(n-2)(n-3)} \qquad (1.4.32)$$

$$\doteq \frac{7n}{30} + \frac{7H_n}{60} + \frac{14}{90}, \qquad (1.4.33)$$

where $H_n = \Sigma_{\ell=1}^{n}(1/\ell)$ and $H_n^{(2)} = \Sigma_{\ell=1}^{n}(1/\ell^2)$.

Proof We will sketch an outline of the proof. Details are given in Appendix 1.2. Assume without loss of generality that $i<j$. We expand $E(f_i f_j)$ as follows:

$$E(f_i f_j) = \sum_{r=1}^{n}\sum_{s=1}^{n} \text{Pr (location i fills at time r and}$$

$$\text{location j fills at time s)} \cdot E(f_i f_j \mid r,s) \qquad (1.4.34)$$

$$= \sum_{r=1}^{n-1}\sum_{s=r+1}^{n} \text{Pr (location i fills at time r and}$$

$$\text{location j fills at time s)} \cdot E(f_i f_j \mid r,s,r<s)$$

$$+ \sum_{r=s+1}^{n}\sum_{s=1}^{n-1} \text{Pr (location i fills at time r and}$$

$$\text{location j fills at time s)} \cdot E(f_i f_j \mid r,s,r>s). \qquad (1.4.35)$$

We consider the case $r<s$ first. Consider the locations in which the first $r-1$ arrivals are placed. Let m be the number of arrivals placed in locations 1 through $i-1$ and let p be the number of

arrivals placed in locations $i+1$ through $j-1$. Thus, the remaining $r-1-m-p$ arrivals are placed in locations $j+1$ through n. Expanding, we have

$E(f_i f_j \mid r,s,r<s)$

$$= \sum_{m=0}^{r-1} \sum_{p=0}^{r-1-m} Pr(m,p) \quad E(f_i \mid r,s,r<s,m,p) \cdot E(f_j \mid r,s,r<s,m,p)$$

$$= \sum_{m=0}^{r-1} \sum_{p=0}^{r-1-m} \frac{\binom{i-1}{m}\binom{j-i-1}{p}\binom{n-j}{r-1-m-p}}{\binom{n-2}{r-1}} \cdot$$

$$\frac{1}{2}\left(\frac{i-1-m}{n-r+1} + \frac{i-m}{n-r+1} \right) E(f_j \mid r,s,r<s,m,p). \qquad (1.4.36)$$

Consider the arrivals at times $r+1$, ..., $s-1$. Let q be the number of those placed in locations 1 through $j-1$. Then, expanding as before, we have

$$E(f_j \mid r,s,r<s,m,p) = \sum_{q=0}^{s-1-r} \frac{\binom{j-2-m-p}{q}\binom{n-j-(r-1-m-p)}{s-1-r-q}}{\binom{n-r-1}{s-r-1}}$$

$$\cdot \frac{1}{2}\left(\frac{j-2-(m+p+q)}{n-s+1} + \frac{j-1-(m+p+q)}{n-s+1} \right). \qquad (1.4.37)$$

After some manipulation of binomial coefficients detailed in Appendix

1.2, we have

$$E(f_j \mid r,s,r<s,m,p) = \frac{(n-s)(j-2-m-p)}{(n-r-1)(n-s+1)} + \frac{1}{2(n-s+1)}. \qquad (1.4.38)$$

Substituting back into (1.4.36), we have after further manipulation

$$E(f_if_j \mid r,s,r<s) = \frac{1}{2(n-s+1)}\left[\frac{(i-1)(n-r-1)}{(n-r+1)(n-2)} + \frac{1}{2(n-r+1)}\right]$$

$$+ \frac{(n-s)}{(n-s+1)(n-r+1)}\left[\frac{j-2}{2(n-2)} + \right.$$

$$\left. \frac{(i-1)(j-2)(n-r-2)}{(n-2)(n-3)} + \frac{(i-1)(r-1)}{(n-2)(n-3)}\right]. \qquad (1.4.39)$$

Proceeding in an analogous fashion, we can show

$$E(f_if_j \mid r,s,r>s) = \frac{1}{2(n-s+1)(n-r+1)}$$

$$\cdot\left[\frac{(i-1)(n-r)}{(n-2)} + \frac{1}{2}\right] + \frac{1}{(n-s+1)(n-r+1)}\cdot$$

$$\left[\frac{(i-1)(j-1)(n-r)(n-3)-(i-1)(j-3)(n-r)(s-1)}{(n-2)(n-3)}\right.$$

$$\left. + \frac{(j-1)(n-2)-(j-2)(s-1)}{2(n-2)}\right]. \qquad (1.4.40)$$

Substituting into (1.4.35) and summing on r and s, we can obtain

$$
E(f_i f_j) = \frac{ij}{n(n-1)} \left[\frac{2n^2 - 10n}{2(n-2)(n-3)} \right.
$$

$$
\left. - \frac{4H_n(n-3)}{2(n-2)(n-3)} + \frac{12(H_n^2 - H_n^{(2)})}{4(n-2)(n-3)} \right]
$$

$$
+ \frac{i}{n(n-1)} \left[\frac{12n}{2(n-2)(n-3)} + \frac{H_n(n^2 + 2n - 15)}{2(n-2)(n-3)} \right.
$$

$$
\left. - \frac{9(n+1)(H_n^2 - H_n^{(2)})}{4(n-2)(n-3)} \right]
$$

$$
+ \frac{j}{n(n-1)} \left[\frac{-2n^2 + 10n}{2(n-2)(n-3)} + \frac{H_n(n^2 - 9)}{2(n-2)(n-3)} \right.
$$

$$
\left. - \frac{3(n+1)(H_n^2 - H_n^{(2)})}{4(n-2)(n-3)} \right]
$$

$$
+ \frac{1}{n(n-1)} \left[\frac{-12n}{2(n-2)(n-3)} - \frac{H_n(3n^2 - 6n - 9)}{2(n-2)(n-3)} \right.
$$

$$
\left. + \frac{(2n^2 + 5n + 3)(H_n^2 - H_n^{(2)})}{4(n-2)(n-3)} \right].
\tag{1.4.41}
$$

Substituting this expression for $E(f_i f_j)$ into the version of the lemma given by (1.4.13) and using (1.4.14), (1.4.15) and (1.4.16) to evaluate the sums on i and j gives, after simplification,

$$
E(D_h) \approx \frac{(n+1)(14n^4 - 70n^3 + 194n^2 - 160n + 90)}{20n(3n+1)(n-2)(n-3)}
$$

$$+ \ \frac{(n+1)H_n(7n^3 - 10n^2 + 7n + 30)}{20n^2(3n+1)(n-2)}$$

$$- \frac{(n+1)(H_n^2 - H_n^{(2)})(23n^2 + 20n + 33)}{40n(3n+1)(n-2)(n-3)}. \tag{1.4.42}$$

Expanding in a series and saving only the most significant terms yields

$$E(D_h) \doteq 7n/30 + 7H_n/60 + \frac{14}{90}. \tag{1.4.43}$$

1.4.7.   Other distance functions In general, we are not directly concerned with the expected distance between consecutively referenced locations but rather with the expectation of some function of this distance.   It has been shown [1] that the optimal static placement strategy is optimal for any monotone increasing function of distance.   However, assumption of monotonicity is not sufficient to guarantee asymptotic optimality of our heuristic placement strategy. We demonstrate this fact by means of the following simple example:

Define the function h by

$$h(d(i,j)) = \begin{cases} 1 & \text{if } \{i,j\} = \{1,2\}; \\ 0 & \text{otherwise.} \end{cases} \tag{1.4.44}$$

Then h is monotone. The expectation of $h(d(i,j))$ is given by

$$E(h(d(i,j))) = 2E(p_1 p_2) \tag{1.4.45}$$

since all other terms in the sum are zero. Applying Lemma 1.4.1, we have

$$E(h(d(i,j))) \approx 8E(f_1 f_2)/n^2. \tag{1.4.46}$$

For optimal static placement,

$$E(f_1 f_2) = 3/((n + 1)(n + 2)), \qquad\qquad (1.4.47)$$

by (1.4.30). For heuristic placement,

$$E(f_1 f_2) \approx (H_n^2 - H_n^{(2)})/(2n(n-1)), \qquad\qquad (1.4.48)$$

by (1.4.41). Thus heuristic placement is asymptotically suboptimal by a factor proportional to $\lg^2 n$.

For any linear function of distance, asymptotic optimality of heuristic placement is easily seen to hold. This observation provides a reasonable assurance that the heuristic will do an adequate job of minimizing seek time on a disk.

1.4.8. Concluding remarks For the problem we have considered in which users log on to a computing system and must be allocated disk space when they log on, one could apply two different tests of optimality. Fortunately, the heuristic placement was able to pass the stronger test of optimality, in which we compared with the optimal static placement strategy when the frequencies associated with all users are known a priori. It may be that stronger optimality statements could be made if one considers the weaker test, in which we restrict ourselves to the class of algorithms that must take placement decisions in a step-by-step fashion as arrivals occur.

Lemma 1.4.1 and Theorem 1.4.1 do not depend on the assumption of a frequency distribution for the f_t's. This is in accordance with the well-known result that the average distance for randomly generated seeks is roughly $n/3$. For the other placement strategies, the result depends on the assumed frequency distribution.

The heuristic placement strategy can, of course, be used when customers are also allowed to depart from the system since the allocation strategy is stated only in terms of the current memory occupancy. An open problem in this regard is analysis of placement strategies which attempt to exploit storage utilizations which are less than 100 percent and which fluctuate as a result of the arrival and departure mechanism.

1.5. Record arrangement to minimize head travel (unequal record size)

1.5.1. Introduction So far, we have assumed that all the records are of equal size. In this section, we consider the more general case when records can have different lengths. We still assume that record requests are served in a FIFO fashion and that consecutive accesses are independent. The records now have access probabilities $\{p_1,...,p_n\}$, $\sum_{i=1}^{n} p_i = 1$ and corresponding lengths $\{\ell_1,...,\ell_n\}$. The objective is again to allocate the records to minimize the head travel.

The distance between record i and record j now depends not only on the number of records between them, as in Section 1.2, but also on their lengths. This added complexity makes the problem much harder. In fact, we shall prove that this problem is NP-Complete [6,12]. To this end, we need a more formal description of the problem.

An allocation or arrangement of the records is a permutation of the indices 1 to n and is denoted by $\pi = (\pi_1,...,\pi_n)$, where π_i is the index of the record assigned to the i-th position from the left. The expected head travel $D(\pi)$ of a record access is again

$$D(\pi) = \sum_{i=1}^{n} \sum_{j=1}^{n} p_{\pi_i} p_{\pi_j} d(i,j), \qquad (1.5.1)$$

where $d(i,j)$ is the distance traveled in accessing the record at position j, given that the record at position i was last accessed.

Consider the problem of allocating a set of records to a magnetic tape. The length of a record represents units of distance the record occupies. The distance function $d_T(i,j)$ is easily seen to be

$$d_T(i,j) = \begin{cases} \displaystyle\sum_{k=i+1}^{j-1} \ell_{\pi_k} & \text{for } i<j; \\[2em] \displaystyle\sum_{k=j}^{i} \ell_{\pi_k} & \text{for } i \geq j. \end{cases} \qquad (1.5.2)$$

Substituting (1.5.2) into (1.5.1) and simplifying, we derive the expected head travel function $D_T(\pi)$ to be

$$D_T(\pi) = \sum_{i=1}^{n} p_{\pi_i} \ell_{\pi_i} + 2 \sum_{i=2}^{n-1} \ell_{\pi_i} \left(\sum_{j=1}^{i-1} p_{\pi_j} \right) \left(\sum_{j=i+1}^{n} p_{\pi_j} \right). \qquad (1.5.3)$$

More specifically, from the distance function $d_T(i,j)$, we obtain $d_T(i,i) = \ell_{\pi_i}$ for $1 \leq i \leq n$ and $d_T(i,j) + d_T(j,i) = \ell_{\pi_i} + \ell_{\pi_j} + 2 \sum_{k=i+1}^{j-1} \ell_{\pi_k}$ for $1 \leq i < j \leq n$. Substituting this into (1.5.1), we obtain

$$D_T(\pi) = \sum_{i=1}^{n} \sum_{j=1}^{n} p_{\pi_i} p_{\pi_j} d_T(i,j)$$

$$= \sum_{i=1}^{n} p_{\pi_i}^2 d_T(i,i) + \sum_{i=1}^{n} \sum_{j=i+1}^{n} p_{\pi_i} p_{\pi_j} [d_T(i,j) + d_T(j,i)]$$

$$= \sum_{i=1}^{n} p_{\pi_i}^2 \ell_{\pi_i} + \sum_{i=1}^{n} \sum_{j=i+1}^{n} p_{\pi_i} p_{\pi_j} (\ell_{\pi_i} + \ell_{\pi_j} + 2 \sum_{k=i+1}^{j-1} \ell_{\pi_k})$$

$$= \left[\sum_{i=1}^{n} p_{\pi_i}^2 \ell_{\pi_i} + \sum_{i=1}^{n} \sum_{j=i+1}^{n} p_{\pi_i} p_{\pi_j} (\ell_{\pi_i} + \ell_{\pi_j}) \right]$$

$$+ 2 \left[\sum_{i=1}^{n} \sum_{j=i+1}^{n} \sum_{k=i+1}^{j-1} p_{\pi_i} p_{\pi_j} \ell_{\pi_k} \right].$$

Rearranging terms and changing the order of summation, we obtain (1.5.3).

If the storage device is a magnetic disk, the length of a record represents the number of cylinders the record occupies. The distance function $d_D(i,j)$ is given by

$$d_D(i,j) = \begin{cases} \left(\displaystyle\sum_{k=i+1}^{j-1} \ell_{\pi_k} \right) + 1 & \text{for } i < j \\[2ex] \left(\displaystyle\sum_{k=j}^{i} \ell_{\pi_k} \right) - 1 & \text{for } i \geq j. \end{cases} \tag{1.5.4}$$

Substituting (1.5.4) into (1.5.1) and simplifying, we derive the expected head travel function $D_D(\pi)$ to be

$$D_D(\pi) = \sum_{i=1}^{n} p_{\pi_i} (\ell_{\pi_i} - p_{\pi_i}) + 2 \sum_{i=2}^{n-1} \ell_{\pi_i} \left(\sum_{j=1}^{i-1} p_{\pi_j} \right) \left(\sum_{j=i+1}^{n} p_{\pi_j} \right).$$

$$\tag{1.5.5}$$

Derivation of the above formula is similar to the derivation of the formula for $D_T(\pi)$ and hence will be omitted.

If $D_D(\pi)$ is expressed in terms of $D_T(\pi)$, then the formula

$$D_D(\pi) = D_T(\pi) - \sum_{i=1}^{n} p_{\pi_i}^2$$

relates the two problems. Since the difference between the two expected head travel functions is independent of the arrangement, an optimal arrangement for one problem will be an optimal arrangement for the other. Thus, it is sufficient to study one of these two expected head travel functions. We choose to study the function $D_T(\pi)$. Note that the expected head travel function studied in Section 1.2 was a special case of $D_D(\pi)$ with $\ell_{\pi_k} = 1$ for all k.

To simplify our notation, we shall assume that the records have been reindexed so that $\pi_i = i$ for all $1 \le i \le n$. With this notation, the expected head travel function $D(\pi)$ is simply written as

$$D(\pi) = \sum_{i=1}^{n} p_i \ell_i + 2 \sum_{i=2}^{n-1} \ell_i \left(\sum_{j=1}^{i-1} p_j \right) \left(\sum_{j=i+1}^{n} p_j \right). \qquad (1.5.6)$$

An optimal arrangement S_o is an arrangement which satisfies $D(S_o) \le D(S)$ for all possible arrangements S. We are interested in devising fast algorithms which will determine an optimal arrangement for any given set of records.

Finding an optimal arrangement for a set of equal-sized records is a relatively easy task. As seen in Section 1.2, an optimal arrangement can be obtained by arranging the records so that the access probabilities form an "organ-pipe arrangement." That is, the record with highest access probability is placed in the middle and records with successively lower probabilities are placed adjacently on alternate sides. Finding an optimal arrangement for a set of equal-access-probability records is equally simple. One can easily verify from the objective function that an optimal arrangement can be obtained by arranging the records so that the reciprocals of record lengths form an organ-pipe arrangement (i.e., the shortest record is placed in the middle and successively longer ones are placed adjacently on alternate sides). These results seem to indicate that an optimal arrangement for the general case can be obtained by arranging the records so that the ratios p_i/ℓ_i form an organ-pipe arrangement. This view does not appear to carry one very far, however, as we shall show in the sequel that finding an optimal arrangement is NP-complete.

1.5.2. Characteristics of optimal arrangements We begin by giving some characterizations of an optimal arrangement. In addition to simplifying our proof of NP-completeness, these results can be quite useful when branch-and-bound techniques are used to obtain exact solutions. First, we derive a formula for the change in expected head travel when two records are interchanged.

Lemma 1.5.1 Let π' be obtained from π by interchanging the records at positions t and t', where $1 \leq t < t' \leq n$. Then we have

$$D(\pi') - D(\pi) = 2[D_1(t,t')R_1(t,t') + D_2(t,t')R_2(t,t')], \quad (1.5.7)$$

where

$$D_1(t,t') = p_t - p_{t'},$$

$$D_2(t,t') = \sum_{i=1}^{t-1} p_i - \sum_{i=t'+1}^{n} p_i,$$

$$R_1(t,t') = \sum_{i=t+1}^{t'-2} \sum_{j=i+1}^{t'-1} R_3(i,j),$$

$$R_2(t,t') = \sum_{j=t}^{t'-1} (R_3(j,t') + R_3(t,j))$$

and

$$R_3(u,v) = p_u \ell_v - p_v \ell_u.$$

Proof By (1.5.6), we can write $D(\pi)$ as

$$D(\pi) = \sum_{i=1}^{n} p_i \ell_i + 2\left\{ \sum_{i=1}^{t-1} \ell_i E_1(i) E_2(i) \right.$$

$$+ \ell_t E_1(t) E_2(t) + \sum_{i=t+1}^{t'-1} \ell_i E_1(i) E_2(i)$$

$$\left. + \ell_{t'} E_1(t') E_2(t') + \sum_{i=t'+1}^{n} \ell_i E_1(i) E_2(i) \right\},$$

where $E_1(i) = \sum_{j=1}^{i-1} p_j$ and $E_2(i) = \sum_{j=i+1}^{n} p_j$. Now $D(\pi')$ can be expressed as

$$D(\pi') = \sum_{i=1}^{n} p_i \ell_i + 2\left\{ \sum_{i=1}^{t-1} \ell_i E_1(i) E_2(i) + \ell_{t'} E_1(t) [E_2(t) + p_t - p_{t'}] \right.$$

$$+ \sum_{i=t+1}^{t'-1} \ell_i [E_1(i) - p_t + p_{t'}][E_2(i) + p_t - p_{t'}]$$

$$\left. + \ell_t [E_1(t') - p_t + p_{t'}] E_2(t') + \sum_{i=t'+1}^{n} \ell_i E_1(i) E_2(i) \right\}.$$

Subtracting $D(\pi)$ from $D(\pi')$ and combining terms gives

$$D(\pi')-D(\pi) = 2\left\{\ell_{t'}D_2(t,t')\sum_{j=t}^{t'-1}p_j - \ell_t D_2(t,t')\sum_{j=t+1}^{t'}p_j\right.$$

$$+ \left(\sum_{i=t+1}^{t'-1}\ell_i\right)D_2(t,t')(p_t-p_{t'})$$

$$\left. + (p_t-p_{t'})\left[\sum_{i=t+1}^{t'-1}\ell_i\left(\sum_{j=t+1}^{i-1}p_j - \sum_{j=i+1}^{t'-1}p_j\right)\right]\right\},$$

where $D_2(t,t') = \sum_{i=1}^{t-1}p_i - \sum_{i=t'+1}^{n}p_i$. If the order of summations is changed so that

$$\sum_{i=t+1}^{t'-1}\ell_i\sum_{j=t+1}^{i-1}p_j = \sum_{i=t+1}^{t'-1}p_i\sum_{j=i+1}^{t'-1}\ell_j$$

and

$$\sum_{i=t+1}^{t'-1}\ell_i\sum_{j=i+1}^{t'-1}p_j = \sum_{i=t+1}^{t'-1}p_i\sum_{j=t+1}^{i-1}\ell_j,$$

and terms are combined to make differences of the form $p_i\ell_j - p_j\ell_i$, then $D(\pi')-D(\pi)$ becomes

$$D(\pi')-D(\pi) = 2[D_1(t,t')R_1(t,t') + D_2(t,t')R_2(t,t')],$$

where

$$D_1(t,t') = p_t - p_{t'},$$

$$D_2(t,t') = \sum_{i=1}^{t-1}p_i - \sum_{i=t'+1}^{n}p_i,$$

$$R_1(t,t') = \sum_{i=t+1}^{t'-2} \sum_{j=i+1}^{t'-1} R_3(i,j),$$

$$R_2(t,t') = \sum_{j=t}^{t'-1} (R_3(j,t') + R_3(t,j))$$

and

$$R_3(u,v) = p_u \ell_v - p_v \ell_u. \qquad \square$$

As a corollary of Lemma 1.5.1, we have the following formula for the change in the expected head travel when two adjacent records are interchanged.

Corollary 1.5.1 Let π' be obtained from π by interchanging the records at positions t and t+1, where $1 \leq t \leq n - 1$. Then we have

$$D(\pi') - D(\pi) = 2 \left(\sum_{i=1}^{t-1} p_i - \sum_{i=t+2}^{n} p_i \right) (p_t \ell_{t+1} - p_{t+1} \ell_t). \qquad (1.5.8)$$

From Corollary 1.5.1, we can see that the expected head travel is lowered by interchanging the records at positions t and t+1 if $p_t/\ell_t < p_{t+1}/\ell_{t+1}$ and $\sum_{i=1}^{t-1} p_i > \sum_{i=t+2}^{n} p_i$ or if $p_t/\ell_t > p_{t+1}/\ell_{t+1}$ and $\sum_{i=1}^{t-1} p_i < \sum_{i=t+2}^{n} p_i$. If $p_t/\ell_t = p_{t+1}/\ell_{t+1}$, there is no change in the expected head travel when the two records are interchanged. Thus, it follows that if $p_i/\ell_i = p_j/\ell_j$ for all $1 \leq i, j \leq n$, then all arrangements give the same value.

The record(s) with the highest p_i/ℓ_i ratio play an important role in the optimal arrangement. Our next result shows that these records must be placed contiguously in an optimal arrangement. That is, if there are $r+1$ records with the highest p_i/ℓ_i ratio, then they must be placed in positions h, $h+1$,..., $h+r$ for some $1 \leq h \leq n - r$. Moreover, the optimal arrangement is in a class of arrangements which we call the "bell-shaped" arrangements. An arrangement is bell-shaped if there exists a position $h(1 \leq h \leq n)$ such that $p_1/\ell_1 \leq ... \leq p_h/\ell_h \geq ... \geq p_n/\ell_n$. As can be seen, the arrangement is bell-shaped with respect to the p_i/ℓ_i ratios.

Lemma 1.5.2 Let π_o be an optimal arrangement of a set of records with access probabilities $\{p_1,...,p_n\}$ and the corresponding lengths $\{\ell_1,..,\ell_n\}$. Let there be $r+1$ records with the highest p_i/ℓ_i ratio. Then we have

a) the records with the highest p_i/ℓ_i ratio are placed in positions h, $h+1$,...,$h+r$ in π_o for some $1 \leq h \leq n - r$,

b) $\displaystyle\sum_{i=1}^{h+r-1} p_i \geq \sum_{i=h+r+2}^{n} p_i$,

c) $\displaystyle\sum_{i=1}^{h-2} p_i \leq \sum_{i=h+1}^{n} p_i$

and

d) $p_1/\ell_1 \leq ... \leq p_{h-1}/\ell_{h-1} \leq p_h/\ell_h \geq p_{h+1}/\ell_{h+1} \geq ... \geq p_n/\ell_n$.

Proof We proceed to prove part a) by contradiction. Assume that π_o is an optimal arrangement which does not satisfy a). Let x and y be the leftmost and rightmost positions respectively in π_o such that $p_x/\ell_x = p_y/\ell_y = \max \{p_i/\ell_i\}$. Let u and v be the leftmost and rightmost positions respectively in π_o such that $p_u/\ell_u < \max \{p_i/\ell_i\}$, $p_v/\ell_v < \max \{p_i/\ell_i\}$ and $x < u \leq v < y$. If $\displaystyle\sum_{i=1}^{u-2} p_i < \sum_{i=u+1}^{n} p_i$, then by Corollary 1.5.1, interchanging the records at positions u-1 and u will give a smaller expected head travel. On the other hand, if $\sum_{i=1}^{u-2} p_i \geq \sum_{i=u+1}^{n} p_i$, then we must have $\sum_{i=1}^{v-1} p_i > \sum_{i=v+2}^{n} p_i$. Again, by Corollary 1.5.1, we obtain a smaller expected head travel by interchanging the records at positions v and v+1. Thus, π_0 cannot be an optimal arrangement.

Part b) is obtained from the observation that if it were not true, then interchanging the records at positions h+r and h+r+1 would give a smaller expected head travel. Part c) is obtained similarly, this time interchanging the records at positions h−1 and h. Finally, part d) is proved using an argument similar to that in a).

$\square$

The results in Lemma 1.5.2 reduce greatly the number of arrangements that need to be examined in a search for optimal arrangements. Specifically, if there are r+1 records with the highest p_i/ℓ_i ratio, then the number of arrangements that need to be examined is at most $2^{(n-r-2)}$. This number may be further reduced by effective use of b) and c) in Lemma 1.5.2. This is a significant improvement over the brute force approach where n!/2 arbitrary arrangements need to be examined to find the optimal arrangement. Although there appears to be a lot of structure in the optimal arrangement, the problem of finding it seems to be quite difficult. Specifically, we show that the language recognition version of this problem is NP-complete. We define the ALLOCATION problem as follows:

ALLOCATION Given a number K and a set of records with access probabilities $\{p_1,...,p_n\}$ and lengths $\{\ell_1,...,\ell_n\}$, is there an arrangement π of the records such that $D(\pi) \leq K$?

We shall reduce the PARTITION problem to the ALLOCATION problem. The PARTITION problem has been shown to be NP-complete [6,12] and is defined as follows:

PARTITION Given a set of integers $A = \{a_1,...,a_n\}$, is there a partition (A_1,A_2) of the integers in A such that $\sum\limits_{a_i \in A_1} a_i = \sum\limits_{a_i \in A_2} a_i$?

Theorem 1.5.1 The ALLOCATION problem is NP-complete.

Proof It is easy to see that the ALLOCATION problem is in NP. To complete the proof, we shall show that the PARTITION problem is polynomially reducible to the ALLOCATION problem.

Given an instance $A = \{a_1,...,a_n\}$ of the PARTITION problem, we construct an instance of the ALLOCATION problem as follows: Let there be $n+1$ records with access probabilities $p_i = a_i/z$ $(1 \leq i \leq n)$ and $p_{n+1} = a_{n+1}/z$, where $a_{n+1} = 1 + \max\limits_{1 \leq i \leq n} \{a_i\}$ and $z = \sum\limits_{i=1}^{n+1} a_i$. Let the lengths of the records be given by $\ell_i = a_i$ $(1 \leq i \leq n)$ and $\ell_{n+1} = x/2$, where $x = \min\limits_{1 \leq i \leq n} \{a_i\}$. Finally, we choose $K = K_1 + 2(K_2 + K_3)/z^2$, where $K_1 = (\sum\limits_{i=1}^{n} a_i^2 + xa_{n+1}/2)/z$, $K_2 = \sum\limits_{i=1}^{n-1} \sum\limits_{j=i+1}^{n} \sum\limits_{m=j+1}^{n+1} a_i a_j a_m$, $K_3 = (x/2 - a_{n+1})g^2$ and $g = (\sum\limits_{i=1}^{n} a_i)/2$. It is clear that this transformation can be done in polynomial time. We need to show that the PARTITION problem has a solution if and only if the ALLOCATION problem has a solution.

The ALLOCATION problem generated is a very special one in terms of the ratios p_i/ℓ_i. It can easily be seen that $p_i/\ell_i = 1/z$ for $1 \leq i \leq n$ and $p_{n+1}/\ell_{n+1} = 2a_{n+1}/(xz) > 1/z$. Therefore, p_{n+1}/ℓ_{n+1} is the highest such ratio, and any arrangement π can be represented as $\pi = (b_1,...,b_u, n + 1, c_1,...,c_v)$, where $b_1,...,b_u$ are the indices of the records to the left of the record R_{n+1}, $c_1,...,c_v$ are the indices of the records to the right of R_{n+1} and $u+v=n$.   Moreover, since $p_i/\ell_i = p_j/\ell_j$ for all $1 \leq i$, $j \leq n$, any arrangement π does not depend on how records to the left (or right) of R_{n+1} are arranged, other than how they are split between the left and right sides of R_{n+1}.

If the expected head travel function is used with the values for this particular problem, then the formula for the cost of an arrangement π of the generated ALLOCATION problem is

$$D(\pi) = K_1 + 2(K_2 + K_4)/z^2, \tag{1.5.9}$$

where

$$K_4 = (x/2-a_{n+1})g'(\pi)g''(\pi),$$

$$g'(\pi) = \sum_{i=1}^{u} a_{b_i},$$

$$g''(\pi) = \sum_{i=1}^{u} a_{c_i}$$

and K_1 and K_2 are defined as before.   The derivation of this formula is as follows:

If the values for the generated probabilities and lengths are substituted into the first term of formula (1.5.6), then it is clear that

$$\sum_{i=1}^{n+1} p_i \ell_i = \left(\sum_{i=1}^{n} a_i^2 + xa_{n+1}/2 \right)/z = K_1.$$

If an arrangement of the generated problem is denoted by

$\pi = (b_1,...,b_u,n + 1,c_1,...,c_v)$, then the second term of formula (1.5.6) can be denoted by T_2 and can be written as

$$T_2 = (2/z^2)\left\{ \sum_{i=1}^{u} a_{b_i}\left(\sum_{j=1}^{i-1} a_{b_j} \right) \right.$$

$$\cdot\left(\sum_{j=i+1}^{u} a_{b_j} + a_{n+1} + g''(\pi) \right) + xg'(\pi)g''(\pi)/2$$

$$\left. + \sum_{i=1}^{v} a_{c_i}(g'(\pi) + a_{n+1} + \sum_{j=1}^{i-1} a_{c_j})(\sum_{j=i+1}^{v} a_{c_j}) \right\}$$

$$= (2/z^2)\left\{ \sum_{i=1}^{u} a_{b_i} \sum_{j=1}^{i-1} a_{b_j} \sum_{j=i+1}^{u} a_{b_j} + \sum_{i=1}^{u} a_{b_i} \sum_{j=1}^{i-1} a_{b_j}(a_{n+1} + g''(\pi)) \right.$$

$$+ xg'(\pi)g''(\pi)/2 + g'(\pi) \sum_{i=1}^{v} a_{c_i} \sum_{j=i+1}^{v} a_{c_j} + a_{n+1}\sum_{i=1}^{v} a_{c_i} \sum_{j=i+1}^{v} a_{c_j}$$

$$\left. + \sum_{i=1}^{v} a_{c_i} \sum_{j=1}^{i-1} a_{c_j} \sum_{j=i+1}^{v} a_{c_j} \right\},$$

where $g'(\pi) = \sum_{i=1}^{u} a_{b_i}$ and $g''(\pi) = \sum_{i=1}^{v} a_{c_i}$. If the order of summation is changed so that

$$\sum_{i=1}^{u} a_{b_i} \sum_{j=1}^{i-1} a_{b_j} = \sum_{i=1}^{u} a_{b_i} \sum_{j=i+1}^{u} a_{b_j},$$

$$\sum_{i=1}^{u} a_{b_i} \sum_{j=1}^{i-1} a_{b_j} \sum_{j=i+1}^{u} a_{b_j} = \sum_{i=1}^{u} a_{b_i} \sum_{j=i+1}^{u} a_{b_j} \sum_{m=j+1}^{u} a_{b_m}$$

and

$$\sum_{i=1}^{v} a_{c_i} \sum_{j=1}^{i-1} a_{c_j} \sum_{j=i+1}^{v} a_{c_j} = \sum_{i=1}^{v} a_{c_i} \sum_{j=i+1}^{v} a_{c_j} \sum_{m=j+1}^{v} a_{c_m},$$

then by gathering terms, T_2 becomes

$$T_2 = (2/z^2) \left\{ \sum_{i=1}^{u} a_{b_i} \sum_{j=i+1}^{u} a_{b_j} \sum_{m=j+1}^{u} a_{b_m} + \sum_{i=1}^{u} a_{b_i} \sum_{j=i+1}^{u} a_{b_j}(a_{n+1} + g''(\pi)) \right.$$

$$+ xg'(\pi)g''(\pi)/2 + g'(\pi) \sum_{i=1}^{v} a_{c_i} \sum_{j=i+1}^{v} a_{c_j}$$

$$\left. + a_{n+1} \sum_{i=1}^{v} a_{c_i} \sum_{j=i+1}^{v} a_{c_j} + \sum_{i=1}^{v} a_{c_i} \sum_{j=i+1}^{v} a_{c_j} \sum_{m=j+1}^{v} a_{c_m} \right\}$$

$$= (2/z^2) \left\{ \sum_{i=1}^{u} a_{b_i} \sum_{j=i+1}^{u} a_{b_j} \sum_{m=j+1}^{u} a_{b_m} \right.$$

$$+ \sum_{i=1}^{u} a_{b_i} \sum_{j=i+1}^{u} a_{b_j}(a_{n+1} + g''(\pi))$$

$$+ g'(\pi)a_{n+1}g''(\pi) + g'(\pi) \sum_{j=1}^{v} a_{c_j} \sum_{m=j+1}^{v} a_{c_m}$$

$$+ a_{n+1} \sum_{j=1}^{v} a_{c_j} \sum_{m=j+1}^{v} a_{c_m} + \sum_{i=1}^{v} a_{c_i} \sum_{j=i+1}^{v} a_{c_j} \sum_{m=j+1}^{v} a_{c_m}$$

$$\left. + xg'(\pi)g''(\pi)/2 - a_{n+1}g'(\pi)g''(\pi) \right\}$$

$$= (2/z^2) \left\{ \sum_{i=1}^{n-1} \sum_{j=i+1}^{n} \sum_{m=j+1}^{n+1} a_i a_j a_m + g'(\pi)g''(\pi)(x/2 - a_{n+1}) \right\}.$$

Therefore, $D(\pi)$ becomes

$$D(\pi) = K_1 + T_2$$

$$= K_1 + (2/z^2) \left\{ \sum_{i=1}^{n-1} \sum_{j=i+1}^{n} \sum_{m=j+1}^{n+1} a_i a_j a_m + g'(\pi)g''(\pi)(x/2 - a_{n+1}) \right\}$$

$$= K_1 + 2(K_2 + K_4)/z^2.$$

Observe that K_1 and K_2 are independent of the arrangement π. Thus, to minimize $D(\pi)$, we need to minimize K_4. Since $x < 2a_{n+1}$, K_4 will be minimized if $g'(\pi)g''(\pi)$ is maximized. Since $g'(\pi) + g''(\pi) = \sum_{i=1}^{n} a_i$, $g'(\pi)g''(\pi)$ achieves the maximum if and only if $g'(\pi) = g''(\pi) = (1/2)\sum_{i=1}^{n} a_i$. Therefore, $D(\pi)$ achieves the minimum value K if and only if $g'(\pi) = g''(\pi)$. It then follows that the PARTITION problem has a solution if and only if the ALLOCATION problem has a solution.

□

1.5.3. Heuristics and performance bounds Since the ALLOCATION problem is NP-complete, there is a need for devising good approximation algorithms which compute near-optimal solutions in an acceptable amount of computing time. To further motivate the importance of heuristics, we show that for any given number of records, an arbitrary arrangement can perform arbitrarily poorly in comparison with an optimal arrangement.

Theorem 1.5.2 Let π' and π'' be any two arrangements of a set of records with access probabilities $\{p_1,...,p_n\}$ and lengths $\{\ell_1,...,\ell_n\}$. Then we have

$$D(\pi')/D(\pi'') \leq (1 + p_{min})/(2p_{min}),$$

where $p_{min} = \min_{1 \leq i \leq n} \{p_i\}$. Moreover, for every odd $n \geq 3$, there are sets of records for which the ratio $D(\pi')/D(\pi'')$ can approach $1/(2p_{min}) + p_{min}/2$ arbitrarily closely.

Proof Let p'_i and p''_i denote the access probabilities of records assigned to the i-th position in the arrangements π' and π'' respectively, and let ℓ'_i and ℓ''_i denote the corresponding lengths. Since $\sum_{i=1}^{n} p'_i \ell'_i = \sum_{i=1}^{n} p''_i \ell''_i$, we have

$$\frac{D(\pi')}{D(\pi'')} = 1 + \frac{D(\pi')-D(\pi'')}{D(\pi'')}$$

$$= 1 + \frac{2\sum_{i=2}^{n-1}\ell'_i\left(\sum_{j=1}^{i-1}p'_j\right)\left(\sum_{j=i+1}^{n}p'_j\right) - 2\sum_{i=2}^{n-1}\ell''_i\left(\sum_{j=1}^{i-1}p''_j\right)\left(\sum_{j=i+1}^{n}p''_j\right)}{\sum_{i=1}^{n}\ell'_ip'_i + 2\sum_{i=2}^{n-1}\ell''_i\left(\sum_{j=1}^{i-1}p''_j\right)\left(\sum_{j=i+1}^{n}p''_j\right)}$$

$$\leq 1 + \frac{2\sum_{i=2}^{n-1}\ell'_i\left(\sum_{j=1}^{i-1}p'_j\right)\left(\sum_{j=i+1}^{n}p'_j\right)}{\sum_{i=1}^{n}\ell'_ip'_i}. \tag{1.5.10}$$

Now

$$\left(\sum_{j=1}^{i-1} p'_j\right)\left(\sum_{j=i+1}^{n} p'_j\right) \leq \left(\frac{1-p'_i}{2}\right)^2$$

$$= \frac{p'_i(1/p'_i - 2 + p'_i)}{4}$$

$$\leq \frac{p'_i(1/p_{min} - 2 + 1)}{4}$$

$$= \frac{p'_i(1/p_{min} - 1)}{4}. \qquad (1.5.11)$$

Substituting (1.5.11) into (1.5.10), we obtain

$$\frac{D(\pi')}{D(\pi'')} \leq 1 + \frac{(1/p_{min} - 1)\sum_{i=2}^{n-1} \ell'_i p'_i}{2\sum_{i=1}^{n} \ell'_i p'_i}$$

$$\leq 1 + \frac{(1/p_{min} - 1)}{2}$$

$$= \frac{1 + p_{min}}{2p_{min}}.$$

To show that the ratio $D(\pi')/D(\pi'')$ can approach $1/(2p_{min}) + p_{min}/2$ arbitrarily closely, we consider the set of $n = 2m+1$ records with access probabilities

$\{e,(1-e)/(n-1),...,(1-e)/(n-1)\}$ and the corresponding lengths $\{x/e,1,...,1\}$, where e is smaller than $(1-e)(n-1)$ and x is a large positive number. Let π'' be the arrangement where the records are arranged as listed above. We have $D(\pi'') = x + (1-e) + 2f(e,n)$, where $f(e,n)$ is a function of just e and n. Let π' be the arrangement where the record with access probability e is placed in the middle. We have $D(\pi') = x + (1-e) + [x(1-e)^2]/(2e) + 2g(e,n)$, where $g(e,n)$ is again a function of e and n only. By choosing x large enough, the ratio $D(\pi')/D(\pi'')$ can be made to approach $1/(2e) + e/2$ arbitrarily closely. Since $e = \min_{1\leq i\leq n}\{p_i\}$, we have the desired result.

$\square$

Theorem 1.5.2 shows that an arbitrary arrangement can perform quite poorly in comparison with an optimal arrangement. Since it is known from Lemma 1.5.2 that an optimal arrangement is a bell-shaped arrangement, it is interesting to see how an arbitrary bell-shaped arrangement might compare with an optimal arrangement. Before we derive this result, we need to introduce a different notation for representing bell-shaped arrangements and their expected head travel.

We shall index the records $R_1,..,R_n$ so that $p_1/\ell_1 \geq p_2/\ell_2 \geq ... \geq p_n/\ell_n$. With this indexing, any bell-shaped arrangement can be represented by an n-tuple $\beta = (b_1,...,b_n)$, where $b_1 = 1$ and

$$b_i = \begin{cases} 1 & \text{if record } R_i \text{ is placed to the right of } R_1; \\ 0 & \text{if record } R_i \text{ is placed to the left of } R_1 \end{cases}$$

for i=2,...,n. Since $p_i/\ell_i \geq p_{i+1}/\ell_{i+1}$ for $1\leq i<n$, there exist n

nonnegative numbers, $d_j(1 \leq j \leq n)$, such that ℓ_i can be expressed as $\ell_i = p_i(\sum_{j=1}^{i} d_j/p_j)$ for each $1 \leq i \leq n$. With these notations, we can rewrite the expected head travel function as follows:

$$D(\beta) = \sum_{i=1}^{n} \left((d_i/p_i) \sum_{j=i}^{n} p_j(p_j + 2g_j) \right), \qquad (1.5.12)$$

where $g_j = b_j[E(j) + V_2(j)]V_1(j) + (1-b_j)[E(j) + V_1(j)]V_2(j)$,

$$E(j) = \sum_{k=1}^{j-1} p_k,$$

$$V_1(j) = \sum_{k=j+1}^{n} b_k p_k$$

and

$$V_2(j) = \sum_{k=j+1}^{n} (1-b_k)p_k.$$

The above formula can be obtained by a direct substitution of $\ell_i = p_i(\sum_{j=1}^{i} d_j/p_j)$ into the expected head travel formula given in (1.5.6). We shall omit the derivation of this formula, trusting that readers can derive it without any difficulties. Using this formula, we can now bound the performance of an arbitrary bell-shaped arrangement with respect to an optimal arrangement.

Theorem 1.5.3 Let β' and β'' be any two bell-shaped arrangements of a set of n records. Then we have

$$D(\beta')/D(\beta'') \leq 1 + n/2.$$

Proof   Let $\beta' = (b'_1,...,b'_n)$ and $\beta'' = (b''_1,...,b''_n)$ be any two bell-shaped arrangements of a set of n records. Then we have

$$\frac{D(\beta')}{D(\beta'')} = 1 + \frac{D(\beta') - D(\beta'')}{D(\beta'')}$$

$$= 1 + \frac{2[\sum\limits_{i=1}^{n} (d_i/p_i)E(i)W_1(i)W_2(i)]}{\sum\limits_{i=1}^{n} \left((d_i/p_i)\sum\limits_{j=i}^{n} p_j(p_j + 2g''_j) \right)}, \qquad (1.5.13)$$

where $W_1(i) = \sum\limits_{j=i}^{n} (b''_j - b'_j)p_j,$

$$W_2(i) = \sum\limits_{j=i}^{n} (1 - b''_j - b'_j)p_j,$$

$$g''_j = b''_j[E(j) + V''_2(j)]V''_1(j)$$

$$+ (1 - b''_j)[E(j) + V''_1(j)]V''_2(j),$$

$$E(j) = \sum\limits_{k=1}^{j-1} p_k,$$

$$V''_1(j) = \sum\limits_{k=j+1}^{n} b''_k p_k$$

and

$$V''_2(j) = \sum\limits_{k=j+1}^{n} (1 - b''_k)p_k.$$

To derive formula (1.5.13), all we need to show is

$$D(\beta') = D(\beta'') = 2\sum_{i=1}^{n} (d_i/p_i)E(i)W_1(i)W_2(i). \qquad (1.5.14)$$

Substituting β' and β'' into formula (1.5.12) and forming the difference $D(\beta') - D(\beta'')$, we obtain

$$D(\beta') - D(\beta'') = 2\sum_{i=1}^{n} (d_i/p_i)\sum_{j=i}^{n} p_j(g'_j - g''_j), \qquad (1.5.15)$$

where

$$g'_j = b'_j[E(j) + V'_2(j)]V'_1(j)$$

$$+ (1 - b'_j)[E(j) + V'_1(j)]V'_2(j),$$

$$g''_j = b''_j[E(j) + V''_2(j)]V''_1(j) +$$

$$(1 - b''_j)[E(j) + V''_1(j)]V''_2(j),$$

$$V'_1(j) = \sum_{k=j+1}^{n} b'_k p_k,$$

$$V'_2(j) = \sum_{k=j+1}^{n} (1 - b'_k)p_k,$$

$$V''_1(j) = \sum_{k=j+1}^{n} b''_k p_k$$

and

$$V''_2(j) = \sum_{k=j+1}^{n} (1-b''_k)p_k.$$

If the facts that $b'_i + (1 - b'_i) = 1$ and $b''_i + (1-b''_i) = 1$ for all i are used, then

$$g'_j = E(j)V'_3(j) + V'_2(j)V'_1(j)$$

and

$$g''_j = E(j)V''_3(j) + V''_2(j)V''_1(j),$$

where

$$V'_3(j) = \sum_{k=j+1}^{n} [b'_k b'_j + (1-b'_j)(1-b'_k)]p_k$$

and

$$V''_3(j) = \sum_{k=j+1}^{n} [b''_k b''_j + (1-b''_j)(1-b''_k)]p_k.$$

Thus, $g'_j - g''_j$ becomes

$$g'_j - g''_j = E(j)[V'_3(j) - V''_3(j)] + V'_2(j)V'_1(j) - V''_2(j)V''_1(j).$$

If the second half of this is expanded and the fact that $a^2 - b^2 = (a - b)(a + b)$ is used, then

$$V'_2(j)V'_1(j) - V''_2(j)V''_1(j) = -F_1(j)F_2(j),$$

where $F_1(j) = \sum\limits_{k=j+1}^{n} (b''_k - b'_k)p_k$ and $F_2(j) = \sum\limits_{k=j+1}^{n} (1-b''_k - b'_k)p_k.$ It is not difficult to verify that

$$V'_3(j) - V''_3(j) = (1 - b''_j - b'_j)F_1(j) + (b''_j - b'_j)F_2(j).$$

If all of the above are used, then $g'_j - g''_j$ becomes

$$g'_j - g''_j = E(j)[(1 - b''_j - b'_j)F_1(j)$$

$$+ (b''_j - b'_j)F_2(j)] - F_1(j)F_2(j).$$

Substituting the above into formula (1.5.15), changing the order of summation so that

$$\sum_{j=i}^{n} p_j \sum_{k=1}^{j-1} p_k[(1 - b''_j - b'_j)F_1(j) + (b''_j - b'_j)F_2(j)]$$

$$= \sum_{k=1}^{i-1} p_k \sum_{j=i}^{n} p_j[(1 - b''_j - b'_j)F_1(j) + (b''_j - b'_j)F_2(j)]$$

$$+ \sum_{k=i}^{n-1} p_k \sum_{j=k+1}^{n} p_j[(1 - b''_j - b'_j)F_1(j) + (b''_j - b'_j)F_2(j)]$$

and combining terms gives

$$D(\beta') - D(\beta'') = 2 \sum_{i=1}^{n} (d_i/p_i)\{E(i)[Q_1(i) + Q_2(i)]$$

$$+ \sum_{k=i}^{n-1} p_k[Q_1(k + 1) + Q_2(k + 1)] - \sum_{k=i}^{n} p_k F_1(k)F_2(k)\}, \qquad (1.5.16)$$

where $Q_1(j) = \sum_{\ell=j}^{n} p_\ell(1 - b''_\ell - b'_\ell)F_1(\ell)$ and $Q_2(j) = \sum_{\ell=j}^{n} p_\ell(b''_\ell - b'_\ell)F_2(\ell).$

If the order of summations in $Q_1(j)$ is changed so that

$$Q_1(j) = \sum_{\ell=j}^{n} p_\ell (1-b''_\ell - b'_\ell) \sum_{k=\ell+1}^{n} (b''_k - b'_k) p_k$$

$$= \sum_{\ell=j}^{n} p_\ell (b''_\ell - b'_\ell) \sum_{k=j}^{\ell-1} p_k (1-b''_k - b'_k)$$

and using the observation that $(b''_\ell - b'_\ell)(1-b''_\ell - b'_\ell) = 0$ for all $1 \le \ell \le n$, then we have

$$Q_1(j) + Q_2(j) = F_1(j-1)F_2(j-1).$$

Substituting the above into formula (1.5.16), we obtain

$$D(\beta') - D(\beta'') = 2 \sum_{i=1}^{n} (d_i/p_i)\{E(i)F_1(i-1)F_2(i-1)$$

$$+ \sum_{k=i}^{n-1} p_k F_1(k)F_2(k) - \sum_{k=i}^{n} p_k F_1(k)F_2(k)\}$$

$$= 2 \sum_{k=1}^{n} (d_i/p_i)E(i)F_1(i-1)F_2(i-1)$$

$$= 2 \sum_{i=1}^{n} (d_i/p_i)E(i)W_1(i)W_2(i)$$

since $W_1(i) = F_1(i-1)$ and $W_2(i) = F_2(i-1)$. This completes the derivation of (1.5.13).

Since one of the terms $(b''_j - b'_j)$ and $(1-b''_j - b'_j)$ must be zero for each $1 \leq j \leq n$, we have $W_1(i)W_2(i) \leq (\sum_{j=i}^{n} p_j/2)^2$. By Cauchy's

inequality, we have $\left(\sum_{j=i}^{n} p_j/2\right)^2 \leq (n-i+1)\left(\sum_{j=i}^{n} p_j^2\right)/4$. Therefore,

$W_1(i)W_2(i) \leq (n-i+1)(\sum_{j=i}^{n} p_j^2)/4$. Substituting this inequality into

formula (1.5.13), along with the observation that $E(i) \leq 1$ for all

$1 \leq i \leq n$, we derive

$$\frac{D(\beta')}{D(\beta'')} = 1 + \frac{2[\sum_{i=1}^{n} (d_i/p_i)E(i)W_1(i)W_2(i)]}{\sum_{i=1}^{n} \left((d_i/p_i)\sum_{j=i}^{n} p_j(p_j + 2g''_j) \right)}$$

$$\leq 1 + \frac{2[\sum_{i=1}^{n} (d_i/p_i)(n-i+1)(\sum_{j=i}^{n} p_j^2)/4]}{\sum_{i=1}^{n} \left((d_i/p_i)\sum_{j=i}^{n} p_j(p_j + 2g''_j) \right)}$$

$$\leq 1 + \frac{n[\sum_{i=1}^{n} ((d_i/p_i)\sum_{j=i}^{n} p_j^2)]}{2[\sum_{i=1}^{n} \left((d_i/p_i)\sum_{j=i}^{n} (p_j^2 + 2p_j g''_j) \right)]}$$

$$\leq 1 + n/2. \qquad\qquad \square$$

Since an optimal arrangement is a bell-shaped arrangement, the

bound in Theorem 1.5.3 also serves as a bound for the performance of

an arbitrary bell-shaped arrangement with respect to an optimal

arrangement. Although the bound appears to be quite large, we have been unable to find examples for which the ratio is larger than 2. Through a detailed case analysis, we have shown that the bound is in fact 2 for all $n \leq 4$, and we conjecture that it holds for all n.

In addition to the bell-shaped arrangements, we have studied a couple of heuristics which are intuitively quite appealing. The first one arranges the records so that the ratios p_i/ℓ_i form an organ-pipe arrangement. Since the arrangement obtained from this heuristic is a bell-shaped arrangement, the bound in Theorem 1.5.3 also applies to this heuristic. The worst-case example we have found for this heuristic achieves a ratio of 2. The second heuristic that we considered constructs two arrangements and chooses the better of the two as the final arrangement. The first is an organ-pipe arrangement by access probabilities and the second is an organ-pipe arrangement by the reciprocals of record lengths. We have shown that the worst-case performance of this heuristic with respect to optimal solutions is bounded above by $\min \{a^2/b^2, c/d\}$, where $a = \max \{p_i\}$, $b = \min\{p_i\}$, $c = \max \{\ell_i\}$, and $d = \min \{\ell_i\}$. However, we feel that this may not be a tight bound, as the worst-case example we have found achieves a ratio of 1.1447. The difficulties we encountered in deriving a tight bound for this heuristic lie in the fact that there appears to be no apparent relationship between the two arrangements.

We note that the two heuristics mentioned above are incomparable in the sense that there are examples in which one heuristic performs better than the other, and conversely. Surprisingly, the worst-case example we have been able to find for the second heuristic has a performance ratio far less than that of the first one. We have done some experiments using randomly generated access probabilities and record lengths to get a feel for the average performance of these two heuristics. Both heuristics perform quite well in comparison with optimal solutions, with the first heuristic outperforming the second in 19 out of 20 cases.

1.6. Schedules to minimize head travel in a batched processing environment

1.6.1. Introduction One thing in common throughout all previous sections is that requests for records are processed sequentially, i.e., one request at a time on the FIFO basis. In this section, we consider the accessing of batched requests; we process a fixed number (a batch) of requests at a time. The advantage of batched processing has been discussed thoroughly in [19]. We make the same assumption as before, namely, consecutive accesses are independent and the frequencies are known. Our objective is to minimize the expected head travel for a batch.

In this model, two problems arise immediately. First, for a given arrangement of the records, what is a good scheduling algorithm (or rule for short) for the head movement? Second, what is a good arrangement of the records?

We shall address ourselves primarily to the first problem since we believe that the organ-pipe arrangement is the best arrangement for most reasonable rules. In fact, we shall prove this for two simple rules.

1.6.2. Formulation of the problem Let the locations of a linear storage be labeled $1,2,...,n$ from left to right. We use a row n-vector to represent the arrangement of records, e.g., $(R_1,...,R_n)$ means record R_i is at location i for all i. Let p_i be the access probability of record R_i

for $i=1,2,...,n$. Then $\Sigma_{i=1}^{n} p_i = 1$. At time t, b requests are generated (with repetitions allowed) according to these probabilities. Let $L_1 \leq L_2 ... \leq L_b$, $1 \leq L_i \leq n$ be the b locations where the requests are made. From now on, L_1, L_b will be referred to as the left and right extremes respectively and will be written as L and R. Suppose the current head location is x, $1 \leq x \leq n$. A rule specifies the order in which the head goes through $L_1, L_2, ..., L_b$, starting from x. The head stops when all locations have been visited. Let the stopping location be y. The location y will be the starting location for the next batch, i.e., for time $t+1$. Let $d(x,y)$ denote the distance traveled by the head from x to y, whose expected value is our cost. We are interested only in rules whose cost has a definite value - for example, rules whose behavior can be modeled by a Markov chain. A more formal definition of rules will be given later. Our objective is to find rules with as small a cost as possible. In general, we denote the cost by C or by $C(R_1,...,R_n)$ if the record arrangement $(R_1,...,R_n)$ needs emphasis.

1.6.3. Two simple rules We now propose and analyze two simple rules called the *Leftist* and *Alternating* rules.

Leftist rule. From the current head location x, move to the extreme L; then sweep across to the right extreme R and stop.

A *Rightist* rule can be similarly defined - that is, the head moves to the right first and then sweeps left.

Alternating rule. When the time t is odd, use Leftist rule. Otherwise, use Rightist rule.

Let $COST_L$, $COST_R$, $COST_A$ be the cost functions of the Leftist, Rightist and Alternating rules respectively. Also, define

$$\lambda_i = \text{Prob}(L \geq i) = \left(\sum_{j=i}^{n} p_j \right)^b,$$

$$\rho_i = \text{Prob}(R \leq i) = \left(\sum_{j=1}^{i} p_j \right)^b.$$

By symmetry, $\text{COST}_L = \text{COST}_R$ (see Corollary 1.6.1). We shall derive closed form expressions for COST_L and COST_A.

Lemma 1.6.1 $E(\text{RANGE}_b) = E(R-L) = \sum_{i=1}^{n-1} (1 - \lambda_{i+1} - \rho_i).$

Proof Define

$$I_j = \begin{cases} 1 & \text{if record } R_j \text{ is at L or R; or is inbetween;} \\ 0 & \text{otherwise.} \end{cases}$$

Then $E(\text{RANGE}_b) = \left[\sum_{j=1}^{n} E(I_j) \right] - 1 = \left[\sum_{j=1}^{n} \text{Prob}(I_j = 1) \right] - 1.$
But

$$\text{Prob}(I_j = 1) = 1 - \left(\sum_{i=1}^{j-1} p_i \right)^b - \left(\sum_{i=j+1}^{n} p_i \right)^b;$$

the result follows from substitution.

$\square$

Theorem 1.6.1

$$\text{COST}_L = E(\text{RANGE}_b) + \sum_{i=1}^{n-1} (1 + \lambda_{i+1})(1 - \rho_i) + \sum_{i=1}^{n-1} \lambda_{i+1} \rho_i \qquad \text{(a)}$$

$$= 2E(\text{RANGE}_b) + 2 \sum_{i=1}^{n-1} \lambda_{i+1} \rho_i \qquad \text{(b)}$$

$$= 2 \sum_{i=1}^{n-1} (1-\lambda_{i+1})(1-\rho_i). \tag{c}$$

Proof Let L and R be the left and right extremes for the current batch and R_0, the right extreme for the previous batch. $COST_L$ consists of moving from R_0 to L and then from L to R; hence

$$COST_L = E(RANGE_b) + E(|R_0-L|). \tag{1.6.1}$$

Note that

$$E(|R_0-L|) = \sum_{r=1}^{n} \sum_{s=1}^{n} |r - s| \cdot Prob(R_0 = r, L = s), \tag{1.6.2}$$

$$Prob(R_0 = r) = Prob(R_0 \le r) - Prob(R_0 \le r - 1) = \rho_r - \rho_{r-1}, \tag{1.6.3}$$

$$Prob(L = s) = \lambda_s - \lambda_{s+1}. \tag{1.6.4}$$

Since R_0 and L are independent,

$$E(|R_0 - L|) = \sum_{r=1}^{n} \sum_{s=1}^{n} |r - s| \cdot (\rho_r - \rho_{r-1})(\lambda_s - \lambda_{s+1})$$

$$= \sum_{r=1}^{n} (\rho_r - \rho_{r-1}) \sum_{s=1}^{n} |r - s| (\lambda_s - \lambda_{s+1}). \tag{1.6.5}$$

The inner sum $= |r - 1|\lambda_1 + \sum_{s=1}^{n-1}(|r - s - 1| - |r - s|)$ $\lambda_{s+1} + |r - n|\lambda_{n+1} = |r - 1| - \sum_{s=1}^{r-1}\lambda_{s+1} + \sum_{s=r}^{n-1}\lambda_{s+1}$ since

$\lambda_1 = 1$, $\lambda_{n+1} = 0$ and

$$|r - s - 1| - |r - s| = \begin{cases} -1 & \text{if } r > s; \\ 1 & \text{if } r \leq s. \end{cases}$$

After substituting into (1.6.5), we further simplify the expression by splitting the sum, changing the index and recombining. Noting that $\rho_0 = 0$ and $\rho_n = 1$, we obtain the expression for $E(|R_0 - L|)$ as specified in (a). Equations (b) and (c) follow from straightforward manipulation and Lemma 1.6.1.

$\square$

Corollary 1.6.1 $COST_L$ is symmetric, i.e., $COST_L$ remains the same if we replace p_i by p_{n-i+1} for $i=1,...,n$. Consequently, $COST_L = COST_R$.

Proof Note only that ρ_i and λ_{i+1} are now replaced by λ_{n-i+1} and ρ_{n-i} respectively. The formula in Theorem 1.6.1(b) becomes $2\sum_{i=1}^{n-1} \rho_{n-i} \lambda_{n-i+1}$. By replacing i by $n-i$ and reversing the order of summation, the original formula is obtained.

$\square$

Theorem 1.6.2

$$COST_A = E(RANGE_b) + \sum_{i=1}^{n-1} \rho_i(1-\rho_i) + \sum_{i=1}^{n-1} \lambda_{i+1}(1-\lambda_{i+1}) \qquad \text{(a)}$$

$$= \sum_{i=1}^{n-1} (1-\rho_i^2-\lambda_{i+1}^2) \qquad \text{(b)}$$

$$= E(RANGE_{2b}).   \text{(c)}$$

Proof The cost of accessing a batch using this rule consists of first, either going from the left extreme of the previous batch (L_0) to the left extreme of the current batch (L) or going from the previous right extreme (R_0) to the current right extreme (R). Each possibility has probability $\frac{1}{2}$. Second, a sweep across the batch is needed, requiring a move of $E(RANGE_b)$. Therefore

$$COST_A = E(RANGE_b) +$$

$$\frac{1}{2}(E(|L - L_0|) + E(|R - R_0|)).   \text{(1.6.6)}$$

Following the reasoning in Theorem 1.6.1, we have

$$E(L - L_0|) = \sum_{s=1}^{n} (\lambda_s - \lambda_{s+1}) \sum_{m=1}^{n} |s - m|(\lambda_m - \lambda_{m+1}),$$

$$E(|R - R_0|) = \sum_{r=1}^{n} (\rho_r - \rho_{r-1}) \sum_{u=1}^{n} |r - u|(\rho_u - \rho_{u-1}).$$

These are simplified as in Theorem 1.6.1, giving

$$E(|L - L_0|) = 2\sum_{s=1}^{n-1} \lambda_{s+1}(1 - \lambda_{s+1}), \quad E(|R - R_0|) = 2\sum_{r=1}^{n-1} \rho_r(1 - \rho_r).$$

Substituting into (1.6.6) proves part (a). Part (b) is obtained by straightforward manipulation. Part (c) is derived by noting $\rho_r^2 = \left(\sum_{i=1}^{r} p_i\right)^{2b}$ and $\lambda_s^2 = \left(\sum_{i=s}^{n} p_i\right)^{2b}$ so (b) is exactly the formula for $E(RANGE_{2b})$.

□

Next, we shall show that $COST_L$ (hence $COST_R$) and $COST_A$ are both minimized when the record arrangement is the organ-pipe arrangement.

Define an interchange operation, which, given an arrangement $(R_1,...,R_n)$, creates a new arrangement as follows: For every $i \leq \lfloor n/2 \rfloor$, R_i and R_{n-i+1} are interchanged if and only if $p_i > p_{n-i+1}$. Similarly, a reverse interchange operation creates a new arrangement by interchanging R_{i+1} and R_{n-i+1} if and only if $p_{i+1} < p_{n-i+1}$. Record R_1 is ignored.

Lemma 1.6.2 The organ-pipe arrangement minimizes the cost function, C, of a rule if C satisfies the following conditions for every $n \geq 1$:

(1) C is symmetric, i.e., $C(R_1,...,R_n) = C(R_n,...,R_1)$.

(2) If $p_n = 0$, then $C(R_1,...,R_{n-1},R_n) = C(R_1,...,R_{n-1})$.

(3) Given any arrangement $(R_1,...,R_n)$, let $(R'_1,...,R'_n)$ be the arrangement created by a reverse interchange operation. Then $C(R_1,...,R_n) \geq C(R'_1,...,R'_n)$.

Proof We first show that a reverse interchange operation will not increase the cost function. Consider any arrangement $(R_1,...,R_n)$ and let $(R'_1,...,R'_n)$ be the arrangement created by a reverse interchange operation. Consider the arrangement $(R_1,...,R_n, R_{n-1})$, where R_{n+1} has zero probability. Using conditions (1) and (2), we have $C(R_1,...,R_n) = C(R_1,...,R_n,R_{n+1}) = C(R_{n+1},R_n,...,R_1)$. Performing an interchange operation on $(R_{n+1},R_n,...,R_1)$ produces $(R_{n+1},R'_n,...,R'_1)$ since R_1 is compared with a record of zero probability and will not be moved. Therefore

$$C(R_{n+1}, R_n, \ldots, R_1) \geq C(R_{n+1}, R'_n, \ldots, R'_1)$$

$$= C(R'_1, \ldots, R'_n, R_{n+1}) = C(R'_1, \ldots, R'_n),$$

proving that a reverse interchange operation will not increase the cost function.

It is clear that we can "sort" any initial arrangement into the organ-pipe arrangement by using a sufficiently long alternating sequence of interchange and reverse interchange operations. Since each step will not increase the cost, the cost of the organ-pipe arrangement must be less than or equal to that of any other arrangement, proving the lemma.

$$\square$$

Lemma 1.6.3 If $f(x)$ is concave $(f''(x) \leq 0)$ on an interval $[a,b]$, then for any $a \leq x \leq y \leq b$ and $\varepsilon > 0$, $f(x) + f(y) \geq f(x - \varepsilon) + f(y + \varepsilon)$. (Of course, we must also have $x - \varepsilon$, $y + \varepsilon$ in $[a,b]$.)

Proof Since $f''(x) \leq 0$, $f'(x)$ is decreasing on $[0,1]$. By the mean value theorem, for some u such that $x - \varepsilon \leq u \leq x$,

$$f(x) - f(x - \varepsilon) = \varepsilon \cdot f'(u) \geq \varepsilon \cdot f'(x)$$

and for some v such that $y \leq v \leq y + \varepsilon$,

$$f(y + \varepsilon) - f(y) = \varepsilon \cdot f'(v) \leq \varepsilon \cdot f'(y).$$

Then

$$f(x)-f(x-\varepsilon)\geq\varepsilon\cdot f'(x)\geq\varepsilon\cdot f'(y)\geq f(y+\varepsilon)-f(y). \qquad \square$$

Theorem 1.6.3 The organ-pipe arrangement minimizes $COST_L$.

Proof We show that Lemma 1.6.2 holds. Clearly, condition (2) is satisfied. Corollary 1.6.1 verifies condition (1). To verify condition (3), let $k = \lfloor (n-1)/2 \rfloor$ and rewrite the formula in Theorem 1.6.1 (b) as

$$COST_L = 2\sum_{i=1}^{k}\left[\left(1-\left(\sum_{j=1}^{i}p_j\right)^b\right)\left(1-\left(\sum_{j=i+1}^{n}p_j\right)^b\right)\right.$$

$$\left.+ \left(1-\left(\sum_{j=1}^{n-i}p_j\right)^b\right)\left(1-\left(\sum_{j=n-i+1}^{n}p_j\right)^b\right)\right]$$

$$+ 2\left(1-\left(\sum_{j=1}^{n/2}p_j\right)^b\right)\left(1-\left(\sum_{j=n/2+1}^{n}p_j\right)^b\right),$$

where the last term is included only if n is even. This last term can be written as $x+x$ and then is in the same form as the others with $i=n/2$.

Now consider the term for any $i \leq n/2$. Let

$s=$ sum of the probabilities of the records in $\{R_1,...,R_i\}$ that are not moved by an interchange operation.

$t=$ sum of the probabilities of the records in $\{R_1,...,R_i\}$ that are moved.

$u=$ sum of the probabilities of the records in $\{R_{n-i+1},...,R_n\}$ that are not moved.

$v=$ sum of the probabilities of the records in $\{R_{n-i+1},...,R_n\}$ that are moved.

w=sum of the probabilities of the records in $\{R_{i+1},...,R_{n-i}\}$.

An interchange operation interchanges the t-records with the v-records. Let T be this term before the interchange operation and let T' be the term after the operation. Then

$$T = (1-(s + t)^b)(1-(u + v + w)^b)$$

$$+ (1-(s + t + w)^b)(1-(u + v)^b),$$

$$T' = (1-(s + v)^b)(1-(u + t + w)^b)$$

$$+ (1-(s + v + w)^b)(1-(u + t)^b).$$

Since s+t+u+v+w=1, these can be rewritten as

$$T = (1-(s + t)^b)(1-(1 - s - t)^b)$$

$$+ (1-(s + t + w)^b)(1-(1 - s - t - w)^b),$$

$$T' = (1-(s + v)^b)(1-(1 - s - v)^b)$$

$$+ (1-(s + v + w)^b)(1-(1 - s - v - w)^b).$$

It is easy to verify that the function $f(x) = (1-x^b)(1-(1 - x^b))$ is concave over [0,1]. Lemma 1.6.3 is used with x=s+t, y=s+t+w and $\varepsilon = t - v$. (Note that by the definition of the interchange operation, t>v, so $\varepsilon>0$.) Thus, each term is decreased by an interchange operation; therefore, $COST_L$ is decreased, verifying condition (3) of Lemma 1.6.2 and proving the theorem.

$\square$

Theorem 1.6.4 The organ-pipe arrangement minimizes COST_A.

Proof The proof proceeds as in Theorem 1.6.3. Conditions (1) and (2) of Lemma 1.6.2 are easily verified. To verify condition (3), the formula in Theorem 1.6.2 (b) is rewritten as

$$\text{COST}_A = \sum_{i=1}^{k} \left[1-\left(\sum_{j=1}^{i} p_j\right)^{2b} - \left(\sum_{j=i+1}^{n} p_j\right)^{2b} \right.$$

$$\left. + 1-\left(\sum_{j=1}^{n-i} p_j\right)^{2b} - \left(\sum_{j=n-i+1}^{n} p_j\right)^{2b} \right] + 1-\left(\sum_{j=1}^{n/2} p_j\right)^{2b} - \left(\sum_{j=n/2+1}^{n} p_j\right)^{2b},$$

where $k = \lfloor (n-1)/2 \rfloor$ and the last term is included *only if* n is even.

Now consider any term for $i \leq n/2$ and define s,t,u,v and w as in Theorem 1.6.3. Let T be the term before the interchange operation and let T' be the term after the operation. Then

$$T = 1-(s + t)^{2b}-(1 - s - t)^{2b}$$

$$+ 1-(s + t + w)^{2b}-(1 - s - t - w)^{2b},$$

$$T' = 1-(s + v)^{2b}-(1 - s - v)^{2b}$$

$$+ 1-(s + v + w)^{2b}-(1 - s - v - w)^{2b}.$$

The function $1 - x^{2b}-(1 - x)^{2b}$ is concave over $[0,1]$ and Lemma 1.6.3 is used with $x=s+t$, $y=s+t+w$ and $\varepsilon = t - v$ to prove the theorem.

□

Corollary 1.6.2 $E(\text{RANGE}_b)$ is minimized by the organ-pipe arrangement.

Proof Theorem 1.6.4 shows $E(RANGE_{2b})$ is minimized by the organ-pipe arrangement. The proof also works if an odd number is used instead of 2b.

□

Next we prove a simple result which compares $COST_A$, $COST_L$ and the minimum cost.

Theorem 1.6.5 $E(RANGE_{2b}) \leq 2 \cdot E(RANGE_b)$.

Proof Using Lemma 1.6.1, we have

$$E(RANGE_{2b}) - 2 \cdot E(RANGE_b) = \sum_{i=1}^{n-1} 1 - (1 - \lambda_{i+1})^2 - (1 - \rho_i)^2.$$

Consider any term in the sum and let $x = \sum_{j=i+1}^{n} p_j$; then this term equals $1 - (1 - x^b)^2 - (1 - (1 - x)^b)^2$, which is nonpositive for x in $[0,1]$. Since all terms are nonpositive, we have $E(RANGE_{2b}) - 2 \cdot E(RANGE_b) \leq 0$.

□

Corollary 1.6.3

(1) $COST_A \leq COST_L = COST_R$

for any record arrangement.

(2) $C_{min} \leq C_A \leq 2 \cdot C_{min}$, where C_{min} is the minimum cost for any rule and any record arrangement; C_A is $COST_A$ when the organ-pipe arrangement is used.

Proof From Theorems 1.6.1(b), 1.6.2(c) and 1.6.5, $COST_L \geq 2 \cdot E(RANGE_b) \geq E(RANGE_{2b}) = COST_A$.

From Corollary 1.6.2, $E(RANGE_b)$ is minimized by the organ-pipe arrangement. Let this minimum value be E_0. Then clearly, $E_0 \leq C_{min}$. Therefore, by Theorems 1.6.2(c) and 1.6.5, $C_A \leq 2 \cdot E_0 \leq 2 \cdot C_{min}$.

$\square$

Therefore, the Alternating rule is better than the Leftist or Rightist rule and is never more than twice larger than the minimum.

1.6.4. The Nearest rule We now study a slightly more complicated rule. Later we shall see that this belongs to a family of rules called B-optimal rules. In fact, this rule is a 1-optimal rule.

Nearest rule. From the current head location, move to the closer of the two extremes; then sweep across to the other extreme and stop. In case of a tie, choose either extreme.

Analysis of this rule is harder than for previous rules because it is difficult to calculate the probability that the head will be at a given position after accessing a batch. For the previous rules, this was simple. It was either the probability that the given position was the right extreme, or one-half times the probability that it was either a left or a right extreme. In the Nearest rule, we know that the head position must be an extreme, but which extreme depends on the previous head position.

The head position can be described by a Markov chain where the i-th state $(i=1,...,n)$ corresponds to having the head at location i. Such a chain is irreducible and aperiodic and hence approaches a unique steady state distribution, $s = (s_1,..,s_n)$. (For definitions of terms pertaining to Markov chains, see, for example, [10]. Note that s is a row vector.) This can be found by solving the equation $sP = s$, or equivalently, $s(P - I) = 0$, where P is the transition matrix of the chain, I is the identity matrix and 0 is a row vector of zeros.

Let p_{xy} = Prob (head ends up at y | head starts at x). Then the transition matrix is $P = [p_{xy}]$. To compute p_{xy}, recall that record R_i is at location i, and L, R are the left and right extremes respectively. Then we have

$$\text{for } x = y, \ p_{xy} = (p_x)^b,$$ (1.6.7)

$$\text{for } x<y, \ p_{xy} = \text{Prob}(R = y, L \geq 2x - y)$$

$$-\frac{1}{2}\text{Prob}(R = y, L = 2x - y),$$ (1.6.8)

$$\text{for } x>y, \ p_{xy} = \text{Prob}(L = y, R \leq 2x - y)$$

$$-\frac{1}{2}\text{Prob}(L = y, R = 2x - y).$$ (1.6.9)

Note that

$$\text{Prob}(L = u, R \leq r) = \left(\sum_{i=u}^{r} p_i\right)^b - \left(\sum_{i=u+1}^{r} p_i\right)^b,$$ (1.6.10)

$$\text{Prob}(L \geq u, R = r) = \left(\sum_{i=u}^{r} p_i\right)^b - \left(\sum_{i=u}^{r-1} p_i\right)^b$$ (1.6.11)

and

$$\text{Prob}(L = u, R = r) = \text{Prob}(L = u, R \leq r)$$

$$-\text{Prob}(L = u, R \le r - 1), \qquad (1.6.12)$$

where we consider $p_i = 0$ if $i < 1$ or $i > n$. Substituting (1.6.10), (1.6.11), (1.6.12) into (1.6.7), (1.6.8), (1.6.9) yields p_{xy} and hence the transition matrix P.

Note that if L and R are equidistant from x, the rule randomly chooses L or R with probability $\frac{1}{2}$. This is why the second terms in (1.6.8), (1.6.9) have to be subtracted; otherwise they are counted twice.

Although P assumes such a simple form, to solve for s symbolically appears intractable even for simple cases, such as a uniform distribution (i.e., $p_i = 1/n$, for all i). However, given a distribution, n, and b, the resulting system of equations is easily solved by computer using numerical techniques, giving s. Let COST_N be the cost of the Nearest rule. Then

$$\text{COST}_N = E(\text{RANGE}_b)$$

$$+ \sum_{i=1}^{n} \sum_{u \le r} s_i \cdot \text{Prob}(L = u, R = r) \cdot \min\,(\,|\,x - u\,|\,,\,|\,x - r\,|\,).$$

Such a calculation was done for several distributions, and the results are shown in Table 1.6.3. To simplify the computation, symmetric versions of Zipf's distribution,

$$p_i = p_{n-i+1} = 1/(2((n/2) - i + 1)H), \text{ where } H = \sum_{i=1}^{n/2} \frac{1}{i},$$

and the exponential distribution,

$$p_i = p_{n-i+1} = r^{(n/2)-i}/(1 - r^{n/2}) \text{ with } r = 0.9$$

were used. (Note that the records are in the organ-pipe arrangement.)

For comparison, we did the same calculation for the Leftist
and Alternating rules (Tables 1.6.1 and 1.6.2).

Table 1.6.1

Asymptotic cost for the Leftist rule

	n b	100	200	300
Uniform Zipf Expo	5	133.389 73.584 58.114	266.803 134.738 60.303	400.210 192.346 60.327
Uniform Zipf Expo	10	163.603 107.014 80.964	327.256 200.347 84.836	490.897 289.465 84.882
Uniform Zipf Expo	15	174.950 126.223 94.276	349.976 239.489 99.594	524.982 348.565 99.660

Table 1.6.2
Asymptotic cost for the Alternating rule

		n		
b		100	200	300
Uniform		81.802	163.628	245.449
Zipf	5	53.507	100.174	144.733
Expo		40.482	42.418	42.441
Uniform		90.443	180.936	271.418
Zipf	10	69.393	132.831	194.279
Expo		51.784	55.093	55.136
Uniform		93.498	187.072	280.629
Zipf	15	77.139	149.290	219.704
Expo		58.156	62.615	62.677

Table 1.6.3
Asymptotic cost for the Nearest rule

		n		
b		100	200	300
Uniform		80.753	161.529	242.299
Zipf	5	52.135	97.409	140.588
Expo		39.977	41.972	41.999
Uniform		90.408	180.869	271.317
Zipf	10	68.728	131.211	191.617
Expo		51.698	55.121	55.168
Uniform		93.498	187.070	280.626
Zipf	15	76.870	148.515	218.327
Expo		58.136	62.726	62.795

From these results and intuition, one would expect $COST_N \leq COST_A$ for all distributions, n, and b. Surprisingly, this is not the case. In Appendix 1.3, we show that there exists a distribution, n, and b such that $COST_N > COST_A$.

Whether or not the organ-pipe arrangement minimizes $COST_N$ is still an open question, but we strongly believe the answer is affirmative.

1.6.5. B-Optimal rules We propose a family of rules called B-optimal rules. When B=1, we have the Nearest rule. When B=∞, we have the optimal rule. The latter case will be discussed separately later since it requires a completely different approach.

Before proceeding further, it is worth mentioning why the Nearest rule is not optimal and what exactly the difficulty is in determining an optimal rule. Although successive batches are assumed to be independent, the final head position for accessing the current batch is the initial head position for the next batch. Some positions, namely, those near where we expect the extremes to be, are more "advantageous" as final head positions, as the expected cost for accessing the next batch will be smaller. An optimal rule must consider this effect in deciding how to access the current batch and must go to the extreme that is farther from the initial head position (rather than to the closer one) if the advantage of ending at the closer extreme outweighs the additional cost of moving to the farther extreme rather than to the closer one.

Consider the situation where the initial head location is x and exactly B batches of b records are to be accessed. A B-optimal rule is a rule which minimizes the expected total distance traveled by the head starting from x going through the B batches of requests. We define the cost of a B-optimal rule as the expected total distance divided by B.

Obviously, when $B=1$, if L and R are the left and right extremes respectively of the batch and x is the head location, then a 1-optimal rule would be to move the head from x to the closer of L and R and then sweep across to the other extreme if necessary. But this is exactly the Nearest rule.

Before we can show rules to be optimal, we have to define what is meant by "rule." The most general definition is that a rule gives a sequence of positions for the head to pass through, given the current head position and the extremes of the current and all previous batches. A rule may be "nondeterministic," giving probabilities that different sequences should be followed. The following lemmas restrict to a more manageable class the form a B-optimal rule can take.

Lemma 1.6.4 If a rule is B-optimal, then immediately after accessing all the records in a given batch, the head must be at an extreme.

Proof If the last record access is not an extreme, clearly records on both sides of this record (the two extremes) must have already been accessed and we must have already passed through this record to get from one side to the other. The move into this position can then be deleted, giving a rule of lower cost, a contradiction.

□

In the following lemma, the total cost for accessing the B batches is divided among the batches. The cost for accessing a batch begins immediately after the last record in the previous batch is accessed and ends immediately after the last record in this batch is accessed.

Lemma 1.6.5 If a rule is B-optimal, it must access a batch by moving directly to an extreme and then sweeping across to the other extreme (if necessary).

Proof Since all the records are accessed, both extremes must be accessed. Call the first extreme to be accessed the first extreme and the other the second extreme. If this rule is B-optimal, the first extreme can be accessed only once. Otherwise, a rule which behaves like this rule but deletes any movement between accesses to the first extreme will still access all the records (since both extremes are accessed) and have lower cost: a contradiction.

Thus, the rule must move to one extreme and then to the other. If it does not do so directly, a rule which does so will still access all records but have lower cost: again, a contradiction.

□

Lemma 1.6.6 For every rule whose decisions depend on previous batches, there is a rule with equal cost whose decisions depend only on the current batch.

Proof Since the batches are independent, a rule which ignores the previous batches will cost the same as one that does not.

□

Note that a rule satisfying the previous lemmas is expressible as a sequence, $d_B(x;s,r), d_{B-1}(x;s,r),...,d_1(x;s,r)$ of *decision functions*, where $d_i(x;s,r)$ is the probability that the rule moves left when its head is currently at x for accessing the i-th batch from the last batch with extremes s and r. A rule is *deterministic* if for every i,x,s and r, $d_i(x;s,r)$ is either zero or one. We now prove that nondeterministic rules are no better than deterministic rules.

Lemma 1.6.7 For every nondeterministic rule, there is a deterministic rule with smaller or equal cost.

Proof Let M be a nondeterministic rule with cost, $COST_M$. We show how to eliminate one nondeterministic decision. The process is then repeated until a deterministic rule is obtained. Choose any $d_i(x;s,r)$ which is neither zero nor one, and let $COST_L$ be the expected cost assuming a left move is made at $d_i(x;s,r)$ and $COST_R$ be that assuming a right move. Clearly,

$$COST_M = d_i(x;s,r) \cdot COST_L + (1 - d_i(x;s,r)) \cdot COST_R,$$

and at least one of $COST_L$ and $COST_R$ must be less than or equal to $COST_M$. Therefore, there is a rule, making a deterministic choice at $d_i(x;s,r)$, that has cost less than or equal to rule M. Continuing in this manner eventually results in a deterministic rule with cost less than or equal to $COST_M$.

□

Note that now all decision functions can be restricted to 0-1 function, meaning only a finite number of rules might possibly be B-optimal.

A final lemma guarantees that an optimal rule is optimal no matter what the initial head position is. This is important; conceivably one rule might be better than another from one position but poor from another.

Lemma 1.6.8 An optimal rule is optimal for every initial head position.

Proof (The proof is by induction on B.) For $B=0$, the proof is trivial, so consider any B and let $r_1,r_2,...,r_n$ be rules that are optimal from positions 1,2,...,n. These rules must all have the same cost if the first batch is not counted, because they must all use a $(B-1)$-optimal rule to access the remaining batches, which, by induction, is optimal for all head positions. A new rule which accesses the first batch using r_i when it starts at position i $(1 \leq i \leq n)$ and then uses a $(B-1)$-optimal rule to access the remaining batches will have the same cost as r_i when it starts at position i $(1 \leq i \leq n)$ and hence is optimal for all head positions.

$$\square$$

To define the class of B-optimal rules, we need a sequence of functions, $C_B(x)$ for $B=0,1,...$, defined by:

$$C_0(x) = 0 \text{ for } 1 \leq x \leq n,$$

$$C_B(x) = \sum_{s \leq r} \text{Prob}(L = s, R = r) \cdot \min \quad [\, |x - s| + C_{B-1}(r),$$
$$|x - r| + C_{B-1}(s)] + E(\text{RANGE}_b) \text{ for } 1 \leq x \leq n \text{ and } B=1,2,... .$$

Recursive rule. Let i be the number of batches remaining to be accessed and x the current head position. To access this batch, we have the following rule:

    (1) Move to the left extreme; then sweep across to the right if $|x - L| + C_{i-1}(R) < |x - R| + C_{i-1}(L)$.

    (2) Move to the right; then sweep left if $|x - L| + C_{i-1}(R) > |x - R| + C_{i-1}(L)$.

    (3) Do either if $|x - L| + C_{i-1}(R) = |x - R| + C_{i-1}(L)$.

The optimality of this rule and $C_B(x)$ is proven in the following theorem:

Theorem 1.6.6 $C_B(x)$ is the optimal cost for accessing B batches, with the head starting at x. The Recursive rule is indeed B-optimal. (Thus, it has cost $C_B(x)/B$.)

Proof (The proof is by induction on B.) For B=0, the proof is trivial. Assume then for all x that $C_B(x)$ is the optimal cost for accessing B batches from x and consider a rule accessing B+1 batches from some position y. By Lemmas 1.6.4 and 1.6.5, an optimal rule can access these batches only by either:

(1) moving to the left extreme, sweeping across to the right and then accessing the remaining B batches in an optimal manner with head starting at R (total cost is $|y - L| + E(RANGE_b) + C_B(R)$), or

(2) moving to the right initially (total cost is $|y - R| + E(RANGE_b) + C_B(L)$).

Since the (B+1)-optimal rule always chooses the option with the smallest cost, it must be optimal, and therefore $C_B(x)$ must be the optimal cost.

□

Several comments can be made on $C_B(x)$. First, it indicates how advantageous it is to have the head at a given position. The B-optimal rules take this into consideration when accessing a batch; a rule is willing to spend more than the minimum head movement on the current batch (by moving to the farther extreme first) if $C_B(x)$ indicates that the difference will be made up on subsequent batches. The shape of $C_B(x)$ is also quite interesting; at first glance one might expect the best position to be near the center of the storage. This, of course, is not the best, as is clearly shown by $C_B(x)$ (see Figure 1.6.1, where $C_1(x)$ for the uniform distribution with $n=100$ and $b=5$ is plotted). The best locations are near the edges (if b is not too small) because that is the probable location of the extremes.

A final note is that B-optimal rules are not necessarily good rules for accessing long sequences of batches, especially if B is small. Such rules pay too little attention to the position of the head, concentrating only on minimizing head movement. As an example, the

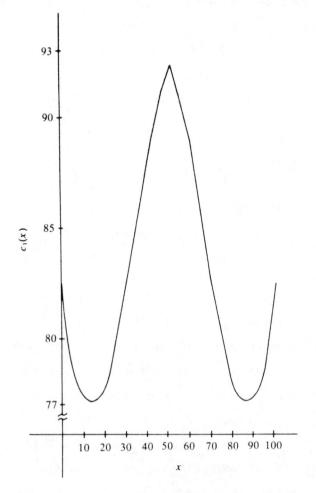

Figure 1.6.1

Nearest rule (a 1-optimal rule) can be outperformed by even the Alternating rule (see Appendix 1.3) if a large number of batches is to be retrieved.

1.6.6. An ∞-Optimal rule We now define and prove correct a procedure to calculate an ∞-optimal rule for any given arrangement $(R_1,..,R_n)$. An ∞-optimal rule is defined in a manner similar to the B-optimal rules. If $COST_B^r(x)$ is the cost of accessing B batches starting from head position x and using rule r, then the expected *asymptotic cost* of rule r $(COST(r))$ is defined to be $\lim_{B \to \infty} COST_B^r(x)/B$. An ∞-optimal rule has expected asymptotic cost which is less than or equal to that of any other rule.

We previously defined a rule for accessing B batches as a sequence of B decision functions. Though we could define a rule for accessing an infinite number of batches to be an infinite sequence of decision functions, we will restrict our attention to uniform rules that consist of one decision function, which is used to access all batches. It can, in fact, be proven that this restriction is not harmful; by considering only uniform rules we do find the ∞-optimal rule (over all rules). However, we omit the proof since it is long and technical. Besides, this fact is intuitively quite clear. Since the batches are independent and (unlike the case with a finite number of batches) each batch will have an infinite number following, there is no intuitive justification for using different decision functions for accessing two different batches.

We note in passing that the sequences of head positions for a uniform rule is described by a Markov chain which is closed and irreducible, and hence it approaches a steady state distribution. If p_i is the steady state probability that the head is at position i, and c_i is the expected cost of accessing a batch from position i, then the expected asymptotic cost is given by $\sum_{i=1}^{n} p_i c_i$. The fact that this is equivalent to the original definition can be shown in a manner similar to that used in Lemma 1.6.10. Note also that an ∞-optimal rule is optimal in the original sense, as described in Subsection 1.6.2.

To develop an algorithm to determine an ∞-optimal rule for a given set of probabilities, we use the idea of "discrete dynamic programming" developed by Blackwell [3].

The situation in discrete dynamic programming is as follows: we are given a system with T states (labeled 1,...,T). At any time, the system is in exactly one state. At intervals of time, we are required to choose any one of a given set of A actions (labeled 1,...,A) to be performed. The cost of performing action a in state t is given by c(t,a). (We will assume all costs are nonnegative.) After an action is performed, the system moves to a new state. The probability that action a will cause the system to move from state t to t' is denoted by $p(t \to t' \mid a)$. A decision function, f, is a function from $\{1,...,T\}$ into $\{1,...,A\}$ where f(t) specifies the action to be performed in state t. A policy $\pi = (f_1, f_2,...,)$ is a sequence of decision functions where f_i is used to determine the i-th decision.

The correspondence between this terminology and the original problem should be clear: a state corresponds to an ordered triple (x, ℓ, r), where x is the current head position and ℓ and r are the extremes of the current batch. There are only two actions: one for moving first to the left extreme and then sweeping across to the right, and another for moving right first. (Note that when we apply an action in a given state, only the x of the next state is determined: ℓ and r are chosen probabilistically.) The correspondence for costs and probabilities follows directly.

The procedure for calculating the ∞-optimal rule starts with an arbitrary rule (we choose the Nearest rule) and iteratively improves it. At each iteration we assume the current rule will be used to access all batches except the first and then calculate the best rule for accessing the first batch. A subsequent theorem shows that the asymptotic cost for this rule is less than or equal to that for the original rule. This new rule is then used on the next iteration, and we continue iterating until the new rule and the current rule are identical. The procedure for calculating the ∞-optimal rule is given below.

1. Make the Nearest rule the "current" rule.

2. Calculate $f_B(x)$ (the cost of accessing B batches with the head starting at position x) for the "current" rule. $f_B(x)$ is iteratively calculated for B=1,2,..., using the formula

$$f_0(x) = 0$$

$$f_B(x) = \sum_{\ell,r} \text{Prob}(L = \ell, R = r) \cdot \delta(x,\ell,r),$$

where

$$\delta(x,\ell,r) = \begin{cases} |x - \ell| + (r - \ell) + f_{B-1}(r) & \text{if the current rule goes to } \ell \text{ first with the head at } x \text{ and extremes } \ell \text{ and } r; \\ |x - r| + (r - \ell) + f_{B-1}(\ell) & \text{if it goes to r first.} \end{cases}$$

The calculation continues until we reach a B such that $f_B(x) - f_{B-1}(x)$ is nearly constant with respect to x.

3. Calculate the "new" rule as follows:
   For each x, ℓ and r, if

$$|x - r| - |x - \ell| + \lim_{B \to \infty} [f_B(\ell) - f_B(r)] < 0,$$

the "new" rule should move to the right extreme first with head at x and extremes ℓ and r. If this quantity is nonnegative, the rule should move left first. (Note that $\lim_{B \to \infty} [f_B(\ell) - f_B(r)]$ is closely approximated by $f_B(\ell) - f_B(r)$ for some large B.)

4.   If the new rule is the same as the current rule, stop. This rule is the ∞-optimal rule. Otherwise, set the "current rule" to be the "new rule" and go to step 2.

This procedure was used to find the ∞-optimal rule for several n and b. The results are shown in Table 1.6.4. The difference between the cost of the ∞-optimal rule and that of the Nearest rule is

Table 1.6.4

Table of cost for the ∞-optimal rule

assuming a uniform distribution

b \ n	100	200
5	80.713	161.452
10	90.394	180.839
15	93.496	187.067

extremely small (compare Tables 1.6.3 and 1.6.4); in all cases it is less than 0.05%. This, however, is to be expected for such large values of b. The extremes and the initial head position will almost always be near 1 and n, and an ∞-optimal rule will rarely have a chance to make a decision differing from that of the Nearest rule (moving to the farther extreme will rarely be "advantageous"). However, even if b is very small, the difference between the costs of the two rules is still very small. For n=100, b=2 and assuming a uniform distribution, the cost for the ∞-optimal rule is 54.971 as opposed to 55.036 for the Nearest rule, a difference of only .1%.

The correctness of this procedure is proven below. In these proofs, we need to distinguish between rules where one initially has lower cost, but asymptotically both have the same cost. Therefore, we need the following definition:

If c_i is the cost incurred at time i, the expected cost weighted by β (for $\beta<1$) is $\sum_{i=1}^{\infty} \beta^{i-1} c_i$.

The following notations are convenient:

Definition 1.6.1 If f is a decision function and π is a policy, then

$c(f)$ is the column vector whose i-th component is $c(i,f(i))$.

$p(t,a)$ is the row vector whose i-th component is $p(t \to i \mid a)$.

$Q(f)$ is the matrix whose (i,j)-th entry is $p(i \to j \mid f(i))$ (state transition matrix).

$w^{(\beta)}(\pi)$ is a column vector whose i-th component is the expected cost weighted by β for using policy π if the system is initially in state i. (When the dependence on β is not important, the superscript will be dropped.)

$w(f,\pi)$ will denote the vector of costs for using f followed by π.

We denote the i-th component of a vector x by x_i. We say $x \leq y$ if and only if $x_i \leq y_i$ for every i and $x < y$ if and only if $x \leq y$ and there exists an i such that $x_i < y_i$.

Let $f^{(n)}$ denote the (finite) policy where f is successively applied n times and $f^{(\infty)}$ the policy $(f,f,...)$. Note that in this notation, a policy π is uniform if and only if $\pi = f^{(\infty)}$ for some f.

Finally, if $\pi = (f_1,f_2,...)$, let shift (π) denote the policy $(f_2,f_3,...)$.

Lemma 1.6.9 Let $\pi = (f_1,f_2,...)$ be a policy; then $w(\pi) = c(f_1) + \beta Q(f_1)w$ (shift (π)).

Proof The (n-1)-step transition matrix is given by $Q(f_1)Q(f_2)...Q(f_{n-1})$, and multiplying by $c(f_n)$ will give the vector of cost for the n-th decision. Hence

$$w(\pi) = \sum_{n=1}^{\infty} \beta^{n-1} \cdot (Q(f_1)Q(f_2)...Q(f_{n-1}))c(f_n).$$

Then

$$w(\text{shift}(\pi)) = \sum_{n=1}^{\infty} \beta^{n-1}(Q(f_2)Q(f_3)...Q(f_n))c(f_{n+1}),$$

and the lemma clearly follows.

□

Theorem 1.6.7 Let f be a decision function and π a policy; then

(a) If $w(f,\pi) < w(\pi)$, then $w(f^{(\infty)}) < w(\pi)$

(b) If $w(f,\pi) > w(\pi)$, then $w(f^{(\infty)}) > w(\pi)$, and

(a)' and (b)': (a) and (b) also hold if < and > are replaced by $\leq$ and $\geq$ respectively.

Proof We first prove by induction that

   Claim: $w(f^{(n+1)}, \pi) < w(f^{(n)}, \pi)$ for all $n \geq 1$.

For $n = 1$, use Lemma 1.6.9 to obtain

$$w(f^{(1)}, \pi) = c(f) + \beta Q(f) w(\pi), \quad w(f^{(2)}, \pi) = c(f) + \beta Q(f) w(f, \pi).$$

By hypothesis, $w(f, \pi) < w(\pi)$, and since all entries in $Q(f)$ are nonnegative, we conclude that $Q(f) w(f, \pi) < Q(f) w(\pi)$ and hence $w(f^{(2)}, \pi) < w(f^{(1)}, \pi)$. The inductive step is proved in exactly the same manner, establishing the claim.

   By applying Lemma 1.6.9 n times, we obtain

$$w(f^{(n)}, \pi) = \sum_{i=1}^{n} \beta^{i-1} Q^i(f) c(f) + \beta^n w(\pi)$$

for any n. Since $\beta^{i-1} Q^i(f) c(f)$ is nonnegative for all i, the summation is monotonically nondecreasing with respect to n. Hence it obviously has $w(f^{(\infty)}) = \sum_{i=1}^{\infty} \beta^{i-1} Q(f) c(f)$ as its limit as $n \to \infty$. Since $\beta < 1$, the second term approaches zero, and therefore, $\lim_{n \to \infty} w(f^{(n)}, \pi) = w(f^{(\infty)})$. From the claim, $w(f^{(n)}, \pi)$ is decreasing with n. Hence, $w(f^{(\infty)}) < w(f, \pi) < w(\pi)$, proving (a). The proof of (b) is identical except that all inequalities are reversed. Finally, (a)$'$ and (b)$'$ are proved by noting that if $w(f, \pi) = w(\pi)$, then $w(f^{(\infty)}) = w(\pi)$ (again, a simple proof by induction).

$\square$

Lemma 1.6.10 For any two policies $f^{(\infty)}$ and $g^{(\infty)}$, the following holds:

If $\lim_{\beta \to 1} [w_t^{(\beta)}(g^{(\infty)}) - w_t^{(\beta)}(f^{(\infty)})] \geq 0$ for all t, then $COST(g^{(\infty)}) \geq COST(f^{(\infty)})$.

Proof Consider any state t and let $c_i(f)$ and $c_i(g)$ be the cost of applying $f^{(\infty)}$ and $g^{(\infty)}$ respectively at time i, starting in state t. We have then $\lim_{\beta \to 1} \left[\sum_{i=1}^{\infty} \beta^{i-1}(c_i(g) - c_i(f)) \right] \geq 0$. Letting x_f and x_g be the steady state costs for $f^{(\infty)}$ and $g^{(\infty)}$, we decompose the cost into steady state and transient parts.

$$c_i(f) = x_f - \delta_i(f); \quad c_i(g) = x_g - \delta_i(g).$$

Using the theory of Markov chains, it can be shown that the δ_i can be written in the following form:

$$\delta_i(f) = p_1(i)\lambda_1^i + p_2(i)\lambda_2^i + ... + p_k(i)\lambda_k^i,$$

where each p_j is a polynomial in i and each λ_j is a complex number with modulus strictly less than one. It is easily seen that $\sum_{i=1}^{\infty} \delta_i(f)$ and $\sum_{i=1}^{\infty} \delta_i(g)$ do not diverge to $\pm\infty$. Therefore,

$$\lim_{\beta \to 1} \left[\sum_{i=1}^{\infty} \beta^{i-1}(c_i(g) - c_i(f)) \right]$$

$$= \lim_{\beta \to 1} \left[\sum_{i=1}^{\infty} \beta^{i-1}(x_g - x_f) - \sum_{i=1}^{\infty} \beta^{i-1}(\delta_i(g) - \delta_i(f)) \right].$$

We now claim that $x_g \geq x_f$. Otherwise, $x_g < x_f$ and the first term in the above approaches $-\infty$, while the second is bounded, violating the assumption that the limit is nonnegative.

Now consider $COST(g^{(\infty)}) - COST(f^{(\infty)})$. By definition, this equals

$$\lim_{B \to \infty} \frac{\sum_{i=1}^{B} c_i(g) - c_i(f)}{B} = \lim_{B \to \infty} \frac{(\sum_{i=1}^{B} x_g - x_f) - (\sum_{i=1}^{B} \delta_i(g) - \delta_i(f))}{B}.$$

Since the second term is bounded, this equals $x_g - x_f$, which is nonnegative. Hence $COST(g^{(\infty)}) \geq COST(f^{(\infty)})$.

$\square$

We now define an algorithm for calculating the ∞-optimal rule. The strategy is one of iterative improvement; we begin with any policy $f^{(\infty)}$ and then calculate for each state the cost of performing a given action at the first time instant, assuming that $f^{(\infty)}$ will be used thereafter. This defines for each state t a set $Impr(t,f)$ of actions that is an improvement upon performing $f(t)$ at the first time instant. This gives rise to a policy $(g,f^{(\infty)})$ which is better than $f^{(\infty)}$. Theorem 1.6.6 guarantees that $g^{(\infty)}$ is better than $f^{(\infty)}$, and we therefore use $g^{(\infty)}$ for our next iteration. This process continues until $Impr(t,f) = \phi$ for every t. In this case, $f^{(\infty)}$ is the optimal rule.

The formula for calculating $Impr(t,f)$ is given in the following theorem. To determine if action a is an improvement over $f(t)$, we calculate for every pair of states x and y the probability that a will send the system to state x and $f(t)$ will send it to state y, multiplied by "advantage" of starting in state x over state y when using policy $f^{(\infty)}$. This is summed over pairs, and $c(t,a) - c(t,f(t))$ is added to reflect the difference in cost between performing action a and $f(t)$. If the result is negative, a will be an improvement over $f(t)$.

Theorem 1.6.8 Let $Impr(f,t) = \{a \mid [c(t,a) - c(t,f(t))] +$
$[\sum_{x,y} p(t \to x \mid f(t)) \cdot p(t \to y \mid a) \cdot \lim_{\beta \to 1} [w_x^{(\beta)}(f^{(\infty)}) - w_y^{(\beta)}(f^{(\infty)})]] < 0\};$
then

(1) If $\text{Impr}(t,f)=\phi$ for all t, then f is optimal.

(2) If for some t $\text{Impr}(t,f)\neq\phi$, then any g such that for all t either $g(t)=f(t)$ or $g(t)\in\text{Impr}(t,f)$ will have $\text{COST}(g^{(\infty)})\leq\text{COST}(f^{(\infty)})$.

Proof We begin by establishing the following claim: The condition in the theorem is equivalent to

$$\lim_{\beta\to 1}\left[w_t^{(\beta)}(g,f^{(\infty)})-w_t^{(\beta)}(f^{(\infty)})\right]<0.$$

Proof of Claim Expanding each term by Lemma 1.6.9 gives

$$\lim_{\beta\to 1}[w_t^{(\beta)}(g,f^{(\infty)})-w_t^{(\beta)}(f^{(\infty)})]$$

$$=\lim_{\beta\to 1}[c(t,a)+\beta p(t,a)w^{(\beta)}(f^{(\infty)})$$

$$-[c(t,f(t))+\beta p(t,f(t))w^{(\beta)}(f^{(\infty)})]]$$

$$=\lim_{\beta\to 1}[[c(t,a)-c(t,f(t))]+\beta[p(t,a)-p(t,f(t))]w^{(\beta)}(f^{(\infty)})].$$

Expanding the product of **p** and **w** gives that the above equals

$$\lim_{\beta\to 1}\{[c(t,a)-c(t,f(t))]$$

$$+\beta\sum_x p(t\to x\mid f(t))\cdot w_x^{(\beta)}(f^{(\infty)})-\beta\sum_y p(t\to y\mid a)\cdot w_y^{(\beta)}(f^{(\infty)})\}$$

Multiplying the first summation by $\Sigma_y p(t\to y\mid a)(=1)$ and the second by $\Sigma_x p(t\to x\mid f(t))$ and then combining the two sums gives that the above equals

$$\lim_{\beta\to 1}\{[c(t,a)-c(t,f(t))]$$

$$+ \beta \sum_{x,y} p(t \to x \mid f(t)) p(t \to y \mid a) \cdot [w_x^{(\beta)}(f^{(\infty)}) - w_y^{(\beta)}(f^{(\infty)})]\},$$

proving the claim.

To prove part (1) of the theorem, consider any decision function, g, and suppose $Impr(t,f) = \phi$ for all t. This means that

$$\lim_{\beta \to 1} [w_t^{(\beta)}(g,f^{(\infty)}) - w_t^{(\beta)}(f^{(\infty)})] \geq 0 \text{ for all t.}$$

Hence there is a β_0 such that

$$w_t^{(\beta)}(g,f^{(\infty)}) - w_t^{(\beta)}(f^{(\infty)}) \geq 0$$

for all t and all β such that $\beta_0 < \beta < 1$. Theorem 1.6.6 then implies that

$$w_t^{(\beta)}(g^{(\infty)}) - w_t^{(\beta)}(f^{(\infty)}) \geq 0$$

for all t and all β such that $\beta_0 < \beta < 1$. Hence $\lim_{\beta \to 1} [w_t^{(\beta)}(g^{(\infty)}) - w_t^{(\beta)}(f^{(\infty)})] \geq 0$ for all t, and Lemma 1.6.10 implies $COST(g^{(\infty)}) \geq COST(f^{(\infty)})$ for any g, and hence $f^{(\infty)}$ is optimal.

To prove part (2) of the theorem, consider the t-th component of any g satisfying the restrictions of part (2). Either (a) g(t) = f(t), in which case $w_t^{(\beta)}(g,f^{(\infty)}) = w_t^{(\beta)}(f^{(\infty)})$ for all $\beta < 1$ and by Lemma 1.6.9, $w_t^{(\beta)}(g^{(\infty)}) \leq w_t^{(\beta)}(f^{(\infty)})$, or (b) $g(t) \in Impr(t,f)$, in which case $\lim_{\beta \to 1} [w_t^{(\beta)}(g,f^{(\infty)}) - w_t^{(\beta)}(f^{(\infty)})] < 0$, implying in a manner like that in the proof of part (1) that $w_t^{(\beta)}(g^{(\infty)}) \leq w_t^{(\beta)}(f^{(\infty)})$. In either case, Lemma 1.6.10 proves that $COST(g^{(\infty)}) \leq COST(f^{(\infty)})$.

□

A more complete list of references for this chapter is given in Section 1.8.

1.7. Appendix 1.1. Another application of vector majorization and Schur function

Consider an m-page program whose pages constitute the set $\{1,2,...,m\}$. Let $\{r_t\}$, $t = 0,\pm1,\pm2,...$ be the program's (page) reference string. $r_t = i$ means that page i is referenced at the t-th reference. Further assume that page i is referenced with probability q_i, $\sum_{i=1}^{m} q_i = 1$, and the references are independently generated. Let N be a given parameter, called the window size. Let $k(\mathbf{q};N,t)$ be the number of distinct values of the set $\{r_{t-N+1},...,r_{t-1},r_t\}$, i.e., the number of distinct pages referenced during the window ending at t. Then $k(\mathbf{q};N,t)$ is a random variable. Since its distribution is independent of t, we can write it as $k(\mathbf{q};N)$ or just $k(\mathbf{q})$. The expected value of $k(\mathbf{q})$ is a measure of locality. For a thorough treatment of memory management, we refer to [5].

Here we are interested mainly in the behavior of this locality measure as a function of the reference probability. A monotonicity property will be proved.

Theorem A.1.1 Let the expected value of $k(\mathbf{q})$ as a function of $\mathbf{q} = (q_1,...,q_m)$ be denoted $E(k(\mathbf{q}))$. Then

$$E(k(\mathbf{q})) \leq E(k(\mathbf{p}))$$

if $\mathbf{q}$ majorizes $\mathbf{p}$, i.e., more skewed reference probabilities imply higher locality.

Proof We can rephrase the problem in terms of the following experiment:

1) Let the set of possible outcomes be $\{1,2,...,m\}$.
2) Outcome i occurs with probability q_i, $\sum_{i=1}^{m} q_i = 1$.

3) N is the number of experiments.

4) $k(\mathbf{q})$ is the number of distinct outcomes.

Let U_i be a random variable defined by

$$U_i = \begin{cases} 1 & \text{if i occurs in one of the N experiments;} \\ 0 & \text{otherwise.} \end{cases}$$

Then

$$k(\mathbf{q}) = \sum_{i=1}^{m} U_i.$$

$$E(k(\mathbf{q})) = \sum_{i=1}^{m} E(U_i)$$

$$= \sum_{i=1}^{m} \Pr[U_i = 1]$$

$$= \sum_{i=1}^{m} \{1 - (1 - q_i)^N\}$$

$$= m - \sum_{i=1}^{m} (1 - q_i)^N$$

Now $\phi(x) = (1 - x)^N$ is convex since

$$\phi'(x) = -N(1 - x)^{N-1}$$

and $\phi''(x) = N(N - 1)(1 - x) \geq 0$

for $0 \leq x \leq 1$.

Thus, by Theorem 1.3.2,

$$\sum_{i=1}^{m} (1 - q_i)^N \geq \sum_{i=1}^{m} (1 - p_i)^N$$

if **q** majorizes **p**. In other words,

$$E(k(\mathbf{q})) \leq E(k(\mathbf{p}))$$

if **q** majorizes **p**.

□

Appendix 1.2. Details of the proof of Theorem 1.4.3

Equation (1.4.37) can be rewritten as

$E(f_j \mid r,s,r<s,m,p)$

$$= \sum_{q=0}^{s-1-r} \frac{\binom{j-2-m-p}{q}\binom{n-j-r+1+m+p}{s-r-1-q}}{\binom{n-r-1}{s-r-1}}$$

$$\cdot \left[\frac{j-2-m-p-q}{n-s+1} + \frac{1}{2(n-s+1)} \right]. \tag{A1.2.1}$$

Using the identities

$$(a - \ell)\binom{a}{\ell} = a\binom{a-1}{\ell} \tag{A1.2.2}$$

and

$$\sum_{\ell=0}^{c} \binom{a}{\ell}\binom{b}{c-\ell} = \binom{a+b}{c} \tag{A1.2.3}$$

and simplifying yields,

$$E(f_j \mid r,s,r<s,m,p) = \frac{(n-s)(j-2-m-p)}{(n-r-1)(n-s+1)} + \frac{1}{2(n-s+1)}. \quad (A1.2.4)$$

Substituting back into (1.4.36) and again using the identity (A1.2.2), we have $E(f_i f_j \mid r,s,r<s)$

$$= \sum_{m=0}^{r-1} \sum_{p=0}^{r-1-m} \frac{(i-1)\binom{i-2}{m}\binom{j-i-1}{p}\binom{n-j}{r-1-m-p}}{(n-r+1)\binom{n-2}{r-1}}$$

$$\cdot \left[\frac{(n-s)(j-2-m-p)}{(n-s+1)(n-r-1)} + \frac{1}{2(n-s+1)} \right]$$

$$+ \sum_{m=0}^{r-1} \sum_{p=0}^{r-1-m} \frac{\binom{i-1}{m}\binom{j-i-1}{p}\binom{n-j}{r-1-m-p}}{2(n-r+1)\binom{n-2}{r-1}}$$

$$\cdot \left[\frac{(n-s)(j-2-m-p)}{(n-s+1)(n-r-1)} + \frac{1}{2(n-s+1)} \right]. \quad (A1.2.5)$$

The following results are easily verified:

$$\sum_{m=0}^{r-1} \sum_{p=0}^{r-1-m} \frac{(i-1)\binom{i-2}{m}\binom{j-i-1}{p}\binom{n-j}{r-1-m-p}}{(n-r+1)\binom{n-2}{r-1}}$$

$$= \frac{(i-1)(n-r-1)}{(n-r+1)(n-2)}, \quad (A1.2.6)$$

$$\sum_{m=0}^{r-1}\sum_{p=0}^{r-1-m} \frac{\binom{i-1}{m}\binom{j-i-1}{p}\binom{n-j}{r-1-m-p}}{2(n-r+1)\binom{n-2}{r-1}} = \frac{1}{2(n-r+1)},$$

(A1.2.7)

$$\sum_{m=0}^{r-1}\sum_{p=0}^{r-1-m} \frac{(m+p)(i-1)\binom{i-2}{m}\binom{j-i-1}{p}\binom{n-j}{r-1-m-p}}{(n-r+1)\binom{n-2}{r-1}}$$

$$= \frac{(i-1)(j-3)(r-1)(n-r-1)}{(n-r+1)(n-2)(n-3)},$$

(A1.2.8)

$$\sum_{m=0}^{r-1}\sum_{p=0}^{r-1-m} \frac{(m+p)\binom{i-1}{m}\binom{j-i-1}{p}\binom{n-j}{r-1-m-p}}{2(n-r+1)\binom{n-2}{r-1}}$$

$$= \frac{(j-2)(r-1)}{2(n-r+1)(n-2)}.$$

(A1.2.9)

Substituting (A1.2.6), (A1.2.7), (A1.2.8) and (A1.2.9) into (A1.2.5), we have

$$E(f_i f_j \mid r,s,r<s)$$

$$= \left[\frac{(n-s)(j-2)}{(n-s+1)(n-r-1)} + \frac{1}{2(n-s+1)} \right]$$

$$\cdot \left[\frac{(i-1)(n-r-1)}{(n-r+1)(n-2)} + \frac{1}{2(n-r+1)} \right]$$

$$-\frac{(n-s)}{(n-s+1)(n-r-1)}\cdot\frac{(i-1)(j-3)(r-1)(n-r-1)}{(n-r+1)(n-2)(n-3)}$$

$$-\frac{(n-s)}{(n-s+1)(n-r-1)}\cdot\frac{(j-2)(r-1)}{2(n-r+1)(n-2)}. \tag{A1.2.10}$$

After elementary algebraic manipulation, (A1.2.10) can be recast in the form

$E(f_i f_j \mid r,s,r<s)$

$$=\frac{1}{2(n-s+1)}\left[\frac{(i-1)(n-r-1)}{(n-r+1)(n-2)}+\frac{1}{2(n-r+1)}\right]$$

$$+\frac{n-s}{(n-s+1)(n-r+1)}$$

$$\left[\frac{j-2}{2(n-2)}+\frac{(i-1)(j-2)(n-r-2)}{(n-2)(n-3)}+\frac{(i-1)(r-1)}{(n-2)(n-3)}\right].$$

$$\tag{A1.2.11}$$

The following form is more convenient for later summation on r and s:

$E(f_i f_j \mid r,s,r<s)$

$$=\left[\frac{(i-1)(j-2)}{(n-2)(n-3)}-\frac{i-1}{(n-2)(n-3)}\right]$$

$$+\frac{1}{n-r+1}\left[\frac{(j-2)}{2(n-2)}-\frac{3(i-1)(j-2)}{(n-2)(n-3)}+\frac{n(i-1)}{(n-2)(n-3)}\right]$$

$$+\frac{1}{n-s+1}\left[\frac{(i-1)}{2(n-2)}-\frac{(i-1)(j-2)}{(n-2)(n-3)}+\frac{(i-1)}{(n-2)(n-3)}\right]$$

$$+ \frac{1}{(n-s+1)(n-r+1)}$$

$$\cdot \left[\frac{1}{4} - \frac{i-1}{n-2} - \frac{j-2}{2(n-2)} + \frac{3(i-1)(j-2)}{(n-2)(n-3)} - \frac{n(i-1)}{(n-2)(n-3)} \right]$$

$$(A1.2.12)$$

We now consider the case r>s. The general outline is the same as the case r<s. Therefore, we simply list the counterparts of (1.4.36), (1.4.37), (A1.2.4), (A1.2.10) and (A1.2.12):

$$E(f_i f_j \mid r,s,r>s) = \sum_{m=0}^{s-1} \sum_{p=0}^{s-1-m} \frac{\binom{i-1}{m}\binom{j-i-1}{p}\binom{n-j}{s-1-m-p}}{\binom{n-2}{s-1}}$$

$$\cdot \frac{1}{2}\left(\frac{j-1-m-p}{n-s+1} + \frac{j-m-p}{n-s+1} \right) E(f_j \mid r,s,r>s,m,p), \quad (A1.2.13)$$

$$E(f_j \mid r,s,r>s,m,p) = \sum_{q=0}^{r-s-1} \frac{\binom{i-1-m}{q}\binom{n-i-s+m}{r-s-1-q}}{\binom{n-s-1}{r-s-1}}$$

$$\cdot \frac{1}{2}\left[\frac{i-1-m-q}{n-r+1} + \frac{i-m-q}{n-r+1} \right] \qquad (A1.2.14)$$

$$= \frac{(i-1-m)(n-r)}{(n-r+1)(n-s-1)} + \frac{1}{2(n-r+1)}, \qquad (A1.2.15)$$

$$E(f_i f_j \mid r,s,r>s) = \left[\frac{j-1}{n-s+1} + \frac{1}{2(n-s+1)} \right]$$

$$\cdot \left[\frac{(i-1)(n-r)}{(n-r+1)(n-2)} + \frac{1}{2(n-r+1)} \right]$$

$$- \frac{(i-1)(n-r)(j-3)(s-1)}{(n-r+1)(n-s+1)(n-2)(n-3)}$$

$$- \frac{(j-2)(s-1)}{2(n-r+1)(n-s+1)(n-2)}, \qquad \text{(A1.2.16)}$$

$$E(f_i f_j \mid r,s,r>s) = \frac{(i-1)(j-1) - 2(i-1)}{(n-2)(n-3)}$$

$$+ \frac{1}{n-r+1} \left[\frac{2(i-1)}{(n-2)(n-3)} \right.$$

$$\left. - \frac{(i-1)(j-1)}{(n-2)(n-3)} + \frac{j-1}{2(n-2)} - \frac{1}{2(n-2)} \right]$$

$$+ \frac{1}{n-s+1} \left[\frac{i-1}{2(n-2)} \right.$$

$$\left. - \frac{3(i-1)(j-1)}{(n-2)(n-3)} + \frac{2n(i-1)}{(n-2)(n-3)} \right]$$

$$+ \frac{1}{(n-r+1)(n-s+1)}$$

$$\cdot \left[\frac{3(i-1)(j-1)}{(n-2)(n-3)} - \frac{2n(i-1)}{(n-2)(n-3)} \right.$$

$$+ \frac{n - 2(j-1)}{2(n-2)} + \frac{1}{4} - \frac{(i-1)}{2(n-2)} \Bigg] . \qquad \text{(A1.2.17)}$$

To perform the indicated summations on r and s, we need the following results:

$$\sum_{r=1}^{n-1} \sum_{s=r+1}^{n} 1 = \sum_{r=s+1}^{n} \sum_{s=1}^{n-1} 1 = (n^2 - n)/2, \qquad \text{(A1.2.18)} .$$

$$\sum_{r=1}^{n-1} \sum_{s=r+1}^{n} \frac{1}{n-r+1}$$

$$= \sum_{r=s+1}^{n} \sum_{s=1}^{n-1} \frac{1}{n-s+1} = \sum_{r=1}^{n-1} \frac{n-r}{n-r+1} = n - H_n, \qquad \text{(A1.2.19)}$$

where

$$H_n = \sum_{\ell=1}^{n} \frac{1}{\ell}, \qquad \text{(A1.2.20)}$$

$$\sum_{r=1}^{n-1} \sum_{s=r+1}^{n} \frac{1}{n-s+1} = \sum_{r=s+1}^{n} \sum_{s=1}^{n-1} \frac{1}{n-r+1}$$

$$= \sum_{r=1}^{s-1} \sum_{s=2}^{n} \frac{1}{n-s+1}$$

$$= \sum_{s=2}^{n} \frac{s-1}{n-s+1} = nH_n - n, \qquad \text{(A1.2.21)}$$

$$\sum_{r=1}^{n-1} \sum_{s=r+1}^{n} \frac{1}{(n-r+1)(n-s+1)} = \sum_{r=s+1}^{n} \sum_{s=1}^{n-1} \frac{1}{(n-r+1)(n-s+1)}$$

$$= \frac{1}{2}\left[\left(\sum_{r=1}^{n}\frac{1}{n-r+1}\right)^2 - \sum_{r=1}^{n}\left(\frac{1}{n-r+1}\right)^2\right]$$

$$= \frac{1}{2}\left(H_n^2 - H_n^{(2)}\right), \tag{A1.2.22}$$

where

$$H_n^{(2)} = \sum_{\ell=1}^{n}\frac{1}{\ell^2}. \tag{A1.2.23}$$

Substituting (A1.2.12) and (A1.2.17) into (A1.2.35), noting that the times for a location to fill are all equally likely so that the probability of a particular pair of times is $(n(n-1))^{-1}$, and using (A1.2.18), (A1.2.19), (A1.2.20) and (A1.2.21), we obtain

$$E(f_i f_j) = \frac{n^2 - n}{2n(n-1)}\left[\frac{(i-1)(j-2)}{(n-2)(n-3)} - \frac{(i-1)}{(n-2)(n-3)}\right.$$

$$+ \frac{(i-1)(j-1)}{(n-2)(n-3)} - \frac{2(i-1)}{(n-2)(n-3)}\right]$$

$$+ \frac{(n-H_n)}{n(n-1)}\left[\frac{j-2}{2(n-2)} - \frac{3(i-1)(j-2)}{(n-2)(n-3)}\right.$$

$$+ \frac{n(i-1)}{(n-2)(n-3)} + \frac{i-1}{2(n-2)}$$

$$- \frac{3(i-1)(j-1)}{(n-2)(n-3)} + \frac{2n(i-1)}{(n-2)(n-3)}\right]$$

$$+ \frac{(nH_n - n)}{n(n-1)} \left[\frac{i-1}{2(n-2)} - \frac{(i-1)(j-2)}{(n-2)(n-3)} \right.$$

$$+ \frac{(i-1)}{(n-2)(n-3)} + \frac{2(i-1)}{(n-2)(n-3)}$$

$$- \frac{(i-1)(j-1)}{(n-2)(n-3)} + \frac{j-2}{2(n-2)} \right]$$

$$+ \frac{(H_n^2 - H_n^{(2)})}{2n(n-1)} \left[\frac{1}{4} - \frac{i-1}{n-2} - \frac{j-2}{2(n-2)} \right.$$

$$+ \frac{3(i-1)(j-2)}{(n-2)(n-3)} - \frac{n(i-1)}{(n-2)(n-3)}$$

$$+ \frac{1}{4} - \frac{i-1}{2(n-2)} + \frac{3(i-1)(j-1)}{(n-2)(n-3)} - \frac{2n(i-1)}{(n-2)(n-3)} + \frac{n-2(j-1)}{2(n-2)} \right].$$

$$(A1.2.24)$$

After some routine algebraic manipulation, (A1.2.24) can be recast in the form

$$E(f_i f_j)$$

$$= \frac{ij}{n(n-1)} \left[\frac{2n^2 - 10n}{2(n-2)(n-3)} - \frac{4H_n(n-3)}{2(n-2)(n-3)} + \frac{12(H_n^2 - H_n^{(2)})}{4(n-2)(n-3)} \right]$$

$$+ \frac{i}{n(n-1)} \left[\frac{12n}{2(n-2)(n-3)} \right.$$

$$+ \frac{H_n(n^2 + 2n - 15)}{2(n-2)(n-3)} - \frac{9(n+1)(H_n^2 - H_n^{(2)})}{4(n-2)(n-3)} \Bigg]$$

$$+ \frac{j}{n(n-1)} \Bigg[\frac{-2n^2 + 10n}{2(n-2)(n-3)} \Bigg.$$

$$+ \frac{H_n(n^2 - 9)}{2(n-2)(n-3)} - \frac{3(n+1)(H_n^2 - H_n^{(2)})}{4(n-2)(n-3)} \Bigg]$$

$$+ \frac{1}{n(n-1)} \Bigg[\frac{-12n}{2(n-2)(n-3)} - \frac{H_n(3n^2 - 6n - 9)}{2(n-2)(n-3)} \Bigg.$$

$$+ \frac{(2n^2 + 5n + 3)(H_n^2 - H_n^{(2)})}{4(n-2)(n-3)} \Bigg]. \tag{A1.2.25}$$

Substituting this expression for $E(f_i f_j)$ into the version of the lemma given by (1.4.13) and using (1.4.14), (1.4.15) and (1.4.16) to evaluate the sums gives

$$E(D_h) \approx \frac{12}{n^2(n-1)(3n+1)}$$

$$\cdot \Bigg\{ \frac{(n^2 - 1)(14n^3 + 35n^2 + 24n + 15)}{240}$$

$$\cdot \Bigg[\frac{2n(n-5)}{2(n-2)(n-3)} - \frac{4H_n}{2(n-2)} + \frac{12(H_n^2 - H_n^{(2)})}{4(n-2)(n-3)} \Bigg]$$

$$+ \frac{(n^2 - 1)(7n^2 + 8n + 3)}{48} \Bigg[\frac{-2n(n-11)}{2(n-2)(n-3)} \Bigg.$$

$$+ \frac{H_n(2n+8)}{2(n-2)} - \frac{12(n+1)(H_n^2-H_n^{(2)})}{4(n-2)(n-3)} \Bigg]$$

$$+ \frac{(n^2-1)n}{3} \Bigg[\frac{-12n}{2(n-2)(n-3)} - \frac{H_n(3n+3)}{2(n-2)}$$

$$+ \frac{(2n^2+5n+3)(H_n^2-H_n^{(2)})}{4(n-2)(n-3)} \Bigg] \Bigg\}. \qquad \text{(A1.2.26)}$$

Collecting terms yields

$$E(D_h) \approx \frac{12(n+1)(14n^4-70n^3+194n^2-160n+90)}{240n(3n+1)(n-2)(n-3)}$$

$$+ \frac{6(n+1)H_n(7n^3-10n^2+7n+30)}{120n^2(3n+1)(n-2)}$$

$$- \frac{3(n+1)(H_n^2-H_n^{(2)})(23n^2+20n+33)}{120n(3n+1)(n-2)(n-3)}, \qquad \text{(A1.2.27)}$$

as required.

Appendix 1.3. Proof of claim

Claim There exists a distribution, n, and b such that $\text{COST}_N > \text{COST}_A$.

Proof We consider an arrangement of 2x records, where the only records with nonzero probability are at positions 1, x and 2x. In addition, we add the restrictions that $p_1 = p_x$. Therefore, specifying one of the three nonzero probabilities (say p_1) will determine them all. Thus, there are three parameters that can be independently varied: x, b and p_1. Later we will choose x and b to be large, and p_{2x} to be small.

Let us reason intuitively why the Nearest rule should have a higher cost than the Alternating rule for this arrangement. Since $p_1 = p_x \approx \frac{1}{2}$ and b is large, the only batches with significant probability are {1,x} (called a *nonfull* batch), and {1,x,2x} (a *full* batch), with the former being much more probable. Since {1,x} is nearly always the received batch, having the head at position 2x is significantly disadvantageous, and the Nearest rule has a much higher probability of being at position 2x. The Alternating rule will be at 2x if and only if its head is currently at 1 and the batch {1,x,2x} is received. The Nearest rule will also move its head to 2x in this case. In addition, it will move to 2x when its head is currently at x and {1,x,2x} is received. (It moves to 1 first since it is closer, and then ends at 2x. The Alternating rule is at x, a right extreme, and hence will move to 2x first, ending at 1.) This argument is a simplification of the actual situation but does motivate the chosen arrangement. The following formalizes this argument.

During the initial analysis, we assume the only possible batches are {1,x} and {1,x,2x}. At the conclusion, we show that other batches can be made so improbable that they can be safely ignored. Let ε be the probability of a full batch. That is,

ε = Prob(batch is {1,x,2x} | batch is {1,x} or {1,x,2x})

$$= [1 - (2p_1)^b - (1 - p_1)^b + p_1^b]/[1 - p_1^b - (1 - p_1)^b],$$

where $0 < p_1 < \frac{1}{2}$. For any b, ε ranges continuously over (0,1) for values of p_1 in $(0, \frac{1}{2})$. We now fix ε at any arbitrary value in (0,1). Later, when b is chosen, p_1 must also be chosen to give the desired value for ε.

Consider the two rules acting on the given arrangement, with their heads starting at the same position. It is easy to see that their movement will be exactly the same until both heads are at position x, the Alternating rule is at a right extreme and a full batch appears. In this case, the Alternating rule moves right first and then left, and the Nearest rule does exactly the opposite. We now analyze the difference in the costs of the two rules for accessing the batches until the heads are again at the same position.

We define a Markov chain of 5 states with the following specifications:

If the heads are at the same position, the chain is in state 0. The other states are defined by:

State	Position for Alternating Rule	Position for Nearest Rule
1	1	2x
2	2x	1
3	1	x
4	x	1

Note that any other pair of head positions is impossible and that if the Alternating rule is at x, it is known to be a right extreme (resulting from the batch {1,x}), and hence this rule's actions are solely determined by the current head position.

It is mechanical to calculate the transition probabilities for each state by observing what each rule will do when its head is in a given position and a full/nonfull batch is received. A state-diagram for this chain is shown in Figure A1.3.1.

Note: each transition has associated "cost" which gives the "advantage" of using the Alternating rule (the second number) in addition to its probability (the first number). More specifically, the second number gives the distance the Alternating rule moves in making the given transition minus that for the Nearest rule. The chain is initially in state 0 and remains there until both heads are at x and a full batch arrives. Let c_i be the expected cost incurred from the time the chain leaves state i until it first enters state 0 (meaning the heads are again together). We, then, are interested in c_0. The c_i satisfy the following system of equations:

$$c_0 = 1 + c_1,$$

$$c_1 = \varepsilon c_2 + (1-\varepsilon)(c_4 - x),$$

$$c_2 = \varepsilon c_1 + (1-\varepsilon)(c_3 + x),$$

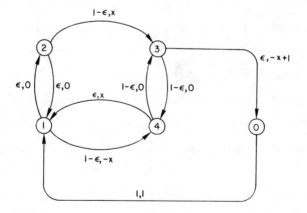

Figure A1.3.1

$$c_3 = (1-\varepsilon)\cdot c_4 + \varepsilon(-x + 1),$$

$$c_4 = (1-\varepsilon)\cdot c_3 + \varepsilon(c_1 + x).$$

These equations are easily seen: for example, consider c_1. With probability ε, the chain goes from c_1 to c_2. In this case, the total cost incurred in going from state 1 to state 0 equals c_2. With probability $1-\varepsilon$ the chain goes to state 4. Here the total cost will be $-x$ (the cost of the transition) plus c_4.

Solving the equations gives $c_0 = -2x(1-\varepsilon)^2 + 2$. Since ε has already been fixed, we can now choose x large enough so that c_0 will be negative.

We now consider the possibility of an "improbable" batch. The first necessity is to show that the probability of an improbable batch (p_I) can be made arbitrarily small by choosing b large enough. Since the "probable batches" are those containing records 1 and 3, or records 1 and 2, but not 3, an improbable batch must consist solely of record 1, or not contain record 1 at all. Hence $p_I = p_1^b + (1 - p_1)^b$. Since $0 < \varepsilon < 1$, we have $0 < p_1 < 1$, and hence $p_I \to 0$ as $b \to \infty$.

A Markov chain that considers all batches as possible can be defined. (Since we are concerned only with the chain's existence and obvious properties, we will not actually specify it.) This chain would have a state for the heads being together and one for each ordered pair of different positions. (In fact, there must be two states for each ordered pair where the Alternating rule is at position x: one for x being a left extreme and another for it being a right.) Now consider b as a parameter. As b is varied, p_1 is always chosen so that ε remains constant. Clearly this chain will be aperiodic and irreducible for any value of b, its "cost" can be solved for, as in the case of the simplified chain in Figure 1.6.2, and the limit of the cost as $b \rightarrow \infty$ will be exactly the cost of the simplified chain (the transition probability of all the "improbable" arcs approaches zero).

Since the cost of the simplified chain is positive, b can be chosen large enough to make the cost of the actual chain positive, proving the claim.

$\square$

1.8. References

[1]   Bergmans, P. P., "Minimizing expected travel time on geometrical patterns by optimal probability rearrangements," Inf. Control **20** (1972), 331-350.

[2]   Bitner, J. R., and Wong, C. K., "Optimal and near-optimal scheduling algorithms for batched processing in linear storage," SIAM J. Comput. **8**, 4 (1979), 479-498.

[3]   Blackwell, D., "Discrete dynamic programming," Annals Math. Stat. **33** (1962), 719-726.

[4]   Cody, R. A., "Allocation algorithms for minimizing expected access costs on drum-like storage devices," Ph.D. Thesis, Dept. of Computer Science, The Pennsylvania State University, University Park, Pa., 1974.

[5]   Coffman, E. G., Jr., and Denning, P. J., *Operating Systems Theory*, Prentice-Hall, Englewood Cliffs, N.J., 1973.

[6]   Garey, M. R., and Johnson, D. S., *Computers and Intractability: A Guide to the Theory of NP-completeness*, W. H. Freeman and Company, San Francisco, 1979.

[7]   Grossman, D. D., and Silverman, H. F., "Placement of records on a secondary storage device to minimize access time," J. ACM **20** (1973), 429-438.

[8]   Gupta, U. I., Lee, D. T., Leung, J.Y.-T., Pruitt, J. W. and
       Wong, C. K., "Record allocation for minimizing seek delay,"
       Theoretical Computer Science **16** (1981), 307-319.

[9]   Hardy, G. H., Littlewood, J. E. and Pólya, G., *Inequalities*,
       Cambridge University Press, Cambridge, England, 1952.

[10]   Hoel, P. B., Port, S. C. and Stone, C. J., *Introduction to
       Stochastic Processes*, Houghton Mifflin, Boston, 1972.

[11]   IBM Corp, IBM VM/370: Introduction, File No. S370-20,
       Order No. GC20-1800-1, IBM Corp., White Plains, N. Y.

[12]   Karp, R. M., "Reducibility among combinatorial problems," in
       Complexity of Computer Computations, R. E. Miller and J. W.
       Thatcher, Eds., Plenum Press, New York, 1972, 85-103.

[13]   Knuth, D. E., *The Art of Computer Programming*, Vol. III,
       Addison-Wesley, Reading, Ma., 1973.

[14]   Kollias, J. G., "An estimate of seek time for batched searching
       of random or index sequential structured files," Comput. J. **21**,
       2 (1978), 122-123.

[15]   Marshall, A. W., Olkin, I. and Proschan, F., "Monotonicity of
       ratios of means and other applications of majorization," in
       Inequalities, O. Shisha, Ed., Academic Press, New York, 1967.

[16]   McKellar, A. C., and Wong, C. K., "Dynamic placement of
       records in linear storage," J. ACM **25** (1978), 421-434.

[17]   Ostrowski, A., "Sur quelques applications des fonctions convexes et concaves au sens de I. Schur," J. Math. Pures Appl. **31** (1952), 253-292.

[18]   Pratt, V. R., "An N log N algorithm to distribute N records optimally in a sequential access file," in *Complexity of Computer Computations*, R. E. Miller and J. W. Thatcher, Eds., Plenum Press, New York, 1972, 111-118.

[19]   Schneiderman, B., and Goodman, V., "Batched searching of sequential and tree structured files," ACM Trans. Database Syst. **1** (1976), 268-275.

[20]   Schur, I., "Uber eine Klasse von Mittelbildungen mit Anwendungen auf die Determinatentheorie," Sitzber. Berl. Math. Ges. **22** (1923), 9-20.

[21]   Teorey, T. J., "Properties of disk scheduling policies in multiprogrammed computer systems," in Fall Jt. Computer Conf., Vol. 41, Pt. 1, 1972, 1-11.

[22]   Teory, T. J., and Pinkerton, T. B., "A comparative analysis of disk scheduling policies," Commun. ACM **15**, 3 (1972), 177-184.

[23]   Vaquero, A., and Troya, J. M., "Placement of records on linear storage devices," in Proc. IFIP Congress 1980, North-Holland, Amsterdam, 1980, 331-336.

[24] Weingarten, A., "The analytical design of real-time disk systems," in Proc. IFIP Congress 1968, North-Holland, Amsterdam, 1968, D131-D137.

[25] Whittaker, E. T., and Watson, G. N., *A Course of Modern Analysis*, University Press, Cambridge, England, 1952.

[26] Wiederhold, G., *Database design*, McGraw-Hill, New York, 1977, 307-310.

[27] Wong, C. K., "Minimizing expected head movement in one-dimensional and two-dimensional mass storage systems," Computing Surveys **12**, 2 (1980), 167-178.

[28] Wong, C. K., and Yue, P. C., "A majorization theorem for the number of distinct outcomes in N independent trials," Discrete Math, **6** (1973), 391-398.

[29] Yue, P. C., and Wong, C. K., "On the optimality of the probability ranking scheme in storage application," J. ACM **20** (1973), 624-633.

2. TWO-DIMENSIONAL STORAGE

2.1. Introduction and basic model

2.1.1. Introduction As mentioned in the preface, online, trillion-bit database systems have been coming into existence. For such large systems, storing all information on disks would be very expensive, while storing on tapes would mean very slow access time. In practice, a two-level storage system is used. All records of the system are permanently stored on a relatively cheap, but slow, mass storage unit. When a record is requested for online use, a copy is made on a disk, and it is this copy that is used for as long as necessary. When the transaction is completed, the copy is returned to the mass storage device, replacing the old copy.

Several two-dimensional storage devices have been designed for such mass storage of information. For example, the IBM 3851 Mass Storage Facility has a very large array of tape cartridges housed in compartments and accessed by an x-y mechanism, as depicted in Figure 2.1.1. In this mechanism the fetch station (and read/write head) moves along the x-axis while the x-axis itself moves simultaneously along a fixed y-axis. To access a particular cartridge, we move the head to the desired location from its last position, mount the cartridge and start processing.

On the other hand, in a recent design of a two-dimensional magnetic bubble memory system [4], the accessing of bubbles is done by moving the bubbles en masse horizontally or vertically (but not simultaneously) relative to a fixed sensor (read/write head). Thus, depending on the system, we may have different access mechanisms, and the time required by the head to travel from one location to

116

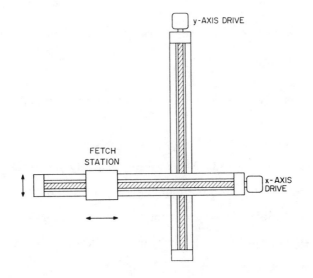

Figure 2.1.1

another may be measured by different distance functions. This added complexity makes algorithmic studies in two-dimensional storage systems much more difficult and challenging.

In this chapter, we are interested mainly in the same kind of problems as in Chapter 1, namely, placement of records to minimize expected head travel. In addition, we also study one aspect of the head scheduling problem in a batched processing environment. Finally, a record permutation problem is discussed; it serves as an introduction to the problems to be discussed in Chapter 3, namely, record permutation, sorting and searching problems in bubble memories.

2.1.2 Basic model Throughout this chapter, we assume the access mechanisms of interest fall in one of three categories: the read/write head can move

(a)   horizontally or vertically, but *not both* simultaneously, at
         uniform speed;

(b)   horizontally, vertically *or both* at uniform speed; and

(c)   in *any direction* at uniform speed.

Thus, the IBM 3851 Mass Storage Facility falls into category
(b), while the two-dimensional bubble system falls into category (a) if
we regard the bubbles as fixed and the sensor as moving.

Also, we represent a two-dimensional storage by a plane with
records located at points with *integral* coordinates $0, \pm 1, \pm 2,...$ only.

Accordingly, the head travel time between any two points in
the plane $\xi = (x,y), \eta = (u,v)$ can be measured by the following
metrics (see Figure 2.1.2):

$$\text{(a)} \quad d_1(\xi,\eta) = |x - u| + |y - v| \tag{2.1.1}$$

$$\text{(b)} \quad d_\infty(\xi,\eta) = \max(|x - u|, |y - v|) \tag{2.1.2}$$

$$\text{(c)} \quad d_2(\xi,\eta) = (|x - u|^2 + |y - v|^2)^{1/2}, \tag{2.1.3}$$

where d_1 is the rectilinear (L_1) metric, d_∞ is the maximum (L_∞) metric and d_2 is the Euclidean (L_2) metric. They belong to the family of L_p

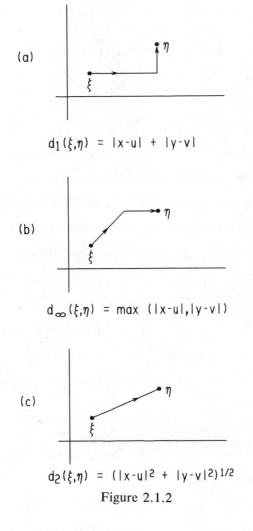

$$(a) \qquad d_1(\xi,\eta) = |x-u| + |y-v|$$

$$(b) \qquad d_\infty(\xi,\eta) = \max(|x-u|,|y-v|)$$

$$(c) \qquad d_2(\xi,\eta) = (|x-u|^2 + |y-v|^2)^{1/2}$$

Figure 2.1.2

metrics:

$$d_p(\xi,\eta) = (|x-u|^p + |y-v|^p)^{1/p} \qquad (2.1.4)$$

for $1 \leq p \leq \infty$. Specifically, (a) corresponds to $p = 1$, (b) to $p = \infty$ and
(c) to $p = 2$.

2.2. Record arrangement to minimize head travel

2.2.1. Introduction In Chapter 1, we studied the problem of positioning records in a linear storage medium in such a way that the expected head travel is minimized. The solution was to place the most frequently accessed record and then repetitively to place the next most frequently accessed record, alternating between the position immediately to the left of those already placed and the position immediately to the right (the organ-pipe arrangement).

In this section, we consider a generalization of this problem in which the storage medium is an infinite two-dimensional rectangular array of storage cells, and it is desired to minimize the expected Euclidean distance between consecutively referenced records. It is quite easy to construct examples to show that it is not sufficient to know only the ordering of records by frequency of access in order to construct the optimal solution. Thus, there is no hope of finding as elegant an algorithm for this two-dimensional case as for the one-dimensional case.

The problem we consider is a special case of the quadratic assignment problem, which arises, for example, in various circuit placement problems [9,10].

We consider a heuristic which operates only on the relative frequency with which records are accessed and show that the resulting placement is within an additive constant of optimal. This asymptotically optimal heuristic consists of placing the most frequently accessed record and then filling "shells" of storage cells which are equidistant from the center with a set of next most frequently accessed records.

We then consider the problem of replacing Euclidean distance with rectilinear distance, with distance defined to be the maximum of the difference in the x-coordinates and the difference in the y-coordinates (the maximum metric). In each case, we show that there is an analogue of the "shell" heuristic which is within an additive constant of optimal when the access probabilities are equal. However, a "shell" no longer consists of the set of storage locations equidistant from the center, but rather consists of the set of cells on a contour given by the solution of a differential equation for which we have only been able to obtain numerical solutions. We use these results to show that, in general, there is no heuristic for the maximum and rectilinear metrics which operates only on the relative frequency of access and produces solutions within an additive constant of optimal.

2.2.2. Formulation of the problem Consider a set of n records $R_1, \ldots, R_n$ which are referenced repetitively, where with probability p_i the reference is to R_i and consecutive references are independent. We adopt the convention that the records are numbered such that $p_1 \geq p_2 \geq \ldots \geq p_n$. We wish to place these records into an infinite two-dimensional rectangular array of storage cells such that the expected distance between consecutively referenced records is minimized, i.e., we wish to minimize

$$D(\pi) = \sum_{i,j} p_i p_j d^{(\pi)}(i,j), \qquad (2.2.1)$$

where $d^{(\pi)}(i,j)$ is the Euclidean distance between record R_i and record R_j. We will regard the storage cells as points with integral coordinates in the plane, as mentioned in Subsection 2.1.2, and adjacent cells are assumed to be at unit distance from each other.

Figures 2.2.1(a) and 2.2.1(b) give two examples of optimal placements. These examples show that it is not sufficient to know the relative frequency of access to minimize D; one must have more detailed knowledge of the probabilities of access.

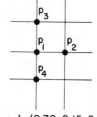

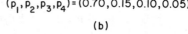

$(p_1,p_2,p_3,p_4)=(0.33,0.32,0.31,0.04)$ $(p_1,p_2,p_3,p_4)=(0.70,0.15,0.10,0.05)$

(a)   (b)

Figure 2.2.1

However, when optimal solutions are not absolutely essential, one may want to use the simple heuristic mentioned in Subsection 2.2.1, namely, filling "shells" of storage cells which are equidistant from the center with a set of records with next largest probabilities. This algorithm depends only on the ordering of the probabilities of access and is subsequently referred to as the "shell" algorithm.

Next we will show that the expected distance between consecutively referenced records resulting from the "shell" algorithm is within an additive constant of that resulting from an optimal placement algorithm.

As confusion is unlikely, we shall drop the arrangement symbol π from now on.

2.2.3.   Analysis of the algorithm   Define

$$\Delta_i = p_i - p_{i+1}, \quad 1 \leq i < n$$

and

$$\Delta_n = p_n$$

so that

$$p_i = \sum_{r=i}^{n} \Delta_r \text{ and } \sum_{r=1}^{n} r\Delta_r = \sum_{i=1}^{n} p_{i=1}.$$

Hence D can be rewritten as

$$D = \sum_{i=1}^{n} \sum_{r=i}^{n} \Delta_r \left(\sum_{j=1}^{n} \sum_{s=j}^{n} \Delta_s \right) d(i,j).$$

Interchanging the orders of summation yields

$$D = \sum_{r=1}^{n} \sum_{s=1}^{n} \Delta_r \Delta_s E_{rs},$$

where

$$E_{rs} = \sum_{i=1}^{r} \sum_{j=1}^{s} d(i,j).$$

The effect of this transformation has been to replace the probabilities by a set of n variables among which there are no ordering constraints. Furthermore, the effect of the placement algorithm has been localized to a term, E_{rs}, which is independent of the access probabilities. For given r and s, there is a placement dependent only on the relative frequency of access which minimizes E_{rs}. However, that placement is incompatible with the placement for some other values of r and s. For example, the shape of Figure 2.2.1(a) minimizes E_{rs} with r = 3, s = 4, whereas Figure 2.2.1(b) is optimal for r = 1, s = 4. Thus, in general, it is not possible to enlarge an optimal solution for n points to an optimal solution for n + 1 points in a straightforward way, which explains why our problem is more difficult than the one-dimensional case.

Let $D(opt)$, $E_{rs}(opt)$ denote the values produced by an optimum placement algorithm (i.e., one which minimizes D) and $D(shell)$, $E_{rs}(shell)$ denote the values produced by the "shell" algorithm. We shall show that

$$E_{rs}(shell) \leq E_{rs}(opt) + crs, \tag{2.2.2}$$

where c is a constant independent of r, s. As a consequence,

$$D(shell) \leq D(opt) + c \sum_{r=1}^{n} \sum_{s=1}^{n} \Delta_r \Delta_s rs = D(opt) + c. \tag{2.2.3}$$

We were unable to find a straightforward proof of (2.2.2), and so we consider the continuous analogue of E_{rs}, for which it is relatively easy to find the optimal solution.

Since $d(i,j) = d(j,i)$, without loss of generality, we can assume $r \leq s$. The problem is then to find two regions ω_0 and ω_1 with areas r and s respectively and $\omega_0 \subset \omega_1$ such that the integral

$$\int_{x \in \omega_1} \int_{y \in \omega_0} d(x,y) \tag{2.2.4}$$

is minimized, where x,y denote points in ω_1, ω_0 respectively, and $d(x,y)$ is the distance between points x and y. The following definition formalizes an obvious geometric property:

Definition 2.2.1   Let ω be any region and L any straight line dividing the plane into A and B. ω is said to have the *covering property with respect to L* if either $I(A \cap \omega) \supset (B \cap \omega)$ or $I(B \cap \omega) \supset (A \cap \omega)$, where

$I(A\cap\omega)$ means the mirror image of $A\cap\omega$ with respect to L. $I(B\cap\omega)$ is similarly defined. (See Figure 2.2.2.)

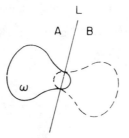

Figure 2.2.2

Lemma 2.2.1 If $\omega_0^*,\omega_1^*(\omega_0^*\subset\omega_1^*)$ form a minimal solution for (2.2.4), then ω_0^*,ω_1^* have the covering property with respect to any straight line L. Furthermore, if L partitions the plane into A and B, and if $I(A\cap\omega_1^*)\supset(B\cap\omega_1^*)$, then $I(A\cap\omega_0^*)\supset(B\cap\omega_0^*)$. Similarly, if $I(B\cap\omega_1^*)\supset(A\cap\omega_1^*)$, then $I(B\cap\omega_0^*)\supset(A\cap\omega_0^*)$.

Appendix 2.1 contains a proof.

Lemma 2.2.2 Any region which has the covering property with respect to any straight line must be a disk.

Proof Let C be the center of mass of the region. (See Figure 2.2.3.) Suppose there exist points α,β on the boundary such that $d(\alpha,C)<d(\beta,C)$. Draw a straight line L through C, bisecting the angle $\alpha C\beta$ and meeting the boundary at γ.

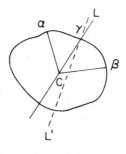

Figure 2.2.3

Let L' be a straight line through γ cutting the region into two parts with equal areas ω_1, ω_2. By the covering property, ω_1, ω_2 should be symmetric images of each other with respect to L'. In particular, L' should go through C; hence, L, L' coincide. Thus, α, β are symmetric with respect to L, a contradiction.

□

Lemma 2.2.3   The minimal solution to (2.2.4) consists of two concentric circles.

Proof   Let $\omega_0{}^*, \omega_1{}^*$ form an optimal solution and $\omega_0{}^* \subset \omega_1{}^*$. By Lemmas 2.2.1 and 2.2.2, they must be circles. It remains to show that they are concentric. Suppose it is not the case. Let C_0, C_1 be the centers of $\omega_0{}^*, \omega_1{}^*$. Let L be the perpendicular bisector of the line segment $C_0 C_1$ (see Figure 2.2.4). With respect to L, the second part of Lemma 2.2.1 is violated: hence, a contradiction.

□

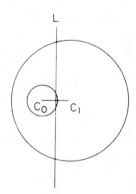

Figure 2.2.4

Let E_{rs}^{cont} denote the optimal value of (2.2.4), i.e.,

$$E_{rs}^{cont} = \int_{x \in \omega_1{}^*} \int_{y \in \omega_0{}^*} d(x,y),$$

where $\omega_1{}^*, \omega_0{}^*$ are concentric circles with areas s, r respectively. We will compare this with the "shell" algorithm and the optimal placement algorithm.

If we look at the first r and s points $(r \leq s)$ in the configuration resulting from the "shell" algorithm, and compute the function $\sum_{i=1}^{r} \sum_{j=1}^{s} d(ij)$, we obtain $E_{rs}(\text{shell})$. Suppose we replace each point by a unit square with center at this point; then we have two regions ω_0, ω_1 with areas r, s respectively, and $\omega_0 \subset \omega_1$. Let

$$E_{rs}^{cont}(\text{shell}) = \int_{x \in \omega_1} \int_{y \in \omega_0} d(x,y).$$

We define the continuous analogue of the optimal placement in the same way and let $E_{rs}^{cont}(\text{opt})$, be the value of the integral in (2.2.4) evaluated over the corresponding regions.

We will show that

$$E_{rs}(\text{shell}) \leq E_{rs}^{cont}(\text{shell}) + \sqrt{2} \, rs$$

by Lemma 2.2.4, that

$$E_{rs}^{cont}(\text{shell}) \leq E_{rs}^{cont} + (4\sqrt{2} + 8\sqrt{\pi}) rs$$

by Lemma 2.2.6, that

$$E_{rs}^{cont} \leq E_{rs}^{cont}(\text{opt}),$$

which is obvious, and that

$$E_{rs}^{cont}(\text{opt}) \leq E_{rs}(\text{opt}) + \sqrt{2} \, rs$$

by Lemma 2.2.5.   Combining these results yields the following theorem:

Theorem 2.2.1 $E_{rs}(\text{shell}) \leq E_{rs}(\text{opt}) + (6\sqrt{2} + 8\sqrt{\pi}) rs$. Consequently,

$D(shell) \leq D(opt) + (6\sqrt{2} + 8\sqrt{\pi})$.

Lemma 2.2.4 $E_{rs}(shell) \leq E_{rs}^{cont}(shell) + \sqrt{2} rs$.

Proof Note only that for any x in the square of R_i and any y in the square of R_j (see Figure 2.2.5),

$$d(i,j) \leq d(x,y) + \frac{\sqrt{2}}{2} + \frac{\sqrt{2}}{2} = d(x,y) + \sqrt{2}.$$

□

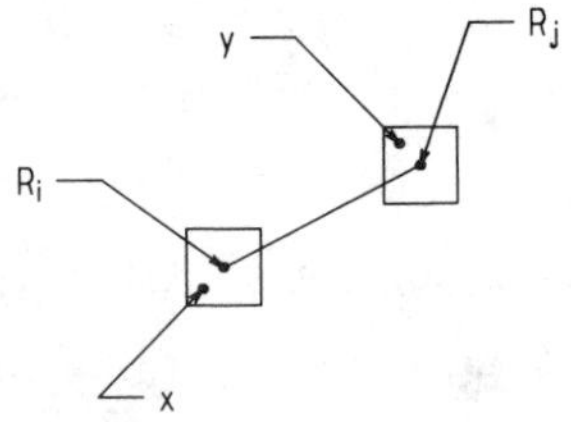

Figure 2.2.5

Although we are showing that the continuous case is bounded by the discrete case, similar argument shows that the following lemma holds:

Lemma 2.2.5 $E_{rs}^{cont}(opt) \leq E_{rs}(opt) + \sqrt{2} rs$.

Next we will prove the following result:

Lemma 2.2.6 $E_{rs}^{cont}(shell) \leq E_{rs}^{cont} + (4\sqrt{2} + 8\sqrt{\pi}) rs$.

Proof   On the regions ω_0, ω_1 for the continuous version of the "shell" algorithm, we superimpose the two concentric circles ω_0^*, ω_1^* with areas r, s respectively, such that their centers 0 coincide with the point where the record R_1 is located, as shown in Figure 2.2.6. (ω_1^* is not shown in the Figure.)

Let us look at ω_0 and ω_0^*. In Figure 2.2.6, the region $\omega_0 - \omega_0^*$ is shaded in one direction and the region $\omega_0^* - \omega_0$ is shaded in another. Let d denote the radius of the largest circle centered at 0 inside ω_0. Let $a = \sqrt{r/\pi}$ be the radius of ω_0^*. Let d_1 denote the radius of the smallest circle centered at 0 outside ω_0. Then

$$d_1 \leq d + \sqrt{2} \text{ and } d \leq a \leq d_1 \leq d + \sqrt{2}. \tag{2.2.5}$$

To see this, let c be the center of the square farthest away from 0. Let d_c be its distance from the center. Then $d_1 \leq d_c + \sqrt{2}/2$ and $d \geq d_c - \sqrt{2}/2$. The first is obvious. To show the second one, assume the contrary; it follows that there exists an empty square, the distance of whose center to 0 is less than d_c, a contradiction to the "shell" algorithm.

Let us classify the regions inside the circle with radius d_1 into 5 classes, as denoted in Figure 2.2.6. Therefore, regions 1, 2, 3 will form the region $\omega_0{}^*$, regions 4, 5 will form the outer annulus A, and regions 2, 3 will form the inner annulus B. Also, area of region 3 equals that of region 4.

To obtain an upper bound on area 4 and hence on area 3 we note that

area $4 \leq$ min (area A, area B).

But min (area A, area B) is maximized when $d_1 - d = \sqrt{2}$ and area A = area B. This occurs when $d_1 - a = \frac{1}{2}(\sqrt{2} - 2a + \sqrt{4a^2 - 2})$. In this case, area A = area B = $\pi\sqrt{2a^2 - 1}$. Therefore,

$$\text{area 3} = \text{area } 4 < \pi\sqrt{2a^2} = \sqrt{2}\pi r. \tag{2.2.6}$$

Let us do exactly the same thing for ω_1 and $\omega_1{}^*$, and call the corresponding regions 1', 2', 3', 4', 5', A' and B'. Also let the radius

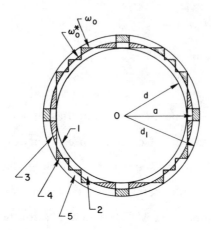

I : INNER DISK
2 : UNION OF ALL UNSHADED REGIONS IN THE INNER ANNULUS
3 : UNION OF ALL SHADED REGIONS IN THE INNER ANNULUS
4 : UNION OF ALL SHADED REGIONS IN THE OUTER ANNULUS
5 : UNION OF ALL UNSHADED REGIONS IN THE OUTER ANNULUS

Figure 2.2.6

of $\omega_1{}^*$ be b. Therefore, $b = \sqrt{s/\pi}$. Thus,

$$E_{rs}^{cont}(\text{shell}) = \int_{124} \int_{1'2'4'} ,$$

$$E_{rs}^{cont} = \int_{123} \int_{1'2'3'} ,$$

$$E_{rs}^{cont}(\text{shell}) - E_{rs}^{cont} = \int_{124} \int_{2'4'} + \int_{124} \int_{1'}$$

$$- \int_{123} \int_{2'3'} - \int_{123} \int_{1'}$$

$$= \int_{124} \int_{2'4'} - \int_{123} \int_{2'3'} + \int_{4} \int_{1'} - \int_{3} \int_{1'}$$

$$\leq \int_{124} \int_{2'4'} + \int_4 \int_{1'} - \int_3 \int_{1'} \; ;$$

area $2'4'$ = area $2'3' \leq \pi b^2 - \pi (b - \sqrt{2})^2 = 2\sqrt{2\pi s} - 2\pi$;

area 124 = r.

Hence,

$$\int_{124} \int_{2'4'} \leq r(2\sqrt{2\pi s} - 2\pi)(a + b + 2\sqrt{2})$$

$$= r(2\sqrt{2\pi s} - 2\pi)(\sqrt{r/\pi} + \sqrt{s/\pi} + 2\sqrt{2})$$

$$\leq (4\sqrt{2} + 6\sqrt{\pi})rs.$$

To bound $\int_4 \int_{1'} - \int_3 \int_{1'}$, we use polar coordinates (ρ',θ') for points in $1'$ and (ρ,θ) for points in A. (Recall that A is an annulus with inner radius a and outer radius d_1).

Let $d(\rho,\theta,\rho',\theta')$ denote the distance from point (ρ,θ) to (ρ',θ'). Let the radius of $1'$ be d'.

For each point (ρ,θ) in A, let

$$I_{\rho,\theta} = \int_{\rho'=0}^{d'} \int_{\theta'=0}^{2\pi} d(\rho,\theta,\rho',\theta')\rho' d\rho' d\theta'.$$

It is easy to show that (i) $I_{\rho,\theta}$ depends on ρ only, and (ii) if $\rho < \hat{\rho}$, then $I_{\rho,\theta} < I_{\hat{\rho},\theta}$. Therefore,

$$I_{\rho,\theta} \leq \int_{\rho'=0}^{d'} \int_{\theta'=0}^{2\pi} d(d_1,0,\rho',\theta')\rho' d\rho' d\theta',$$

and

$$\int_4 \int_{1'} = \int_{\rho=a}^{d_1} \int_{\theta=0}^{2\pi} \rho d\rho d\theta I_{\rho,\theta}$$

$$\leq (\text{area } 4) \int_{\rho'=0}^{d'} \int_{\theta'=0}^{2\pi} d(d_1,0,\rho',\theta')\rho' d\rho' d\theta$$

Similarly,

$$\int_3 \int_{1'} \geq (\text{area } 3) \int_{\rho'=0}^{d'} \int_{\theta'=0}^{2\pi} d(d,0,\rho',\theta')\rho' d\rho' d\theta'.$$

Thus,

$$\int_4 \int_{1'} - \int_3 \int_{1'} \leq (\text{area } 3) \sqrt{2} (\text{area } 1')$$

$$\leq \sqrt{2\pi r} \sqrt{2} s = 2\sqrt{\pi r} \ s.$$

Therefore,

$$E_{rs}^{cont}(\text{shell}) - E_{rs}^{cont} \leq (4\sqrt{2} + 8\sqrt{\pi})rs.$$

□

2.2.4.   Other metrics with uniform distribution The proof in the preceding section goes through practically unchanged for other metrics, although the constants change. The stumbling block is in finding the optimal solution to the continuous problem. Here we consider the special case in which all access probabilities are equal. Thus, we have

$$\Delta_n = \frac{1}{n} \text{ and } \Delta_i = 0, \ 1 \le i < n.$$

Hence, we are concerned only with E_{nn} in (2.2.2) and need only find the optimal continuous solution for the case $r = s = n$. Here we state this continuous problem in a more general form and characterize its optimal solution for the two metrics of interest, namely, the L_1 and L_∞ metrics.

Let $\xi = (x_1, y_1)$, $\eta = (x_2, y_2)$ be any two points in the plane. Recall that the family of L_p metrics are defined as follows:

$$d_p(\xi, \eta) = (\,|\,x_1 - x_2\,|^{\,p} + |\,y_1 - y_2\,|^{\,p})^{1/p}, 1 \le p \le \infty.$$

By $p = \infty$ we mean $d_\infty(\xi, \eta) = \max(\,|\,x_1 - x_2\,|, \ |\,y_1 - y_2\,|)$. For a fixed p and a fixed R, we need to find the solution to the following minimization problem:

$$\underset{\omega \in \Omega}{\min} \ \underset{\xi, \eta \in \omega}{\int \int} d_p(\xi, \eta), \tag{2.2.7}$$

where Ω is the set of all closed regions in the plane with area R.

The following is a necessary condition for an optimal region:

Lemma 2.2.7   Let ω_0 be an optimal region. Let α be a point on the boundary of ω_0. Define

$$P(\alpha) = \int_{\eta \in \omega_0} d_p(\alpha, \eta). \tag{2.2.8}$$

Then $P(\alpha)$ is a constant for all α on the boundary.

Proof   Let β be another point on the boundary (see Figure 2.2.7).

Let ε_α be a region at α inside ω_0 and ε_β a region at β outside ω_0. Assume that ε_α and ε_β both have area ε. Let the new region obtained by removing ε_α from ω_0 and adding ε_β to ω_0 be ω_ε. Then ω_ε has area R.

$$I = \int\int_{\xi,\eta\in\omega_\varepsilon} d_p(\xi,\eta) - \int\int_{\xi,\eta\in\omega_0} d_p(\xi,\eta)$$

$$= \int_{\omega_0}\int_{\omega_0} + \int_{\omega_0}\int_{\varepsilon_\beta} - \int_{\omega_0}\int_{\varepsilon_\alpha}$$

$$+ \int_{\varepsilon_\beta}\int_{\omega_0} + \int_{\varepsilon_\beta}\int_{\varepsilon_\beta} - \int_{\varepsilon_\beta}\int_{\varepsilon_\alpha}$$

$$- \int_{\varepsilon_\alpha}\int_{\omega_0} - \int_{\varepsilon_\alpha}\int_{\varepsilon_\beta} + \int_{\varepsilon_\alpha}\int_{\varepsilon_\alpha} - \int_{\omega_0}\int_{\omega_0} .$$

Noting that terms 5, 6, 8 and 9 are of order ε^2, we have

$$I = 2\left(\int_{\omega_0}\int_{\varepsilon_\beta} - \int_{\omega_0}\int_{\varepsilon_\alpha}\right) + O(\varepsilon^2)$$

$$= 2\left(\varepsilon\int_{\eta\in\omega_0} d_p(\alpha_\varepsilon,\eta) - \varepsilon\int_{\eta\in\omega_0} d_p(\beta_\varepsilon,\eta)\right)$$

$$+ O(\varepsilon^2),$$

where $\alpha_\varepsilon\in\varepsilon_\alpha, \beta_\varepsilon \in\varepsilon_\beta$ are determined by the mean value theorem and $\alpha_\varepsilon \to \alpha, \beta_\varepsilon \to \beta$ as $\varepsilon \to 0$.

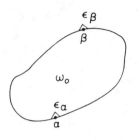

Figure 2.2.7

By optimality,

$$\lim_{\varepsilon \to 0} \frac{\displaystyle\int_{\omega_\varepsilon}\int_{\omega_\varepsilon} - \int_{\omega_0}\int_{\omega_0}}{\varepsilon} = 0.$$

Therefore,

$$\int_{\eta \in \omega_0} d_p(\alpha,\eta) - \int_{\eta \in \omega_0} d_p(\beta,\eta) = 0,$$

as required.

$\square$

The two cases of interest are $p = 1$, the rectilinear metric, and $p = \infty$, the maximum metric. For each of these metrics, we can use Bergmans' [3] methods of proof to show symmetry with respect to horizontal and perpendicular lines as well as lines at $45°$ and $135°$.

We want to find the curve $f(x)$ valid in the first quadrant, as shown in Figure 2.2.8. Then, by symmetry, we can complete the Figure. Because of symmetry about a line at $45°$, $f(f(x)) = x$. Consider any point $(u,v = f(u))$ in the first quadrant and, without loss of generality, let $u \le v$. Then (v,u) is also a point on the curve, as is $(-v,-u)$.

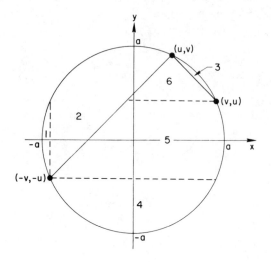

Figure 2.2.8

For the maximum metric, (2.2.8) can now be written as

$$P = \int_{x=-a}^{-v} \int_{y=-f(x)}^{f(x)} (u-x)dydx + \int_{x=-v}^{u} \int_{y=x-u+v}^{f(x)} (u-x)dydx$$

$$+ \int_{x=u}^{v} \int_{y=-x+v+u}^{f(x)} (x-u)dydx$$

$$+ \int_{y=-a}^{-u} \int_{x=-f(y)}^{f(y)} (v-y)dxdy$$

$$+ \int_{y=-u}^{u} \int_{x=y+u-v}^{f(y)} (v-y)dxdy$$

$$+ \int_{y=u}^{v} \int_{x=y+u-v}^{x=-y+v+u} (v-y)dxdy, \tag{2.2.9}$$

where the areas in Figure 2.2.8 are numbered to correspond to the terms in (2.2.9). Performing all integrations not involving f and collecting terms yields

$$P = \int_{x=-a}^{-v} 2(u-x)f(-x)dx + \int_{-v}^{u} (u-x)f(|x|)dx$$

$$+ \int_{u}^{v} (x-u)f(x)dx + \int_{y=-a}^{-u} 2(v-y)f(-y)dy$$

$$+ \int_{y=-u}^{u} (v-y)f(|y|)dy + \frac{1}{3}v^3 + vu^2.$$

We apply the condition of Lemma 2.2.7 by requiring that $dP/du = 0$.
Carrying out the differentiation and collecting terms again yields

$$\int_{x=-a}^{-v} 2f(-x)dx + \int_{x=-v}^{u} f(|x|)dx$$

$$- \int_{x=u}^{v} f(x)dx + 2f'(u)\int_{x=-a}^{-u} f(-x)dx \qquad (2.2.10)$$

$$+ f'(u)\int_{x=-u}^{u} f(|x|)dx + f'(u)(f^2(u)-u^2) = 0.$$

Let the total area surrounded by the curve be R. Then the
area in one quadrant is R/4. In view of the identity

$$R/4 + uf(u) = \int_{0}^{u} f(x)dx + \int_{0}^{v} f(x)dx,$$

(2.2.10) can be converted to

$$(R + 2(f^2(u)-u^2))f'(u) + 8\int_{0}^{u} f(x)dx - 4uf(u) = 0. \qquad (2.2.11)$$

Referring to Figure 2.2.9, it is quite easy to obtain from the rectilinear metric

$$P = 2\int_{x=u}^{a} \int_{y=-f(x)}^{f(x)} (x + y + v)dydx$$

$$+ 2\int_{y=v}^{a} \int_{x=-f(y)}^{f(y)} (x + y + u)dxdy$$

$$+ \int_{x=-u}^{u} \int_{y=-v}^{v} (x + u + y + v)dydx,$$

which after simplification becomes

$$P = 4\int_{x=u}^{a} (x + v)f(x)dx$$

$$+ 4\int_{y=v}^{a} (y + u)f(y)dy + 4uv(u + v).$$

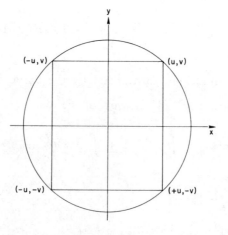

Figure 2.2.9

Differentiating with respect to u and applying Lemma 2.2.7 yields

$$f'(u) \int_{x=u}^{a} f(x)dx + \int_{x=f(u)}^{a} f(x)dx + uf(u)f'(u) + uf(u) = 0.$$

As before, let R be the total area. Noting that

$$\int_{x=u}^{a} f(x)dx = \frac{R}{4} - \int_{0}^{u} f(x)dx$$

and that

$$\frac{R}{4} = \int_{x=u}^{a} f(x)dx + \int_{x=v}^{a} f(x)dx + uf(u),$$

we have

$$f'(u) \left[\frac{R}{4} - \int_{0}^{u} f(x)dx + uf(u) \right] + \int_{0}^{u} f(x)dx = 0. \qquad (2.2.12)$$

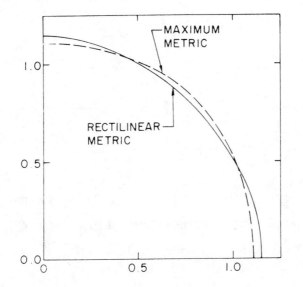

Figure 2.2.10

We have not been able to obtain closed form solutions for
(2.2.11) or (2.2.12). Numerical solutions were obtained and are
shown in Figure 2.2.10 for the case $R = 4$, i.e., the area in each
quadrant is 1. For other values of R, the shape is obtained by linear
scaling.

A priori, one might have been tempted to guess that the square
and diamond were optimal shapes for the maximum and rectilinear
metrics respectively, since each has the property that every point on
the boundary is equidistant from the center. Instead, the shape has
turned out to be quite close to a circle in each case, although it is true
for the maximum metric that the circle is distorted toward the shape of
a square, and for the rectilinear metric, distortion is toward a diamond.

It should be pointed out that (2.2.12) can also be directly
derived from (2.2.11) by means of the following isometry, f, from the
plane with the L_∞ metric, R_∞^2, to the plane with the L_1 metric, R_1^2:

$$
\begin{cases}
x' = \dfrac{y+x}{2} \\[2mm]
y' = \dfrac{y-x}{2},
\end{cases}
\qquad (2.2.13)
$$

where $(x,y) \in R_\infty^2$ and $(x',y') \in R_1^2$. In fact, this linear mapping just
rotates the plane by $45°$ and then shrinks it by a factor of $1/\sqrt{2}$. An
example of this isometry is given in Figure 2.2.11.

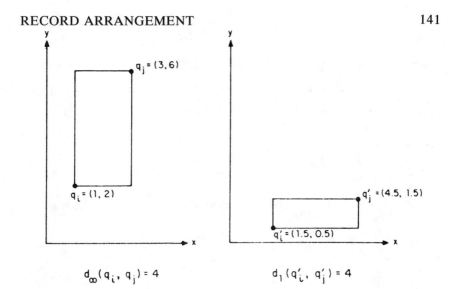

Figure 2.2.11

To prove that (2.2.13) is indeed an isometry, suppose the coordinates of two points q_i and q_j are (x_i, y_i) and (x_j, y_j) respectively and $x_j > x_i, y_j > y_i$ and $x_j - x_i > y_j - y_i$. The distance between their images q_i' and q_j' in R_1^2 is given by $d_1(q_i', q_j') = ((y_j - y_i)/2 + (x_j - x_i)/2) + ((x_j - x_i)/2 - (y_j - y_i)/2)$, which is equal to $x_j - x_i = d_\infty(q_i, q_j)$. Thus, f preserves the distance, i.e., it is an isometry.

2.2.5. Nonexistence of heuristics for the general case In contrast to the Euclidean case, we will show that for the maximum and rectilinear metrics there is no heuristic which operates only on relative frequencies and which is within an additive constant of optimal.

It follows easily from the methods in Subsection 2.2.3 that the optimal solution to the discrete problem is within an additive constant of the optimal solution for the corresponding continuous problem.

Given a continuous solution with total area n, we define a scaled solution with total area 1 by shrinking each area by a factor of $1/n$ and increasing the probability per unit area by a factor of n. Let $D_n(opt)$ be the expected distance for the solution with total area n.

Then the expected distance $D_1(opt)$ for the scaled version is given by $D_n(opt) = \sqrt{n}D_1(opt)$, and the scaled solution is also optimal.

Consider the case

$$p_1 = p \text{ and } p_i = \frac{q}{n-1}, \quad 2 \leq i \leq n,$$

where $p + q = 1$. Then for the corresponding continuous problem,

$$D_1(opt) = 2pqa + q^2b + O(1/\sqrt{n}),$$

where a is the average distance between a point with weight np and a point with weight $nq/(n-1)$, and b is the average distance between points with weight $nq/(n-1)$. Thus,

$$D_n(opt) = \sqrt{n}q(2pa + qb) + O(1).$$

The optimal solutions were obtained in Subsection 2.2.4 for the case $p = 1/n$. Asymptotically for large n, the shapes of these optimal solutions are the shapes which minimize b.

On the other hand, the shape which minimizes a (again asymptotically for large n) is the diamond for the rectilinear metric and the square for the maximum metric. Thus, there is no single shape which simultaneously minimizes a and b. Thus, as p varies from $1/n$ to 1, the shape of the optimal solution varies from the shapes given in Subsection 2.2.4 to the diamond or square.

Suppose that there were a heuristic operating only on relative frequencies for the discrete case. Then for any value of n, this heuristic essentially provides a template for position of the n records, and the shape of this template is independent of p. The continuous analogue of the solution provided by this template would have to be within an additive constant of optimal. But this is a contradiction, since, as argued above, given any shape there is a value of p so that the solution deviates from optimal by a quantity proportional to $\sqrt{n}$.

For the Euclidean metric, of course, the circle simultaneously minimizes a and b.

2.3. Record arrangement to minimize head travel in bounded arrays

2.3.1. Introduction In Section 2.2, we studied the problem of placing records in an infinite plane to minimize the expected head travel in various metrics. This is a realistic model when the number of records is much smaller than the number of storage cells. However, when this is not the case, the bounded nature of the two-dimensional storage array must be taken into consideration. This makes the problem even harder to solve.

In this section, we consider only the maximum metric and study a heuristic based on some enumeration techniques. Similar approach can be applied to the rectilinear as well as the Euclidean metrics. It serves to illustrate the difficulty of the "bounded array" problem and attempts to point out some possible avenues of attack.

2.3.2. Problem formulation Consider n records $R_1,...,R_n$, with access probabilities $p_1 \geq p_2 \geq ... \geq p_n$, $\sum_{i=1}^{n} p_i = 1$. These records are to be placed at the nodes of a finite rectangular grid. The placement strategy is represented by the permutation π, so that the record placed in node i is $R_{\pi(i)}$. Thus, the probability of the head being at node i is equal to $p_{\pi(i)}$.

Suppose d_{ij} denotes the distance between node i and node j.

Then the expected head travel for any placement π is given by

$$D(\pi) = \sum_{i,j} p_{\pi(i)} p_{\pi(j)} d_{ij},$$

where

$$d_{ij} = \max \left(\,|\, x_i - x_j \,|, |\, y_i - y_j \,| \,\right)$$

and (x_i, y_i), (x_j, y_j) are the coordinates of the nodes i and j.

The objective is to find a placement π such that $D(\pi)$ is minimized. As mentioned in Section 2.2, this is a special case of the quadratic assignment problem which has been studied by many authors using mainly integer programming techniques. Readers are referred particularly to the original contribution of Gilmore [9] and the extensive survey of Hanan and Kurtzberg [10]. However, these known techniques are computationally impractical for very large values of n.

As discussed in Chapter 1, the minimization of $D(\pi)$ can be traced back to Hardy, Littlewood and Pólya, who solved in the last chapter of their classic work [11] the one-dimensional case with d_{ij} being the Euclidean distance between i and j . Bergmans [3] was the first one to give an extensive discussion of the two-dimensional infinite grid and presented the pairwise majorizing property (PMP) as a necessary condition for optimality, again using the Euclidean distance for d_{ij}. In this section, however, we are concerned only with finite grids with d_{ij} being the maximum of the distances in the x and y directions.

Fortunately, Bergmans' proof of the optimality condition turns out to be valid for our definition of d_{ij} as well [3]. We therefore have the following result:

Necessary condition for optimality   If an assignment π is optimal, then the following conditions must be satisfied.   For every line α on the plane, consider the subset of all nodes that form symmetric pairs about α. Then all the nodes in this subset that lie on one side of α must have probabilities greater than or equal to those of their symmetric images.

This condition will be referred to as the PMP (pairwise majorizing property).   Note that the one-dimensional case of this condition was already discussed in Lemma 1.2.1.   Recall that in the one-dimensional case, an optimal assignment is readily obtained, as shown in Figure 2.3.1.

NODES:

$n-1$ $\quad$ 4 $\quad$ 2 $\quad\vdots\quad$ 1 $\quad$ 3 $\quad$ 5 $\qquad$ n

p_{n-1} ... p_4 $\quad p_2$ $\vdots$ p_1 $\quad p_3$ $\quad p_5$ ... p_n

$\alpha_1\,\alpha_2$

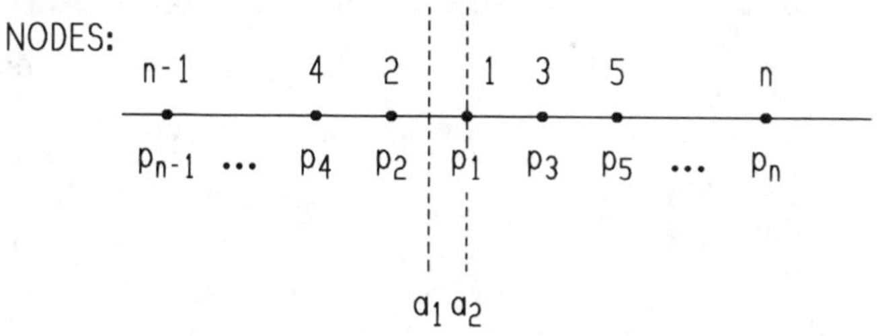

Figure 2.3.1

Recall that in the one-dimensional case, an optimal assignment is readily obtained, as shown in Figure 2.3.1.   It is optimal because using α_1 as a symmetry axis, we have to ensure $p_{\pi(1)} \ge p_{\pi(2)}$, $p_{\pi(3)} \ge p_{\pi(4)}$,..., and using α_2 as a symmetry axis, we have to ensure $p_{\pi(2)} \ge p_{\pi(3)}$, $p_{\pi(4)} \ge p_{\pi(5)}$,..., where the nodes are labeled as in the diagram and the majorizing side is picked arbitrarily.   Thus, $\pi(i) = i$ gives an optimal assignment.   The only alternative to this assignment is the mirror image assignment, i.e.,

$$p_n \cdots p_5 p_3 p_1 p_2 p_4 \cdots p_{n-1}.$$

In the two-dimensional case, this alternating pattern must also be true for all points lying in a straight line according to the same argument. In addition, the same ordering must be maintained for all parallel lines. A placement satisfying all these conditions will be referred to as a PMP configuration. An example of a PMP configuration is given in Figure 2.3.2. It is important to note that PMP configurations are not unique. Furthermore, the optimum is dependent not only on the ranking, but also on the exact values of $\{p_i\}$. An example will be given in Subsection 2.3.4. Theoretically, one can generate and search through all PMP configurations and obtain an optimal solution. Unfortunately, the computational complexity of such a process is prohibitively large. The idea of considering PMP configurations, however, does lead to the establishment of a tight lower bound for the cost function. Based on this, a natural heuristic will then be shown to be nearly optimal.

2.3.3. Enumeration of PMP configurations

Here we assume for simplicity that the grid consists of squares, $n = K \times K$, and K is odd. We also assume that $p_1 > p_2 > \cdots > p_n$.

We shall represent each PMP configuration by a one-to-one mapping π which assigns to node m an item with probability ranking $r = \pi(m)$, and denote the inverse mapping by p, i.e., $p(r) = m$. We also introduce the following naming convention for the nodes (see Figure 2.3.3). Let the center be numbered 1, the nodes in the innermost shell numbered 2, 3, 4, ..., 9, and then the next shell 10, 11, 12, ..., 25, etc. Within each shell, the nodes are numbered in the order

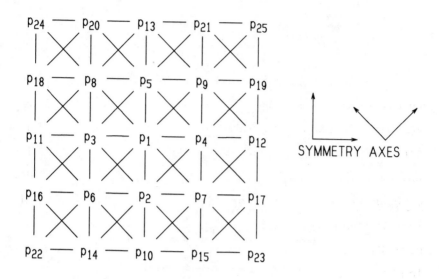

Figure 2.3.2

of

$$a_1a_2a_3a_4b_1b_2b_3b_4b_5b_6b_7b_8\ c_1c_2c_3c_4c_5c_6c_7c_8\ ...z_1z_2z_3z_4,$$

as depicted in Figure 2.3.3.

This naming convention has the merit of being easy to write down and is not dependent on the grid size. It has the side property that the identity mapping $\pi(r) = r$ defines a PMP configuration, which also gives near-optimal performance, as we shall see in Subsection 2.3.5. Since the probability majorization property does not specify which side is the majorizing one, it is clear that any rotation or mirror image of a PMP configuration is also PMP. Therefore, we only consider a set of normalized PMP configurations such that

$$\text{left} > \text{right}, \quad \text{bottom} > \text{top},$$

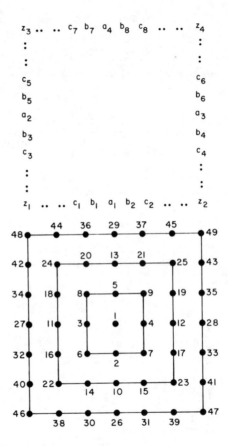

Figure 2.3.3

and for square-meshed grids, since the diagonal lines are also symmetry axes, we require, in addition,

$$\text{bottom left} > \text{top right}, \qquad \text{bottom right} > \text{top left},$$

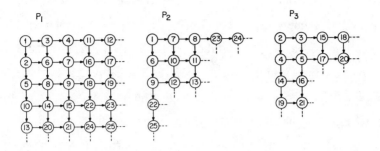

Figure 2.3.4

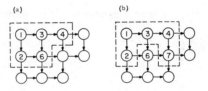

Figure 2.3.5

where the symbol $\succ$ denotes probability majorization, i.e.,

$n_1 \succ n_2$ if and only if $p_{\pi(n_1)} > p_{\pi(n_2)}$.

The PMP requirements are easily expressed in the form of directed graphs.

In Figure 2.3.4, P_1 are the PMP constraints along the horizontal and vertical symmetry axes and $P_2 \cup P_3$ are constraints along the diagonal symmetry axes. The reason for aligning the nodes as in Figure 2.3.4 will be apparent as we examine how these graphs can provide a way of generating PMP configurations iteratively. The rationale is as follows. For every k, the set of nodes assigned to $p_1, p_2, ..., p_k$, namely $S_k = \{p(1), p(2), ..., p(k)\}$, must include all the connecting nodes of the members, i.e., if $x > y > z$, $x \epsilon S_k$ and $z \epsilon S_k$, then $y \epsilon S_k$. For example, for k = 5, the set of nodes $\{1,2,3,4,6\}$ of Figure 2.3.5(a) is feasible as S_k, while the set $\{1,2,3,4,7\}$ of Figure 2.3.5(b) is not because in the latter case, node 6 will have to be assigned to some p_j where j>k, implying in particular that $p_{\pi(6)} < p_{\pi(7)}$ and the constraint $6 > 7$ will be violated. It is easy to see, therefore, that for every k, S_k must be contained by a staircase boundary at the upper left-hand corner of each directed graph. In order to determine the next possible node, i.e., p(k + 1) for assigning p_{k+1}, it suffices to examine only the leading corners of the staircases and select the candidates from $P_1 \cap (P_2 \cup P_3)$. Thus, in the example with $\{p(1), p(2), p(3), p(4), p(5)\} = \{1,2,3,4,6\}$, p(6) must be either 5 or 7 (Figure 2.3.6).

Consequently, if we start at node 1 and increment one node at a time, we can enumerate all possible, normalized PMP mappings by assigning these sequences of nodes to items with descending probabilities. The enumeration procedure is illustrated in the tree diagram of Figure 2.3.7. Once again, we note that the identity map (leftmost path on the tree) is included.

This enumeration procedure has been used to count the possible number of normalized PMP mappings. The result shows that even for n = 25 (i.e., a mere 5 × 5 grid), there are well over 200,000 of them. We can also observe from the above tree structure that this number grows at least exponentially with n. Therefore, an exhaustive comparison for cost optimization leads to insurmountable computations even for medium-size grids. The tree itself, however, is easy to generate since there are numerous identical subtrees, as we will

examine in greater detail in Subsection 2.3.4. Therefore, the tree can
be used for the purpose of heuristic search or heuristic optimization,
which yields suboptimal solutions.

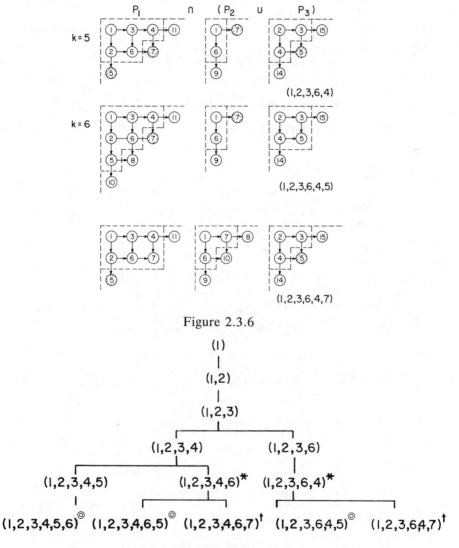

Figure 2.3.6

Figure 2.3.7

2.3.4. Lower bound for cost Since the optimal cost cannot be obtained exactly, it is necessary to have good lower bounds for the evaluation of contending heuristics. The most straightforward way to obtain lower bounds is to consider the quadratic cost function as a linear combination of inner products and invoke the well-known Hardy-Littlewood-Pólya bounds.   Suppose for each i, we order $d_{i1}, d_{i2}, ..., d_{in}$ in ascending order, i.e., $(d_{i1'}, d_{i2'}, ..., d_{in'})$ so that $d_{i1'} \leq d_{i2'} \leq ... \leq d_{in'}$ and compare them with $(d_{11'}, d_{12'}, ..., d_{1n'})$. Recalling that node 1 corresponds to the center of the grid, we see that $d_{ij'} \geq d_{1j'}$ for all i and j'.

Therefore, $p_1 > p_2 > ... > p_n$ implies that

$$D = \sum_{i=1}^{n} p_i \sum_{j=1}^{n} p_j d_{p(i)p(j)} \geq \sum_{i=1}^{n} p_i \sum_{j=1}^{n} p_j d_{1j'} = \sum_{j=1}^{n} p_j d_{1j'}$$

because $\{p_j\}$ and $\{d_{1j'}\}$ are monotonic in the opposite direction [11].

This lower bound is very easy to compute. Unfortunately, it is far too loose to be useful and its tightness also depends very much on the choice of distributions. For example, if n = 9, there are only five normalized PMP configurations, as shown in Figure 2.3.8. Assuming

$(p_1, p_2, p_3, p_4, p_5, p_6, p_7, p_8, p_9)$

$p_8 p_5 p_9$	$p_8 p_6 p_9$	$p_8 p_7 p_9$	$p_8 p_6 p_9$	$p_8 p_7 p_9$
$p_3 p_1 p_4$	$p_3 p_1 p_4$	$p_3 p_1 p_4$	$p_3 p_1 p_5$	$p_3 p_1 p_5$
$p_6 p_2 p_7$	$p_5 p_2 p_7$	$p_5 p_2 p_6$	$p_4 p_2 p_7$	$p_4 p_2 p_6$
D=0.7093	D=0.7037	D=0.7018	D=0.6976	D=0.6957

Figure 2.3.8

$$= (1/2, 1/4, 1/8, 1/16, 1/32, 1/64, 1/128, 1/256, 1/256),$$

we compute the optimal cost to be 0.6957, corresponding to configuration 5. The lower bound, however, gives the value

$$(0 \cdot p_1 + 1 \cdot p_2 + 1 \cdot p_3 + \ldots + 1 \cdot p_9) = 0.5.$$

If we assume $(p_1, p_2, \ldots, p_9) = (1/4, 1/8, 1/8, 1/8, 1/8, 1/16, 1/16, 1/16, 1/16)$, then the cost for the five configurations are $9/8, 145/128, 145/128, 145/128$ and $145/128$ respectively, and the first one is optimal. This clearly shows that the optimum depends on the exact values of $\{p_i\}$. The value of the bound in this case is $3/4$. This bound is loose because the mappings that minimize individual terms are far from being optimal for the sum. In order to obtain a tight bound, we perform a transformation on the double sum as in Section 2.2.

Let E_{rs} be defined for each pair $(r,s), 1 \leq r, s \leq n$, by

$$E_{rs} = \sum_{i=1}^{r} \sum_{j=1}^{s} d_{p(i)p(j)}.$$

Then

$$D = \sum_{r=1}^{n} \sum_{s=1}^{n} \Delta_r \Delta_s E_{rs},$$

where

$$\Delta_r = p_r - p_{r+1}, 1 \leq r < n, \Delta_n = p_n.$$

This transformation is basically the discrete analogue of integration by parts. If each term E_{rs} is minimized by a PMP mapping, then we expect intuitively that the sum will be a better lower bound because the PMP constraints for optimality are explicitly incorporated. Specifically, we write

$$D \geq \sum_{r=1}^{n} \sum_{s=1}^{n} \Delta_r \Delta_s \min_{\substack{p \text{ is PMP}}} E_{rs}$$

The minimization of E_{rs} is a nontrivial task but is much easier computationally than that of D because E_{rs} depends only on the boundaries (graph P_1) which contain the set of nodes assigned to the set of the r largest and the set of the s largest probabilities. These assignments are embodied in a digraph which is reduced from the tree of our enumeration procedure. This graph has fewer nodes and does not fan off exponentially as the tree. For example, in Figure 2.3.9, the three mappings (1,2,3,4,5,6), (1,2,3,4,6,5) and (1,2,3,6,4,5) all represent the same set, which can be assigned to $\{p_1, p_2, p_3, p_4, p_5, p_6\}$, although in different order. These nodes also have identical subtrees. The reduction of nodes in going from the tree to the graph is dramatic, and this reduction makes it possible to minimize E_{rs} by exhaustive comparison. The number of comparisons for each E_{rs} is equal to the number of paths between the r-th and the s-th levels of the graph. By comparing the tree in Figure 2.3.7 and the digraph in Figure 2.3.9, we can readily observe the reduction in computational complexity.

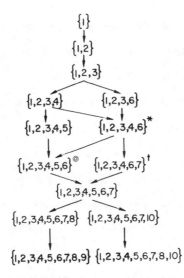

Figure 2.3.9

A great advantage of this bound is that once the set
$\{ \min E_{rs} \}$, $1 \le r \le n, 1 \le s \le n$, has been determined, it can be used again
and again for any values of access probabilities. Therefore, we are not
only able to evaluate any heuristic algorithms for a specific
distribution; we can also study the sensitivity of performance
numerically when the distribution changes. We anticipate that this
bound is not only tight but also robust. The reason is that each E_{rs}
represents the average distance from nodes $p(1)$ through $p(r)$ to nodes
$p(1)$ through $p(s)$ and is optimized for whatever values of r and s by
packing $p_1, p_2, ..., p_t$, $t = \max(r,s)$, as tightly as possible in the
center. This is exactly the underlying property of any good heuristic.
Therefore, the configurations that minimize individual E_{rs} also tend to
minimize the overall cost regardless of the values of p_i's.

2.3.5. Near-optimality of the stepwise minimization algorithm   Since
neither the minimum cost nor the lower bound can be written down in

closed form, numerical studies play an important role. Here we demonstrate how the method described earlier is used to evaluate a heuristic algorithm and show that it is near-optimal under various distributional assumptions. We concentrate on an algorithm which is based on stepwise minimization, and we use only the knowledge of probability ranking.

Stepwise minimization algorithm Let p_1 reside in the center node and assign $p_2, p_3, \ldots, p_n$ iteratively. At each step k, we compare the cost d_{ij} required to move from any legitimate normalized PMP position to the node occupied by p_1, select the minimal one, and place p_k accordingly. If there are ties, consider p_2 and then p_3, if necessary, and so on. As it turns out, we only need the PMP constraints at a few initial steps, and the resulting assignment is unique (i.e., at each k, whenever p_{k-1} is considered, there are no ties). The resulting scheme is shown in Figure 2.3.10.

The distributions we choose for testing purposes consist of a variety of shapes, including convex, concave and combination.

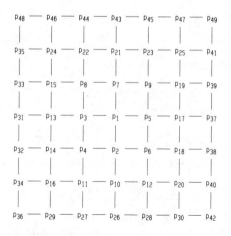

Figure 2.3.10

Specifically, we consider three classes of $\{p_k\}, 1 \leq k \leq n$:

(I) $p_k = \text{const} \cdot k^{-\theta_1}$,

(II) $p_k = \text{cont} \cdot \theta_2^k$,

(III) $p_k = \text{const} \cdot \exp(-k^2/\theta_3^2)$,

where the constants are governed by the condition $\sum_{k=1}^{n} p_k = 1$. Both class I and class II are convex but have different skewedness. Class III is concave for $\theta_3 < (2n)^{1/2}$ and has a half-bell shape otherwise. The actual cost of the stepwise minimization algorithm is compared with the lower bound for different parameter values of $\theta_1, \theta_2, \theta_3$ and different grid sizes. The results are presented in Tables 2.3.1-2.3.3.

As we can see, the actual cost never exceeds the lower bound by more than 0.8% for our test cases, regardless of the distributional shape, parameter value or grid size. Although these are not worst-case bounds, we hope they are at least convincing from a practical standpoint. The stepwise algorithm has a common characteristic with the identity mapping algorithm mentioned in Subsection 2.3.3 since they are both PMP and they both assign higher probabilities to a shell nearer the center. Identical numerical studies have been made on the latter's performance. We observed that the deviations from optimality became more irregular, but were nonetheless within 1-2% of the former. Therefore, the details are not given here.

Finally, we briefly comment on the case of rectangular-mesh grids. First of all, both the bounding procedure and the stepwise algorithm can be used, although the diagonal lines are no longer symmetry axes and the constraints of graphs P_2 and P_3 should be discarded. Thus, the computational complexity should increase

Table 2.3.1
Evaluation of the stepwise minimization algorithm
for Class I distributions

	n = 81			n = 49	n = 25
θ_1	Cost	Bound	Ratio	Ratio	Ratio
1.8	0.9608	0.9594	1.0015	1.0016	1.0019
1.6	1.2167	1.2142	1.0020	1.0022	1.0026
1.4	1.5464	1.5425	1.0025	1.0028	1.0033
1.2	1.9471	1.9412	1.0030	1.0034	1.0041
1.0	2.3949	2.3866	1.0035	1.0039	1.0051
0.8	2.8491	2.8388	1.0036	1.0041	1.0050
0.6	3.2692	3.2581	1.0034	1.0039	1.0047
0.4	3.6302	3.6204	1.0027	1.0031	1.0039
0.2	3.9260	3.9199	1.0016	1.0018	1.0023

Table 2.3.2
Class II distributions

	n = 81			n = 49	n = 25
θ_2	Cost	Bound	Ratio	Ratio	Ratio
1.00	4.1628	4.1628	1.0000	1.0000	1.0000
0.95	2.7181	2.7008	1.0064	1.0062	1.0059
0.90	1.9336	1.9217	1.0062	1.0063	1.0069
0.85	1.5446	1.5353	1.0060	1.0061	1.0065
0.80	1.3071	1.2996	1.0058	1.0058	1.0060
0.70	1.0159	1.0113	1.0046	1.0046	1.0046
0.60	0.8326	0.8304	1.0027	1.0027	1.0027
0.50	0.6968	0.6960	1.0011	1.0011	1.0010

Table 2.3.3
Class III distributions

	n = 81			n = 49	n = 25
θ_3	Cost	Bound	Ratio	Ratio	Ratio
10	1.4760	1.4651	1.0074	1.0074	1.0074
20	2.1348	2.1192	1.0074	1.0074	1.0073
30	2.6347	2.6146	1.0077	1.0073	1.0051
40	3.0394	3.0159	1.0078	1.0065	1.0034
50	3.3448	3.3203	1.0074	1.0053	1.0024
60	3.5586	3.5351	1.0066	1.0042	1.0017
70	3.7051	3.6837	1.0058	1.0034	1.0013
80	3.8067	3.7877	1.0050	1.0032	1.0010

because there should be more nodes in the graph of Figure 2.3.9. The
procedure itself is still valid. Second, the relative positions of the
assignment may change with grid size and with the proportion of the
mesh. For example, in the extreme case of a very flat grid, the
stepwise assignment gives rise to the pattern of Figure 2.3.11, which is
very different from that of Figure 2.3.10. The pattern of Figure
2.3.11 in this case also turns out to be optimal because it is equivalent
to the one-dimensional case. If the x and y directions have unequal
speeds of movement, we can rescale the rectangular grid. For
example, if

$$d_{ij} = \max(|x_i - x_j|, \beta|y_i - y_j|),$$

we can make $\beta = 1$ by replacing βy_i with $y_{i'}$.

We also remark that the ideas of this section can be applied to
other cost functions, e.g., when the cost is a monotonic function of the
Euclidean or the rectilinear distance between two points.

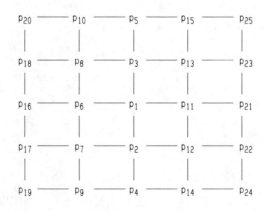

Figure 2.3.11

2.4.   Head scheduling in a batched processing environment

2.4.1.   Introduction   In the last two sections we assumed that the requests to records were processed sequentially, i.e., one request at a time on a first-come-first-served basis.   As in Section 1.6, here we consider again the processing of batched requests, i.e., we process a fixed number (a batch) of requests at a time.

Again, the objective is to minimize the expected head travel for a batch, and two problems need consideration: (a) record placement, (b) head scheduling for processing a batch of requests. Problem (a) depends, among other things, on the solution to (b) and is a very difficult problem.   Intuitively, the "shell" algorithm of Section 2.2 and the enumeration algorithm of Section 2.3 should give very good record arrangements.   Coupled with a good solution to (b), this would result in a nearly optimal expected head travel.

We therefore assume that the records are placed already and consider (b) only.

A given batch of requests specifies a set of storage locations which the head must visit one by one, starting from the stopping location of the last batch.   To minimize the expected head travel, the order of visitation is very important.   Two things must be taken into account: (1) the total distance traveled by the head for the current batch, (2) the final position of the head, which becomes the starting position for the next batch.

Clearly, minimizing only the total distance does not necessarily give an ideal final head position.   In fact, it may push the head so far away from the locations specified by the next batch that the loss in the next batch largely outweighs the gain in the current batch.

In the one-dimensional case, for each batch of requests there were only two directions in which the head could move, namely, left and right. We were able to obtain an optimal algorithm for scheduling the head. However, in the two-dimensional case, the problem becomes much more complicated. If we use the discrete dynamic programming method, as in Section 1.6, the number of states will be too large to be practical. The only reasonable approach is to find a tour of minimum total distance for the current batch and accept the final position of the tour as the starting position for the next batch.

Even this problem is not easy. In fact, it is NP-complete, as will be seen. This section mainly addresses this problem and proposes a fast heuristic. The concept of Voronoi diagram in computational geometry is employed [26,29]. For the Euclidean (L_2) metric, there are many good heuristics for this problem [7] and, it is therefore not considered here. We will only consider the rectilinear (L_1) and maximum (L_∞) metrics here. Furthermore, because of the isometry (2.2.13) of Section 2.2,

$$\begin{cases} x' = \dfrac{y+x}{2} \\[2mm] y' = \dfrac{y-x}{2} \end{cases}$$

which is a linear mapping with rational coefficients from points (x,y) $\in R_\infty^2$, to points (x',y') $\in R_1^2$, the two metrics can be regarded as polynomially equivalent, in the sense that any deterministic polynomial time algorithm for the problem in the L_∞ metric can be applied to solve the same problem in the L_1 metric and vice versa. We therefore need to consider only the L_1 metric from now on.

2.4.2. Statement of the problem and its NP-completeness In general, let R_p^2 denote the plane with the L_p metric:

$$d_p(q_i,q_j) = (\,|\,x_i-x_j\,|^p + |\,y_i-y_j\,|^p)^{1/p},$$

where $q_i = (x_i,y_i)$ and $q_j = (x_j,y_j)$ are points in the plane. We are interested mainly in the case $p = 1$.

Given n points in R_1^2, with one of the points designated as the starting point, we want to find a shortest Hamiltonian path. This problem will be referred to as the Open Path Problem (OPP). In [7] the traveling salesman problem for points in R_1^2 has been shown to be NP-complete. By a slight modification of the proof it can be shown that the so-called "open" traveling salesman problem, i.e., finding a shortest Hamiltonian path without specifying end points, for points in R_1^2, is also NP-complete [16]. To show that the OPP considered here is NP-complete, we note first that it is obviously in NP. Since the open traveling salesman problem is NP-complete, the existence of a polynomial time algorithm for this problem (i.e., NP=P) implies the same for the OPP. On the other hand, if the OPP has a polynomial time algorithm, we can apply it n times to solve the open traveling salesman problem in polynomial time by specifying in turn each point as a starting point and then taking the shortest path of the n solutions.

Due to the difficulty of obtaining an optimal solution to this problem, we shall present two approximation algorithms which run in O(n lg n) time and yield a solution within a factor of 2 of the optimal.

Our proposed heuristics are based on the construction of Voronoi diagrams [26,29] in the L_1 metric. For other applications of the Voronoi diagram, see [29]. Using this diagram one can build a near-optimal path through the given set of points either by construction of a minimum spanning tree or by the closest insertion method, as discussed in [27]. We show that the construction of the Voronoi diagram for n points in a plane with the L_1 (L_∞) metric takes time $O(n \lg n)$. In [20,29] an $O(n \lg n)$ algorithm for constructing the Voronoi diagram for n points in a plane with the L_2 (Euclidean) metric is presented. While our construction follows the same basic approach as in [20,29], it needs some nontrivial modifications. Some new observations are also needed in order to achieve the bound $O(n \lg n)$.

It should also be pointed out that even the intuitively appealing heuristic of moving to the nearest neighbor takes $O(n^2)$ time for our metrics. It is not known if the construction time can be reduced to $O(n \lg n)$.

2.4.3. Voronoi diagrams in the L_1 metric We first introduce some definitions and notations. Given two points q_i and q_j with coordinates (x_i, y_i) and (x_j, y_j) respectively in the plane R_p^2, the bisector $B_p(q_i, q_j)$ of q_i and q_j is the locus of points equidistant from q_i and q_j, i.e., $B_p(q_i, q_j) = \{r \mid r \in R_p^2, d_p(r, q_i) = d_p(r, q_j)\}$. In the Euclidean plane, $B_2(q_i, q_j)$ is the perpendicular bisector of the line segment $\overline{q_i q_j}$. The bisectors of q_i and q_j in different metrics are shown in Figure 2.4.1. If $|x_i - x_j| > |y_i - y_j|$, then $B_1(q_i, q_j)$ has two vertical lines and one line segment (Figure 2.4.1(a)). If $|x_i - x_j| < |y_i - y_j|$, then $B_1(q_i, q_j)$ has two horizontal lines and one line segment (Figure 2.4.1(c)). They are referred to as vertical and horizontal bisectors respectively for short. In the case that $|x_i - x_j| = |y_i - y_j|$, $B_1(q_i, q_j)$ has two unbounded regions (crossed area in Figure 2.4.1(b)) and a line segment. Without creating any significant difference in the following discussion, we shall arbitrarily choose the vertical bisector (the thick lines) as $B_1(q_i, q_j)$. Note that the line segment portion of $B_1(q_i, q_j)$ is of slope ± 1.

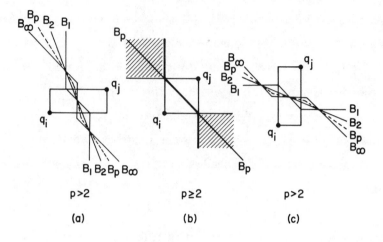

Figure 2.4.1

We now define the generalized notion of Voronoi diagrams [26,29] in the L_p metrics. Given a set $\mathscr{S} = \{q_1, q_2, \ldots, q_n\}$ of n points in R_p^2, the locus of points closer to q_i than to q_j, denoted by $h_p(q_i, q_j)$, is one of the "half-planes" determined by the bisector $B_p(q_i, q_j)$, i.e., $h_p(q_i, q_j) = \{r \mid r \in R_p^2, d_p(r, q_i) \leq d_p(r, q_j)\}$. The locus of points closer to q_i than to any other point, denoted by $V_p(q_i)$, is thus given by $V_p(q_i) = \cap_{i \neq j} h_p(q_i, q_j)$, the intersection of all the half-planes associated with q_i. The region $V_p(q_i)$ is called the *Voronoi polygon* (not necessarily bounded) associated with q_i. The entire set of regions partitions the plane into n regions and is referred to as the *Voronoi diagram* $V_p(\mathscr{S})$ for the set $\mathscr{S}$ of points in the L_p metric. The points at which three or more bisectors meet are called *Voronoi points*. We shall refer to the portion of a bisector between two Voronoi points of a Voronoi polygon as an *edge* of the polygon. An edge of the Voronoi polygon in the $L_1(L_\infty)$ metric can have at most three line segments. Since we shall deal only with the L_1 metric, unless specified otherwise, the subscript p denoting the metric may be dropped without creating confusion. The *body* HB($\mathscr{S}$) of the set $\mathscr{S}$ is defined as the smallest rectangular region that contains the entire set $\mathscr{S}$. Since any two points of $\mathscr{S}$ define a unique rectangle, the body of the set $\mathscr{S}$ can also be defined as HB($\mathscr{S}$) = $\cup_i${HB($\mathscr{S}_i$) | $\mathscr{S}_i$ = {q,r},q,r$\in$ $\mathscr{S}$}, i.e., the union of the bodies of all its 2-subsets (subsets of $\mathscr{S}$ with cardinality 2). In particular, if $\mathscr{S}$ = {q_1,q_2} where q_1,q_2 lie on a line parallel to x- or y-axis, the body HB($\mathscr{S}$) is the line segment $\overline{q_1q_2}$. Figure 2.4.2 shows the Voronoi diagram for a set of 9 points, in which "Δ" denotes a Voronoi point, and the region within the dashed rectangle is the body.

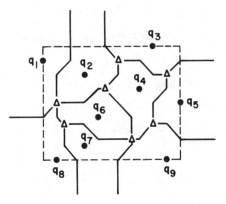

Figure 2.4.2

Several observations need to be made of the Voronoi diagram. First of all, the dual of the diagram is a *planar* graph on the set of n points in which there is an edge between q_i and q_j if the Voronoi polygons $V(q_i)$ and $V(q_j)$ have a common edge $B(q_i,q_j)$ as their border. Since there is a one-to-one correspondence between an edge of the dual and a bisector of the diagram, and a one-to-one correspondence between a region of the dual and a Voronoi point, the number of both bisectors and Voronoi points is O(n). The minimum spanning tree in the L_1 metric can be shown to be a subgraph of the dual of the Voronoi diagram $V(\mathscr{S})$. The proof parallels that of showing the Euclidean minimum spanning tree being embedded in the dual of $V_2(\mathscr{S})$ [29] and hence is omitted here. Second, the closest pair of points can be found in $O(n)$ time if the diagram is available. Since the proof that finding the closest pair of points in the L_2 metric requires at least $O(n \lg n)$ time in the worst case [29] can be carried over to any metric, the construction of the Voronoi diagram must take at least $O(n \lg n)$ time. Third, the diagram outside the body of the set (see Figure 2.4.2) consists only of vertical and horizontal lines. By the definition that the body of the set $\mathscr{S}$ is the union of the bodies of all its 2-subsets and the fact that the bisector $B(q,r)$ of any two points q and r in $\mathscr{S}$ is either vertical or horizontal, this observation follows immediately. We note in passing that the last observation is particularly important in the following discussions.

The Voronoi diagram in the L_1 metric (or metrics other than the L_2) is different from the commonly known Voronoi diagram in the Euclidean metric in that the Voronoi polygons in the former diagram are not *convex*. Convexity plays an important role in the construction of $V_2(\mathscr{S})$ and makes the lower bound $O(n \lg n)$ achievable [20,29]. In the procedure given in [29], the merge process can be accomplished in $O(n)$ time by using the property of convexity of the Voronoi polygon [20]. It is not at all apparent that the same argument can be carried through directly if convexity is no longer available. We shall show in the following that the Voronoi diagram in the L_1 metric can be constructed in $O(n \lg n)$ time by using the above-mentioned properties.

2.4.4. Construction of the Voronoi diagram in the L_1 metric   We shall use a divide-and-conquer technique to construct the Voronoi diagram

$V(\mathscr{S})$. First of all, we presort the data in ascending order of the x-coordinates (and y-coordinates if x-coordinates are equal) and number them 1 through n from left to right. Divide the set $\mathscr{S}$ into two disjoint subsets L and R which contain the leftmost and the rightmost $n/2$ points respectively. Recursively construct the Voronoi diagrams $V(L)$ and $V(R)$ for sets L and R respectively. We shall merge them to form $V(\mathscr{S})$ by constructing a polygonal line T with the property that any point to the left of the line is closer to some point in L and any point to the right is closer to some point in R. After the line is constructed, the portion of $V(L)$ (and $V(R)$) that lies to the right (and left) of the line is discarded, and the resultant $V(\mathscr{S})$ is obtained. Note that the line T can be shown [28] to be monotone with respect to y-axis, i.e., for any three points a, b and c on T, their y-coordinates satisfy either $y(a) \geq y(b) \geq y(c)$ or $y(a) \leq y(b) \leq y(c)$. If one can show that O(n) time suffices to construct the line, then it follows by the recurrence relation $T(n) = 2T(n/2) + O(n)$ that $T(n) = O(n \lg n)$ is enough for the construction of the diagram $V(\mathscr{S})$.

The example shown in Figure 2.4.3 helps illustrate the idea of merging. Consider a set of 18 points numbered from 1 through 18. The left set is $L = \{1,2,..,9\}$ and right set is $R = \{10,...,18\}$. The Voronoi diagrams $V(L)$ and $V(R)$ are shown in short and long dashed lines respectively. The merge process is described as follows. At first, the rightmost point with the smallest index in the set L is found and is denoted by w. Since w is the rightmost point in L, w is on the boundary of the body HB(L) and its associated Voronoi polygon $V(w)$ is unbounded. Consider the horizontal half-line emanating from the point w to infinity in the same direction as the positive x-axis and denote it by **w**. Take any point z on **w**. It is easy to verify that $d(z,w) = \min_{u \in L} d(z,u)$, which implies that the entire half-line **w** is contained in the polygon V(w). Therefore, V(w) is unbounded.

The following process of determining the *starting bisector* is based on the property that any line connecting two points which lie on different sides of T must intersect T. The half-line **w** contains a point z whose x-coordinate is sufficiently large to satisfy the inequality $d(z,w)>d(z,v)$ for some v in R. That is, z lies to the *right* of T. Since w is known to lie to the *left* of T, an intersection point of the line segment $\overline{wz}$ and T is guaranteed to exist. Since T is a collection of bisectors B(u,v) for some u in L and v in R, we shall look for the bisector B(w,s) for some s in R such that it intersects the line segment $\overline{wz}$. We first find the nearest neighbor r of w among the set R, i.e., $d(w,r) = \min_{u \in R} d(w,v)$, i.e., points 8 and 11 respectively in Figure 2.4.3. This step takes O(n) time. r being the nearest neighbor of w, its associated polygon V(r) contains w. We shall scan the edges of V(r) to find which edge the line segment $\overline{wz}$ intersects. Suppose $\overline{wz}$ intersects an edge B(r,r') at a point q. If q is found to lie to the *right* of T, i.e., $d(q,r)<d(q,w)$, then T intersects the line segment $\overline{wq}$ at some point t and B(w,r) is our starting bisector. Otherwise, we do the same by scanning the edges of V(r') to find which edge intersects $\overline{qz}$. Repeat the process until we either find an intersection point which lies to the *right* of T or fail to find one. In either case, we shall use B(w,s) as our starting bisector, where s is the point whose associated polygon V(s) is currently under consideration. The time involved to find the starting bisector is O(n), for each edge of V(R) is examined at most once. As shown in Figure 2.4.3, B(8,14) is the starting bisector, and the construction of T shown in solid lines is carried out in two phases, upward and downward, both using B(8,14) as the starting bisector.

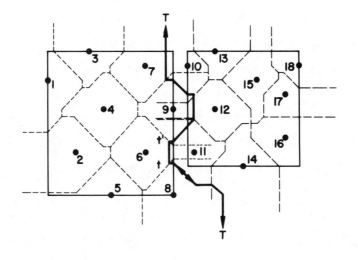

Figure 2.4.3

We remark here that this step for determining the starting bisector of the polygonal line differs from that used in constructing the line in the L_2 metric. In the latter, the starting bisector is determined by the line segments created in forming the union of the convex hulls of L and R [20,29]. We first proceed by moving upward an imaginary point t, following the direction of B(8,11) until we meet B(8,6), at which point, since t is closer to 6 than to 8, we follow the bisector B(6,11), and so on. Continue moving upward until we go out of the body HB(S). The downward phase is similar.

We now show that the construction of T takes O(n) time. Before we proceed, we make the following observation. At any time during the merge process, the imaginary point t always lies in two Voronoi polygons, one in V(L), the other in V(R). Whenever a new Voronoi point is created, we will enter a new Voronoi polygon and follow a new direction determined as follows. Suppose B(a,b) were the bisector that we followed in constructing the polygonal line T and B(b,c) were the bisector that intersects B(a,b). The new direction will be following B(a,c). As one can see, at each step we must determine which edge of the two Voronoi polygons where the imaginary point currently lies intersects the current polygonal line first. To do this we shall use the following scanning scheme: scan the edges of the polygon in V(L) in a *counterclockwise* direction and those of the polygon in V(R) in a *clockwise* direction [20]. This scheme is crucial to make the construction of the polygonal line accomplishable in O(n) time and will be justified later.

Note that when we are in the left (right) body and determining which edge of the polygon in V(L) (V(R)) intersects the polygonal line, the only lines that can interfere with the process are those *horizontal* lines emanating from the opposite body; and those horizontal lines are in order of y-coordinate. Thus, during this process some horizontal lines may be *visited* several times, but the total number of visits is proportional to the number of Voronoi points created. This can be seen as follows. Referring to Figure 2.4.3, suppose we are at the point t in the *left* body HB(L) and in Voronoi polygons V(6) and V(11). The bisector of V(6) which intersects the polygonal line T (i.e., B(6,11)) is determined by examining in counterclockwise fashion the two end points (Voronoi points) of each bisector of the polygon until they lie on different sides of the line T. And the intersecting point of T and the horizontal line from HB(R) (the double-dashed line in Figure 2.4.3) is also determined. A simple comparison decides the first intersecting point. A new Voronoi point will be created and we will enter a new Voronoi polygon. The same process is repeated. For example, t′ is created and we enter polygon V(9). If T meets an edge of the polygon first and we still are in the left body HB(L), the same horizontal line will be revisited again in the next iteration. Thus, the number of times that the horizontal line is visited is proportional to the number of Voronoi points created.

Since the polygonal line is monotone with respect to y-axis, at some point it will either meet the horizontal line first or go out of the body HB(L). If T goes out of the body HB(L) and enters the body HB(R), we have a similar situation as before except we change "left" to "right" and "counterclockwise scan" to "clockwise scan." The case in which T meets the horizontal line first needs more careful investigation. Recall that we are at some point t in the left body HB(L). Suppose that before we find the point t' where T intersects the edge of the polygon, a number of horizontal lines emanating from HB(R) interferes. For detailed illustration, see Figure 2.4.4, where we are following bisector $B(\ell_1, r_1)$ and there are a number of interfering horizontal lines $B(r_1 r_2)$, $B(r_1 r_3)$, etc.

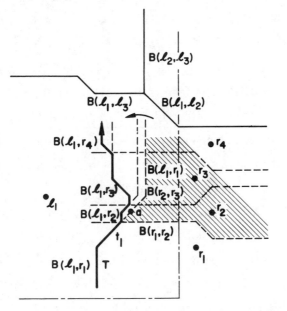

Figure 2.4.4

We claim that some edge of the polygon in V(L) will be visited several times and once it is eliminated from consideration it will never be visited again, i.e., no backtracking is needed. In Figure 2.4.4, we have the situation that T meets the horizontal line first. Before we know that $B(\ell_1 r_1)$ meets $B(r_1,r_2)$ first, we have visited $B(\ell_1,\ell_2)$ once. At point t_1, which is a new Voronoi point on T, we follow the new bisector $B(\ell_1,r_2)$. Again, $B(\ell_1,\ell_2)$ will be revisited. Since both ends of $B(\ell_1,\ell_2)$ lie on the same side of $B(\ell_1,r_2)$, it is eliminated. The next edge $B(\ell_1,\ell_3)$ is visited. Since $B(\ell_1,r_2)$ meets $B(r_2,r_3)$ before it meets $B(\ell_1,\ell_3)$, another Voronoi point t_2 is created and a new bisector $B(\ell_1,r_3)$ is formed. As we can see, each time a new bisector is formed, it is on the left side of the previous bisector, i.e., the portion of $B(\ell_1,r_3)$ in T is to the left of the bisector $B(\ell_1,r_2)$; the portion of $B(\ell_1,r_2)$ in T is to the left of $B(\ell_1,r_1)$. Thus, the possible intersecting edge of the polygon $V(\ell_1)$ moves in a counterclockwise direction. Therefore, no backtracking is needed. To see this, it is sufficient to show that, for example, any point a on $B(\ell_1,r_1)$, where $y(a)>y(t_1)$, lies on the right side of the new bisector $B(\ell_1,r_2)$. Since $d(a,r_2)<d(a,r_1) = d(a,\ell_1)$, it follows that a lies on the right side of $B(\ell_1,r_2)$. In other words, the dotted-line portion of $B(\ell_1,r_2)$ is on the left side of $B(\ell_1,r_1)$. A similar situation occurs if we are in the right body except that the direction of the movement is *clockwise*. This also justifies the scanning scheme mentioned above.

Thus, the number of edge visits in $V(\ell_1)$ is proportional to the number of edges of $V(\ell_1)$ and the number of Voronoi points created. Since the polygonal line is monotone with respect to y-axis, it will eventually meet some edge of the polygon $V(\ell_1)$ and enter a new polygon. At that point, the same process is repeated. Thus, the total number of edge visits in constructing the polygonal line is proportional to the number of bisectors plus the number of Voronoi points on T. Since both of them are $O(n)$, the time for the construction of the polygonal line is $O(n)$. This completes the description of the merge process and verifies that the total construction time for the Voronoi diagram is $O(n \lg n)$, which is optimal in the worst-case sense.

It should be pointed out that [14] gives a completely different method of constructing Voronoi diagrams in the L_1 metric in $O(n \lg n)$ time and [21] extends the method used here to construct Voronoi diagrams in the L_p metric in $O(n \lg n)$ time for arbitrary p.

2.4.5.   Approximation algorithms

1. **Minimum spanning tree method**   Recall that the MST is a subgraph of the Voronoi dual. After we have constructed the Voronoi diagram, we can find its dual in $O(n)$ time. Now we can apply any known minimum spanning tree algorithm [1,32] with time complexity no greater than $O(n \lg n)$ to the dual graph. With the minimum spanning tree obtained we can perform a depth-first search, starting with the specified point, to visit each point once. By the triangle inequality, the total path LENGTH must be smaller than that of traversing the minimum spanning tree edges twice to visit all the points. That is, if MST denotes the total length of the minimum spanning tree, we have LENGTH<2•MST [29]. Since the optimal path is a spanning tree, the total length OPT must be greater than MST. Thus, we have LENGTH<2•OPT. In the worst case, the approximate solution LENGTH may tend to twice the optimal solution. To see this, suppose all the n points are colinear and there are x points on one side of the specified point and n-x-1 points on the other side. Let the distances of the two extreme points to the specified point be d_1 and d_2 respectively. Suppose $d_1 >> d_2$. The

optimal solution would be $2d_2 + d_1$, while the approximate solution could be $2d_1 + d_2$. Therefore, $2d_1 + d_2 \approx 2 \cdot$ OPT.

2. **Closest insertion method** This approach is essentially the same as that given in [27] except that we work on a *path* rather than a *circuit*. We start with a path consisting of a single node, i.e., the specified starting point. At each step, we find the uncontained node k closest to any contained node, i.e., find a minimum $d(m,j)$ such that m is in the path and j is not, and take $k = j$. Then we insert the node k to one of the intervals (p,m) and (m,q), where p, q are in the path and (p,m), (m,q) are edges of the path. Suppose the interval (p,m) is chosen. We replace edge (p,m) by (p,k) and (k,m). To implement this procedure, we shall use an AVL tree [19] as our data structure. Whenever a node k is selected, those edges incident with k in the dual graph of the Voronoi diagram will be added to the tree. Those edges that are already in the tree are excluded. To find the node k, we search through the tree to find the minimum edge (m,j) and delete it from the tree. If both m and j are already in the path, we keep searching and deleting until an edge (m,j) with an end point, say j, not in the path is found. Take $k = j$. Since the total number of edges in the dual graph is $O(n)$, we at most perform $O(n)$ insertions to and deletions from the AVL tree, and the time required is $O(n \lg n)$. This approximation algorithm also yields a solution within a factor of 2 [27], and the bound is tight in the worst case, as described earlier.

2.4.6. Experimental results Here we discuss the expected performance of the approximation algorithms. We assume that the two-dimensional storage arrays are bounded and are represented by the grid points (x,y) in a plane, where x,y are integers and $1 \le x,y \le N$.

We also assume that all of the N^2 grid points are equally likely to be accessed. Suppose at time t a batch A_t of B requests is generated. (Note that multiple requests to a grid point are allowed.) Suppose the last position of the head is $\mathscr{P}$. (For $t = 0$, $\mathscr{P}$ is randomly chosen.) Let U_t denote the total length of the Hamiltonian path with starting point $\mathscr{P}$ determined by the minimum spanning tree method and let W_t denote that by the closest insertion method. Then $U = \lim_{t \to \infty} (\Sigma_t U_t)/t$ is a measure of the expected performance of the minimum spanning tree method. A similarly defined W has the same function for the closest insertion method. Since U and W are very difficult to compute analytically, we resort to simulation. We use a pseudo-random number generator to simulate the random requests. Table 2.4.1 shows the outcomes for different values of N and B. The batched processing is far better than the sequential one, as indicated in Figure 2.4.5. It also shows that the minimum spanning tree approach is better than the closest insertion method.

Table 2.4.1
Comparison of different algorithms

B \ N	15	20	25	30	35	40	
5	50.33	68.01	83.83	98.83	113.41	135.12	Sequential
	33.26	46.06	56.10	65.66	77.21	92.91	Minimum Spanning Tree
	36.77	50.04	63.19	72.95	83.66	98.77	Closest Insertion
10	101.52	131.66	167.22	199.25	227.62	268.97	SQ
	51.08	72.62	88.19	103.91	124.49	145.83	MST
	56.50	75.78	92.88	111.63	128.75	150.96	CI
15	152.30	197.53	249.72	298.95	342.37	399.11	SQ
	66.60	90.62	111.56	136.52	153.98	185.41	MST
	73.38	94.87	118.41	139.93	163.74	190.06	CI

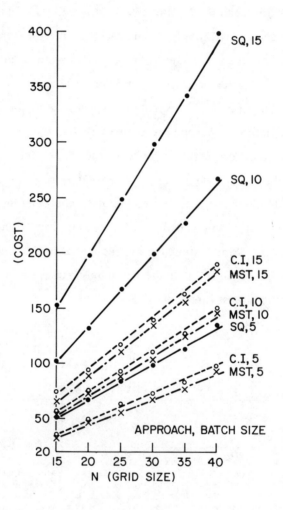

Figure 2.4.5

2.5. Permutation of records using minimum head movement

2.5.1. Introduction So far we have been concerned mainly with the problem of arranging records and scheduling the head in order to minimize its expected travel. In this final section of Chapter 2, we shall deal with a different problem in two-dimensional storage systems, namely, how to rearrange the records in an $n \times n$ grid according to a required permutation so that the total head travel is minimized. In other words, we want to realize an in-place permutation of all the records in a two-dimensional storage system by moving the head around to load/unload the records. The objective is to schedule the head movement so that it can be done in the shortest time. It will later become clear that this problem can be regarded as a forerunner of the problems considered previously. It also serves as an introduction to the topics to be discussed in Chapter 3, where problems of permuting, sorting and searching records in bubble memories will be studied.

We are concerned mainly with the analysis of the general mass storage system shown in Figure 2.5.1. The system is composed of a square $n \times n$ grid of memory "cells," on which a single read/write head is permitted to move to and fro. Each cell contains, uniformly, some memory subsystem with a given capacity; and it is assumed that the read/write head, or its controller, has a fixed number b of "registers" which are each large enough to contain a cell's contents. (Hence, we are concerned with the range of values $1 \leq b \leq n^2$, and the limits $b = 1$ and $b = n^2$ are of particular interest.) In addition to this, the movement of the read/write head is restricted in ways so that the distance between points on the grid (i.e., the amount of time required by the head to move from one point to another) is reflected by the

$L_1, L_2,$ or L_∞ metric on the grid.

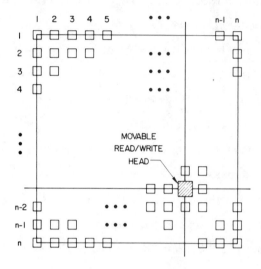

Figure 2.5.1

Note that with $b = 1$ and the L_1 metric the memory system can be made to model an elaborate bubble memory of the type discussed in [4], and with $b = 1$ and the L_∞ metric a tape mass storage system like the IBM 3850 can be modeled. (See Section 2.1.) For most applications a small value of b, such as 1, seems reasonable.

In addition to the grid and read/write head, we assume the existence of a control unit, and some control memory, connected to the head and to the channel making requests on the memory. In the *"online"* mode, requests on the memory are accepted by the control unit and serviced by scheduling a tour for the head (which might be dynamically modified as new requests come in). One problem that might be addressed here is therefore the development of good online scheduling algorithms; if requests are scattered randomly about the grid, then possible solutions might resemble the algorithms already developed for disk-like units (see, e.g., [6,31]). In fact, the memory system here can be regarded as a "four-dimensional drum" — drum with two seek dimensions (each cell containing a track of information).

We will be concerned here with what we call the *"offline,"* or standalone use of this memory, however. Note that, if requests are *not* randomly distributed on the grid, but instead favor given cells over others with a definite probability distribution, then memory performance will be enhanced when all the "popular" cells are located close to one another. With a given access probability distribution, in fact, the best arrangement of the cells for the minimization of average access time is a sort of spiral, with the most popular cells in the center and least popular on the fringes. (This has been discussed in Sections 2.2 and 2.3; the exact nature of the spiral depends on the metric being used, i.e., the restrictions on head movement.) The idea here is that statistics on access frequency might be collected for all the cells while the system is run in online mode; subsequently, the memory system could then be switched offline and the cell contents permuted to realize the spiral organization. In this way average access time in online operation can be reduced, even without a sophisticated scheduling algorithm.

The problem we are addressing is therefore: *What is a good way to realize a permutation of the cell contents in the offline mode?* A solution will permit us to operate the storage system efficiently in the online/offline manner just described and has independent interest as well (it is the two-dimensional generalization of the elevator scheduling problem solved by Karp [19], pp. 358-361). Because of some symmetry considerations, the solution of the problem is somewhat more difficult than might be expected. Below, after suitable definitions and machinery are set up, the average and worst-case costs (i.e., time required to realize a permutation offline, average implying that all permutations are assumed equally likely) are derived for b=1, then $b = n^2$, and finally for intermediate values of b. The "cycle algorithm" analyzed for the b=1 case is asymptotically optimal, so this case may be viewed as resolved (asymptotically at least). For larger b, unfortunately, currently only good algorithms are provided, but these algorithms are shown to give performance within a small constant factor of optimal.

2.5.2. Definitions and general considerations   As just indicated, we are given a square *grid* G, of size n×n, and are concerned with realizing a *permutation* μ selected from P, the set of all permutations of grid points.   Thus, P is the symmetric group on n^2 objects.   The permutation μ indicates how the memory's contents are to be moved: if μ(i) = j, then the contents of cell i are to be moved to cell j. (Cells in the grid may be indexed in any convenient way.) Thus, our problem is to produce an optimal, or near-optimal, *schedule* of head movements and reads or writes (or exchanges) that realizes a given permutation μ. The number of head movements is assumed to be the dominating cost factor, and we will concentrate all of our efforts below on analyzing the movements required by different schedules.   Since each head movement takes, as assumed above, a fixed amount of *time* determined by the $L_p, p = 1,2,\infty$, metric, we will therefore also be studying time requirements of schedules.   Below we will use the terms "head movements" and "time" interchangeably.

Because of the symmetries of the square grid, certain permutations may be effectively realized using fewer head movements than might initially seem necessary.   Consider the realization of the 180° rotation permutation pictured in Figure 2.5.2.

When b=1, if we naively go ahead and move the grid contents around as indicated, then it turns out that we require time of at least $cn^3 + O(n^2)$, where c is the metric-determined constant

$$
c = \begin{cases} 1 & \text{in } L_1 \\[2mm] .76591572... = 1/3[\ell n(1 + \sqrt{2}) + \sqrt{2}] & \text{in } L_2 \\[2mm] 2/3 & \text{in } L_\infty \end{cases}
$$

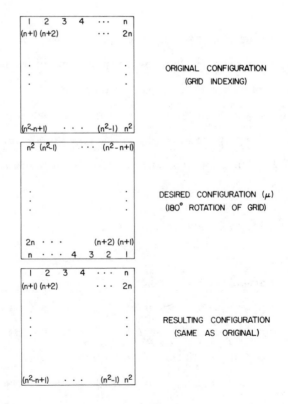

Figure 2.5.2

(The time required is reflected directly by distance under a metric.

Although the L_2 read/write head may seem more powerful than the L_∞ head since it can move in any direction, it really is not since the L_∞ moves simultaneously at uniform speed horizontally and vertically. Thus, to move from (0,0) to (1,1) the L_∞ head takes time 1, while the L_2 head takes time $\sqrt{2}$.) In all three cases this is a great deal of time when one considers that one can get away with *zero* time: if the controller simply remembers that the memory is in the $-180°$ rotated "state," it can translate all future requests on the memory with negligible overhead — and the offline rearrangement never need be made.

We generalize the above idea as follows. Suppose that Cost (π) denotes the least possible cost in time required to (naively) realize the permutation $\pi \in P$. Suppose further that a user requests the memory to be permuted according to $\mu \in P$. Instead of just taking Cost (μ) time, we employ the following more clever approach.

The group S of symmetry operations on the square consists of 8 elements

$$S = \{1,\rho,\rho^2,\rho^3,\tau,\rho\tau,\rho^2\tau,\rho^3\tau\} \subset P,$$

where ρ represents a 90° clockwise rotation and τ a flip about the square's horizontal axis of symmetry, so $\rho^4 = 1, \tau^2 = 1, \rho\tau = \tau\rho^3$, etc. When we say that the grid is in *state* σ we mean the user must apply σ to his conception of the grid's contents to get the actual grid's contents. The grid/state pair (G,σ) is equivalent to the pair $(\sigma'(G), \sigma' \circ \sigma)$ for all $\sigma' \in S$, $\circ$ denoting composition of permutations; the user always thinks of $(\sigma^{-1}(G), 1)$. Note that before Figure 2.5.2 the memory's state σ is 1, since the user's conception of the memory is *correct*, whereas after Figure 2.5.2 the state becomes $\sigma = \mu^{-1} = -180°$ rotation $= \rho^{-2}$.

We may solve the problem posed in the introduction of this section in three steps. Assume that the grid is in state σ and that the user requests a permutation μ to be realized (relative to his perception of the grid's contents); then

(1) Determine which state $\sigma' \in S$ minimizes Cost ($\sigma' \circ \mu \circ \sigma^{-1}$).

(2) Realize $\pi = \sigma' \circ \mu \circ \sigma^{-1}$ directly on the grid.

(3) Mark the grid's state to be σ'.

Note that when the user is kind enough to choose μ as an element of S, this process is trivial, since then one can always find $\sigma' \in$ S such that $\sigma' \circ \mu \circ \sigma^{-1} = 1$, and with any reasonable permuting algorithm we have Cost (1) = 0. In other words, when $\mu \in$ S there is no work to be done except to change the grid's state, as was shown in Figure 2.5.2. The point is, however, that even when μ is not in S, significant savings in time can result by using this approach of choosing the cheapest grid state. We will quantify this statement later.

Now the only remaining difficulty is to exhibit an optimal algorithm which produces head movement schedules for realizing a given permutation π (for example, $\pi = \sigma' \circ \mu \circ \sigma^{-1}$) directly/naively on the grid. Unfortunately, this is not so simple if one wants the algorithm to terminate quickly. Here we want the time to *produce* a schedule for realizing π to be significantly less than the time actually needed to *execute* the schedule by the read/write head. We are assuming that algorithms of moderate time complexity (say, between $O(n^2)$ and $O(n^4)$ steps, where again there are n^2 grid elements) will have this property. Much of the rest of this section is concerned with finding algorithms of moderate complexity for various values of b which produce near-optimal schedules.

It can be shown that the problem of producing an optimal *schedule* of head operations is NP- hard, no matter how large b is (i.e., no matter how many registers the head has), by reducing the following path traveling salesman problem (PTSP) [7,24] to it: given a set of m city coordinates $\{c_1 = (x_i, y_i) \mid i = 1,...,m\}$ where x_i, y_i are integers between 1 and m, find an optimal path through all the cities, i.e., the traveling salesman is not constrained to return to his starting city; he merely is required to visit each city once. Note that except for the L_2 metric we can easily show that the problem is in NP [7]. The reduction is as follows: we construct a set of 2m points $\{p_i, q_i \mid i = 1,...,m\}$ on a suitably large grid, namely,

$$p_i = (4x_i, 4y_i)$$

$$q_i = (4x_i + 1, 4y_i)$$

so n, the grid size, is actually 4 m.

Note that if we can produce an optimal read/write head tour for the permutation

$$\mu = (p_1 q_1)(p_2 q_2) \; \cdots \; (p_m q_m)$$

expressed in cycle notation — so $\mu(p_i) = q_i, \mu(q_i) = p_i$ for all i and $\mu(x) = x$ otherwise — then an optimal tour for the original PTSP can be easily extracted. This reduction works no matter how large b is (since the optimal head tour will always just exchange p_i and q_i before moving on to another pair, so b=1 will always suffice) and no matter which L_p metric is used (the reduction of the L_2 PTSP to the planar Hamiltonian path problem given in [24] generalizes for L_1 and L_∞ as well; see also [7].)

It is therefore clear that the best we can probably do here is to produce a heuristic polynomial algorithm that finds *near*-optimal tours. Fortunately, this is not hard for most permutations, as we shall see. The permutation μ produced in the above reduction is very *sparse* as a permutation, since it leaves most of the grid undisturbed. We shall see that "good" tours for nonsparse permutations can always be found quickly. Interestingly, it is a very rare occurrence for a randomly selected permutation to be sparse; for example, [25] shows

$$\lim_{n \to \infty} \text{Pr} \text{ [random } \mu \epsilon P \text{ does not satisfy}$$

$$\mu(x) = x \text{ for any } x \epsilon G] = 1/e.$$

2.5.3. The case b=1   The case $b=1$, that is, the case that the read/write head contains only one register, is probably the most important for practical applications and will correspondingly be given most of the attention of this section. In this case the contention for the use of the head is extreme - in fact, so extreme that, as we will see, the cost of realizing a permutation is determined almost wholly by the contention and not very much by the precise form of the scheduling algorithm. This simplification permits a thorough analysis of this case, a task which becomes more difficult as b grows large.

We present first a simple but effective algorithm for generating a read/write head schedule in realizing a permutation $\pi \epsilon P$. (Here π is viewed as an "absolute" permutation — symmetry operations on the grid are not taken into consideration.)

Cycle Algorithm

Given $b=1$, permutation π to be realized, head initially in any location x on grid.

Step 1   Determine cycles (orbits) of permutation π

Step 2   Repeatedly

    (a)   schedule the head to permute all the elements in the cycle of its current grid location in the obvious way (i.e., move x to $\pi(x), \pi(x)$ to $\pi(\pi(x))$, etc., until the head returns to point x);

    (b)   *schedule* the head to go to the nearest location whose contents have yet to be moved.

       Although this algorithm is extremely simple-minded, it is clear that the only possible waste in time it might make would come from Step 2(b) since all the moves made in Step 2(a) are necessary when $b=1$. Let CACost (π) denote the cost of realizing π with the cycle algorithm;

$$\text{CACost}(\pi) = \sum_{i \in G} d(i, \pi(i)) + (\text{Cost of Step 2(b) for } \pi),$$

where d is the L_p metric under consideration. The contribution to the total cost from Step 2(a) is directly related to the intrinsic difficulty of the permutation, while that from Step 2(b) is directly dependent on the algorithm. Fortunately, as will be derived below, for most permutations π, $\sum_{i \in G} d(i, \pi(i))$ is of order exactly n^3, whereas we can show

Prop. 1 (Cost of Step (2b) for π) = $O(n^2)$.

Proof   This is easy to show; in fact, the coefficient of n^2 will be less than one. The only observation that need be made is that, in moving from cycle to nearest cycle, the head will traverse the entire grid less than once. And traversing the entire $n \times n$ grid takes time $n^2 + O(n)$.

$\square$

Thus, the Cycle Algorithm is asymptotically optimal for most permutations, although it could conceivably perform badly for "sparse" permutations. As an example of how bad it can get, consider the permutation π of 4 cycles illustrated in Figure 2.5.3, given that the head starts at point a and the L_1 metric is being used.

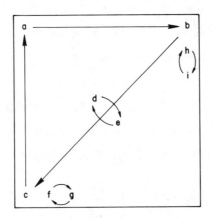

Figure 2.5.3

The cycle algorithm processes π as (abc); (de); (fg); (hi), requiring $8n+0(1)$ head motions. (From a to b to c and back to a, we need $4n$; from a to d, we need n; from d to f, another n; and finally, from f to h, we need $2n$.) However, the optimal method is to process the small cycles while working on the large one, i.e.,

      (a b (hi) (de) (fg) c),

which takes $4n+0(1)$ head motions. It therefore may be worthwhile to consider refinements of the Cycle Algorithm, particularly if head movements are much slower than the computation speed of the control unit (which is devising the head's schedule), as we assume here. One good alternative is the following:

Minimal Spanning Tree/Euler Circuit/Cycle Algorithm

Step 1   Determine cycles of permutation π.

Step 2   Derive distances between cycles of π (i.e., for each pair of cycles C_1, C_2 in π derive $\min_{x \in C_1, y \in C_2} d(x,y)$ and record this in a matrix as the distance between C_1 and C_2).

Step 3   Form a minimal spanning tree for the cycles. This tree corresponds very closely to a "Euler circuit" for π.

Step 4   Traverse the Minimal Spanning Tree (Euler Circuit) in the obvious way. Effectively this changes π to look like one enormous cycle, but a cycle which touches itself.

Note that this algorithm is fairly effective in reducing obvious waste: for the permutation in Figure 2.5.3 it produces the schedule

(a b (hi) c (fg)) (de)

with a cost of $5n + 0(1)$ steps if cycles are joined in one way, and

(a (hi) b (fg) c (de))

with the same cost if they are joined in another (note that this latter schedule is better under the L_2 and L_∞ metrics than the former). However, Step 2 can be extremely expensive, requiring as much as $0(n^4)$ time or $0(n^2)$ words of memory, depending on π's cycle structure. If the cost of Step 2 is not felt to be exorbitant, however, the user may consider enlarging it to capitalize on the fact that the distance between two cycles is often less than the minimum distance between their elements; this was shown in Figure 2.5.3 with the cycles (abc) and (de).

For the rest of this subsection we will assume that the read/write head control unit uses something like the cycle algorithm so that the dominant term in the cost of realizing a permutation depends solely on the permutation. In fact we define

$$\text{Cost}(\pi) = \sum_{i \in G} d(i, \pi(i)),$$

d being again the metric under consideration, since then CACost asymptotically approaches Cost as n grows large, and since this simplification permits us to ignore algorithm structure in the following analyses of costs.

Ignoring for the moment the symmetry operations S mentioned in Subsection 2.5.2, we ask the *average and worst-case values of Cost* (π), where average means that all permutations π are considered equally likely. Essentially then, we are asking how much time we would require to realize permutations offline if we did not worry about "grid states"; this will serve as a basis for comparison when the analysis *with* grid states is made below.

Theorem 2.5.1 Average $\underset{\pi \in P}{[\text{Cost} (\pi)]} = \begin{cases} 2/3 \ n^3 + 0(n), \ L_1 \text{metric} \\ (.5214)n^3 + 0(n^2), \ L_2 \text{ metric} \\ 7/15 \ n^3 + 0(n), \ L_\infty \text{metric} \end{cases}$

Proof For all three metrics we have

$$\begin{aligned} \underset{\pi \in P}{\text{Average} [\text{Cost}(\pi)]} &= \frac{1}{(n^2)!} \sum_{\pi \in P} \sum_{i \in G} d(i, \pi(i)) \\ &= \frac{1}{(n^2)!} \sum_{i \in G} \sum_{\pi \in P} d(i, \pi(i)) \\ &= \frac{1}{(n^2)!} \sum_{i \in G} \sum_{j \in G} N(i,j)d(i,j), \end{aligned}$$

where $N(i,j) = $ [number of permutations $\pi \in P$ such that $\pi(i) = j$]

$$= (n^2 - 1)!$$

so

$$\text{Average}_{\pi}[\text{Cost}(\pi)] = \frac{1}{n^2} \sum_{i \in G} \sum_{j \in G} d(i,j).$$

This sum must now be analyzed independently for each of the three metrics. In all three cases we represent grid points with the matrix-like indexing $i \Longleftrightarrow (i_1, i_2)$, where i_1 and i_2 have values between 1 and n. In the L_1 case we have

$$\frac{1}{n^2} \sum_{i \in G} \sum_{j \in G} d(i,j)$$

$$= \frac{1}{n^2} \sum_{i_1=1}^{n} \sum_{i_2=1}^{n} \sum_{j_1=1}^{n} \sum_{j_2=1}^{n} (|i_1-j_1| + |i_2-j_2|)$$

$$= \frac{1}{n^2} \left(\left(\sum_{i_1=1}^{n} \sum_{j_1=1}^{n} n^2 |i_1-j_1| \right) \right.$$

$$\left. + \left(\sum_{i_2=1}^{n} \sum_{j_2=1}^{n} n^2 |i_2-j_2| \right) \right)$$

$$= 2 \sum_{k,\ell=1}^{n} |k-\ell|.$$

Let Δ denote the *multiset* $\{ |k-\ell|, \; k=1,\ldots,n, \; \ell = 1,\ldots,n \}$. Then it is easy to verify that Δ contains (n) zeroes, $2(n-1)$ ones, $2(n-2)$ twos, ..., and $2(1)$ n-1's. Concisely, if δ is a positive integer less than n, there are $2(n-\delta)$ copies of δ in Δ. Thus, continuing,

$$= 2 \sum_{\delta \in \Delta} \delta$$

$$= 2 \sum_{\delta=1}^{n-1} 2(n-\delta)\delta$$

$$= 2/3(n^3-n) = 2/3n^3 + 0(n),$$

as stated.

In the L_∞ case we find

$$\frac{1}{n^2} \sum_{i \in G} \sum_{j \in G} d(i,j)$$

$$= \frac{1}{n^2} \sum_{i_1,i_2=1}^{n} \sum_{j_1,j_2=1}^{n} \max \left(|i_1-j_1|, |i_2-j_2| \right)$$

$$= \frac{1}{n^2} \sum_{\delta_1 \in \Delta} \sum_{\delta_2 \in \Delta} \max (\delta_1,\delta_2).$$

By carefully manipulating this sum we can show this is

$$= \frac{1}{15n^2} (7n^5 - 5n^3 - 2n)$$

$$= \frac{7}{15} n^3 + 0(n),$$

as stated.

The constant $7/15$ has been independently verified in [30], where it was shown the average L_∞ distance in a square with edge 2 is $14/15$ (implying the average distance in a square of edge 1 is $7/15$).

The L_2 derivation is, unsurprisingly, more complicated. By appealing to the Euler-Maclaurin summation theorem we have

$$\frac{1}{n^2} \sum_{i \in G} \sum_{j \in G} d(i,j) =$$

$$= \frac{1}{n^2} \sum_{i_1,i_2=1}^{n} \sum_{j_1,j_2=1}^{n} \sqrt{|i_1-j_1|^2 + |i_2-j_2|^2}$$

$$= \frac{1}{n^2} \sum_{\delta_1 \in \Delta} \sum_{\delta_2 \in \Delta} \sqrt{\delta_1^2 + \delta_2^2}$$

$$= \frac{1}{n^2} \sum_{\delta_1=1}^{n} \sum_{\delta_2=1}^{n} 2(n-\delta_1)2(n-\delta_2)\sqrt{\delta_1^2 + \delta_2^2} + 0(n)$$

$$= \frac{4}{n^2} \int_0^n \int_0^n (n-x)(n-y)\sqrt{x^2 + y^2}\,dx\,dy + 0(n^2).$$

The double integral can be evaluated as $\frac{4}{n^2} \int_0^n (n - x)F(x,n)dx$, where $F(x,n) = \int_0^n (n-y)\sqrt{x^2 + y^2}\,dy$

$$= \frac{n}{2}x^2 \text{ arcsinh } (n/x) + \frac{n^2}{2}\sqrt{n^2 + x^2}$$

$$- \frac{1}{3}(n^2 + x^2)^{3/2} + x^3/3$$

(fudging at the boundary x=0 is harmless), and by taking the asymptotic behavior of this integral we find that, since *arcsinh* (z) =

$\ell n (z + \sqrt{z^2 + 1})$, we have in closed form

$$\frac{1}{n^2} \sum_{i,j \in G} d(i,j) = \left[\frac{1}{3} \ell n(1 + \sqrt{2}) + \frac{2 + \sqrt{2}}{15} \right] n^3 + 0(n^2)$$

$$= [.52140 \ 54331 \ 64720 \ 67833...]n^3 + 0(n^2),$$

as claimed. This asymptotic form of the average cost agrees well with the exact values for moderate n. For several values the n^3 coefficient

$$\frac{1}{n^3} \left[\frac{4}{n^2} \sum_{\delta_1, \delta_2 = 1}^{n} (n - \delta_1)(n - \delta_2) \sqrt{\delta_1^2 + \delta_2^2} \right]$$

is tabulated in Table 2.5.1, and a polynomial regression on the table shows Average L_2 cost = $(.52140) n^3 - (.66319) n^2 - (2.98662) n + (476.07)$ with small residuals and enormous F-statistics.

□

Table 2.5.1

Asymptotic behavior of average L_2 cost

n	Average L_2 cost$/n^3$
100	0.51471 44257
200	0.51806 59602
300	0.51918 04742
400	0.52007 11123
500	0.52073 85192
1000	0.52096 08787
1500	0.52107 20379

Frequently, the evaluation of average *complexity* is of limited use, since the *standard deviation* can be large, suggesting that behavior much less and much greater than the average will occur reasonably often. It is interesting to note that this is not the case here.

Theorem 2.5.2 Standard Deviation $\underset{\pi \in P}{} [\mathrm{Cost}(\pi)] = O(n^2)$ in all 3 metrics.

Proof Recall Standard Deviation $= \sqrt{\mathrm{Variance}}$, and if we let A = Average[Cost(π)], then

$$\underset{\pi}{\mathrm{Variance}} \; [\mathrm{Cost}(\pi)] = \frac{1}{(n^2)!} \underset{\pi}{\Sigma} \; (\underset{i \in G}{\Sigma} d(i, \pi(i)))^2 - A^2$$

$$= \left(\frac{1}{(n^2)!} \underset{\pi}{\Sigma} \underset{i \in G}{\Sigma} d(i, \pi(i))^2 \right.$$

$$+ \frac{1}{(n^2)!} \underset{\pi}{\Sigma} \underset{i \neq j}{\Sigma} d(i, \pi(i)) d(j, \pi(j)) \left. \right) - A^2$$

$$= \left(\frac{1}{n^2} \underset{i,j}{\Sigma} d(i,j)^2 \right)$$

$$+ \left(\frac{1}{n^2(n^2 - 1)} \underset{\substack{i \neq j \\ k \neq \ell}}{\Sigma} d(i,k) d(j,\ell) \right) - A^2.$$

It can be shown that the second term in this expression is

$$\frac{1}{n^2(n^2-1)} \left[n^4 A^2 - 2 \underset{k}{\Sigma} \left(\underset{i}{\Sigma} d(i,k) \right)^2 + \underset{i,k}{\Sigma} d(i,k)^2 \right],$$

and since we can put

$$A^2 = c_1 n^6 + o(n^6)$$

$$\sum_{i,j} d(i,j)^2 = c_2 n^6 + o(n^6)$$

$$\sum_{k} \left(\sum_{i} d(i,k) \right)^2 = c_3 n^8 + o(n^8)$$

in all 3 metrics we find

$$\text{Variance}_{\pi} [\text{Cost}(\pi)] = \frac{1}{n^2}(c_2 n^6 + o(n^6))$$

$$+ \frac{1}{n^2(n^2-1)}(n^4 A^2 - 2(c_3 n^8 + o(n^8)) + (c_2 n^6 + o(n^6)))$$

$$-A^2$$

$$= n^4(c_2 - 2c_3) + A^2 \left(\frac{1}{1-1/n^2} - 1 \right) + o(n^4)$$

$$= n^4(c_2 - 2c_3) + (c_1 n^6 + o(n^6))(1/n^2 + 1/n^4 + \ldots) + o(n^4)$$

$$= n^4(c_1 + c_2 - 2c_3) + o(n^4).$$

Thus, by taking the square root, we find that the standard deviation of the average cost is $O(n^2)$ in all three metrics. Actually evaluating the leading coefficient $\sqrt{c_1 + c_2 - 2c_3}$ is tedious, but, for example, in the L_1 case (in which case the coefficient is larger than in L_2 or L_∞ since L_1 costs vary more than do the others) we can determine that

$$\text{Standard Deviation}_{\pi \in P}[\text{Cost}(\pi)] = \sqrt{\frac{4}{45}n^4 + O(n^2)}$$

$$= \left(\frac{2\sqrt{5}}{15} \right) n^2 + O(1)$$

$$= (.29814)n^2 + O(1).$$

□

It is thus apparent that the average cost figures given by Theorem 2.5.1 are very good predictors of the running time of a read/write head schedule for a random permutation, especially as n becomes large. We can also get precise bounds on the worst-case running time for any permutation.

Theorem 2.5.3

$$\text{Worst Case}_{\pi \in P} \, [\text{Cost}(\pi)] = \begin{cases} n^3 - n, & n \text{ odd, } L_1 \text{metric} \\ n^3, & n \text{ even, } L_1 \text{metric} \\ \frac{1}{3}[\ell n(1 + \sqrt{2}) + \sqrt{2}]n^3 & \\ \quad + O(n^2), & L_2 \text{ metric} \\ 2/3(n^3 - n), & L_\infty \text{ metric} \end{cases}$$

Proof Letting π be any permutation and p be any point on the grid G, we apply the triangle inequality for the metric d to get the upper bound $\text{Cost}(\pi) = \sum_{i \in G} d(i,\pi(i)) \leq \sum_{i \in G} (d(i,p) + d(p,\pi(i))) = 2 \sum_{i \in G} d(i,p)$.

This right-hand expression is maximized when p is the center of the grid (when n is even, p is not actually a cell location). This gives us the upper bounds stated in the theorem because we can actually find a permutation which attains this upper bound. Note that the $180°$-rotation permutation π shown in Figure 2.5.2 is a worst-case permutation since it satisfies

$$d(i,\pi(i)) = d(i,p) + d(p,\pi(i))$$

for all $i \in G$. Any permutation satisfying this equality for all i must necessarily be a worst-case permutation; also, a simple symmetry argument shows that the only way a permutation π can satisfy this equality is for p to be the grid center. The values stated in the theorem reflect the cost of this permutation in each of the metrics.

□

Up to this point we have ignored the possible savings that are made by taking advantage of the symmetry of the grid, as discussed in Section 2.5.2. In the rest of this section we examine how the symmetry operations affect the average and worst-case cost statistics derived above.

We begin by studying the relative costs of the symmetry permutations themselves. All the necessary information is listed in Figure 2.5.4 and Table 2.5.2, derived in the same manner as in Theorems 2.5.1 and 2.5.2 using the matrix notation

$$\rho((i_1,i_2)) \;=\; (i_2, n + 1 - i_1)$$

$$\tau((i_1,i_2)) \;=\; (n + 1 - i_1, i_2)$$

and so forth for the other members of the group S. The only expressions that present any difficulty are the values of a and b under the L_2 metric, for which we have

$$a \;=\; \sum_{i \in G} d(i,\rho(i)) \;=\; \sum_{k,\ell=1}^{n} \sqrt{|k-\ell|^2 + |n+1-(k+\ell)|^2}$$

$$b \;=\; \sum_{i \in G} d(i,\rho^2(i))$$

$$= \sum_{k,\ell=1}^{n} \sqrt{|n+1-2k|^2 + |n+1-2\ell|^2};$$

in the latter case the techniques of Theorem 2.5.1 can be applied directly, but closed form has not yet been derived for a.

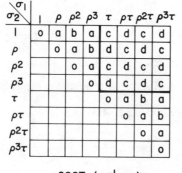

σ_2＼σ_1	I	ρ	ρ^2	ρ^3	τ	$\rho\tau$	$\rho^2\tau$	$\rho^3\tau$
I	o	a	b	a	c	d	c	d
ρ		o	a	b	d	c	d	c
ρ^2			o	a	c	d	c	d
ρ^3				o	d	c	d	c
τ					o	a	b	a
$\rho\tau$						o	a	b
$\rho^2\tau$							o	a
$\rho^3\tau$								o

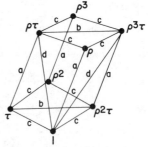

COST $(\sigma_2^{-1} \circ \sigma_1)$

MATRIX IS SYMMETRIC

Figure 2.5.4

We now examine the effect on cost of the symmetry group S. It turns out that symmetry operations do not significantly reduce the *average* running time, but they reduce the *worst-case* running time significantly. We formalize this as follows: given a permutation $\pi\epsilon P$, define the *symmetrized cost SCost* by

$$SCost(\pi) = \min_{\sigma\epsilon S} \; Cost(\sigma\circ\pi).$$

It follows obviously that $SCost(\pi)\leq Cost(\pi)$ for all permutations π. Nevertheless, we have the surprising result of Theorem 2.5.4.

Table 2.5.2
Values of distances in Figure 2.5.4

	a	b	c	d
$d = L_1$ distance	$2/3\,(n^3{-}n)$	$(n^3 {-}n)$, n odd (n^3), n even	$1/2(n^3 {-}n)$, n odd $1/2\,(n^3)$, n even	$2/3\,(n^3{-}n)$
$d = L_2$ distance	$(.54107)\,n^3$ $+\,O(n^2)$	$1/3[\ell n(1{+}\sqrt{2}) + \sqrt{2}]n^3$ $+\,O(n^2)$	$1/2(n^3{-}n)$, n odd $1/2\,(n^3)$, n even	$\sqrt{2}/3\,(n^3{-}n)$
$d = L_x$ distance	$1/2\,(n^3{-}n)$, n odd $1/2\,(n^3)$, n even	$2/3\,(n^3{-}n)$	$1/2\,(n^3{-}n)$, n odd $1/2\,(n^3)$, n even	$1/3\,(n^3{-}n)$

Theorem 2.5.4

$$\text{Average}_{\pi}[SCOST(\pi)] \;=\; \text{Average}_{\pi}[Cost(\pi)] - O(n^2).$$

Proof   Let $f(x) = [$ Number of permutations π such that Cost $(\pi) = x]/(n^2)!$ for any integer x be the "probability density" for Cost (π), with corresponding distribution $F(y) = \sum_{x \le y} f(x)$. The point is that f looks very much like a "spike." If A denotes the average cost as in Theorem 2.5.2, then

$$A \;=\; \sum_{x=0}^{\infty} xf(x),$$

and the variance B^2 is given by

$$B^2 = \sum_{x=0}^{\infty} (x-A)^2 f(x).$$

Using a Chebyshev inequality process, we have for each positive integer $C < A$

$$B^2 \geq \sum_{x=0}^{C} (x-A)^2 f(x)$$

$$\geq (A-C)^2 \sum_{x=0}^{C} f(x) = (A-C)^2 F(C).$$

Thus, $(A-C) \leq B/\sqrt{F(C)}$, for $0 < C < A$. Now note that for every permutation π, SCost (π) is the minimum Cost of the eight translates $\sigma \circ \pi$, with $\sigma \in S$, and of course all of these translates are again permutations. Thus, the distribution function F_S, giving this distribution of costs with S, is at best the left-hand $1/8$ of F (renormalized by a factor of 8). That is, if $\lambda = \max \{ x \mid F(x) \leq 1/8 \}$, then $F_S(x) \leq G(x)$ where

$$G(x) = \begin{cases} 8F(x) & x<\lambda \\ 1 & x\geq\lambda. \end{cases}$$

Correspondingly, if

$$g(x) = \begin{cases} 8F(x) & x<\lambda \\ 1 - 8F(x) & x = \lambda, \\ 0 & x>\lambda \end{cases}$$

then we have the bound

$$A' = \sum_{x>0} xg(x)$$

$$\leq \underset{\pi}{\text{Average}} \ [SCost \ (\pi)] < \sum_{x>0} xf(x) = A.$$

Now it is clear that $A' = \sum_{x>0} x \ g(x) = F^{-1}(1/16)$ since we are finding the average (or midpoint) of the left-hand $1/8$ of F. Then applying the Chebyshev bound derived above for $C = A'$, we find

$$A-A' \leq B/\sqrt{(1/16)} = 4B,$$

so A' is within 4 standard deviations of A; however, from Theorem 2.5.2 we know that B is only of order $O(n^2)$. Thus

$$A-O(n^2) \leq \text{Average} \ [SCost \ (\pi)]<A,$$

which is what was to be proved.

□

Theorem 2.5.4 suggests that using the symmetry operations S will not significantly reduce execution time, on the average. However, we now show that using S does reduce considerably the worst-case time. To do this, we establish first the following lemma.

Lemma 2.5.1   Given $\pi \epsilon P$, we can construct $\pi' \epsilon P$ such that

$$SCost(\pi') = \underset{\sigma \epsilon S}{\text{Average}}[Cost(\sigma o \pi)] + O(n^2).$$

Proof   This statement can be proved, but instead we show the simpler result that we can construct a permutation π' of the $4n \times 4n$ grid having the corresponding property

$$\frac{1}{(4)^3} \ SCost(\pi') \ = \ \underset{\sigma \in S}{Average[Cost(\sigma o \pi)]} \ + \ O(n^2).$$

Since we are not really concerned about the size of n, but only about the form of the worst-case permutation, this shift of grid size is not important.

We construct π' from π by "interleaving" 2 copies of each of the 8 translates $\sigma \ o \ \pi$ of π. We do this by dividing the $4n \times 4n$ grid G' into 16 $n \times n$ subgrids G_{pq}, with p and q being integers between 1 and 4, defined by

$$G_{pq} \ = \ \{(4k_1 \ + \ p, \ 4k_2 \ + \ q) \ | \ 0 \le k_1, \ k_2 \le n-1\}.$$

π' is then constructed as being a permutation mapping each G_{pq} into G_{pq} for all p,q. For each point $(i_1,i_2) = (4k_1 + p, \ 4k_2 + q)$ in G', if $\sigma_{pq}(1 \le p,q \le 4)$ constitutes an enumeration of S such that each element of S appears twice, and if $\sigma_{pq} \ o \ \pi \ (k_1,k_2) \ = \ (\ell_1,\ell_2)$, then we define

$$\pi'((i_1,i_2)) \ = \ (4\ell_1 \ + \ p, 4\ell_2 \ + \ q).$$

In other words, π' is $\sigma_{pq} o \pi$ when restricted to G_{pq}. From this it follows immediately that

$$Cost \ (\pi') = \underset{p,q}{\Sigma} \ 4Cost(\sigma_{pq} o \pi)$$

$$= \ 2 \underset{\sigma \in S}{\Sigma} \ 4Cost(\sigma o \pi)$$

$$= 64 \ \underset{\sigma \in S}{Average \ [Cost(\sigma o \pi)]},$$

where the factor 4 comes from the fact that the grids G_{pq} have a distance of 4 between cells. Moreover, since $\sigma \mathrm{o} S = S$ for all $\sigma \epsilon S$ we know

$$\mathrm{Cost}(\sigma \mathrm{o} \pi') = \mathrm{Cost}(\pi') + O(n^2) \text{ for all } \sigma \epsilon S$$

(where it is understood now that by σ we mean the symmetry operations on the $4n \times 4n$ grid G'), the $O(n^2)$ term resulting from the minor rotations of each of the 4×4 chunks $\{(4k_1 + p, 4k_2 + q) \mid 1 \leq p,q \leq 4\}$ of G' under σ. From this we get

$$\mathrm{SCost}(\pi') = \mathrm{Cost}(\pi') + O(n^2),$$

and the lemma follows.

□

Corollary 2.5.1 $\underset{\pi \epsilon P}{\text{Worst Case}} [\mathrm{SCost}(\pi)] = \underset{\pi \epsilon P}{\text{Worst Case}}[\underset{\sigma \epsilon S}{\text{Average}} [\mathrm{Cost}(\sigma \mathrm{o} \pi)]] + O(n^2)$

Proof Suppose π is worst case, i.e., π maximizes $\mathrm{SCost}\,(\pi)$. Then by Lemma 2.5.1, there exists π' such that

$$\mathrm{SCost}(\pi') = \underset{\sigma \epsilon S}{\text{Average}}[\mathrm{Cost}(\sigma \mathrm{o} \pi)] + O(n^2)$$

$$\geq \mathrm{SCost}(\pi) + O(n^2).$$

Thus, π' is essentially a worst case too. However,

$$\mathrm{SCost}(\pi') = \underset{\sigma \epsilon S}{\text{Average}}[\mathrm{Cost}(\sigma \mathrm{o} \pi')] + O(n^2),$$

so the Corollary is proved.

□

Theorem 2.5.5   Worst Case$[SCost(\pi)] = \alpha n^3 + o(n^3)$,
$\qquad\qquad\qquad\quad {}_{\pi \in P}$

where $\alpha = 0.72096$ for the L_1 metric, $\alpha = .4387826$ for the L_∞ metric and $0.53956 \le \alpha \le 0.6202$ for the L_2 metric.

Proof   By Corollary 2.5.1, it suffices to consider

$$A = \underset{\pi \in P}{\text{Worst Case}}[\underset{\sigma \in S}{\text{Average}}[Cost(\sigma o \pi)]].$$

We study the L_1 metric first.

For convenience of later discussion, we identify the $n \times n$ grid G with the square with vertices $(1,1)$ $(1,-1)$, $(-1,-1)$, $(-1,1)$. Since

$$\underset{\sigma \in S}{\text{Average}}[Cost(\sigma o \pi)] = \frac{1}{8} \sum_{x \in G} \sum_{\sigma \in S} d(x, \sigma o \pi(x)),$$

clearly we can assume without loss of generality that x and $\pi(x)$ are in the same quadrant, i.e., π maps a quadrant into itself. Let $x = (a,b)$ be a point in the first quadrant G_1 and let $\pi(x) = (u,v)$ be its image. Then a, b, u, v, ≥ 0.

$$\sum_{\sigma \in S} d(x, \sigma o \pi(x)) = 2(|u-a| + |v-b| + |u-b| +$$

$$|v-a| + (u + a) + (v + b) + (u + b) + (v + a))$$

$$= 2(d(x,\pi(x)) + d(x,\eta o \pi(x))) + 4(u + v + a + b),$$

where $\eta(u,v) = (v,u)$. Thus,

$$\sum_{x \in G_1} \sum_{\sigma \in S} d(x, \sigma o \pi(x)) = 4 \sum_{x \in G_1} (u + v + a + b)$$

$$+ 2 \sum_{x \in G_1} d(x, \pi(x)) + d(x, \eta\pi(x)).$$

Note that $\sum_{x \in G_1} (u + v + a + b)$ is the same for all π. Hence if we can construct a permutation π from G_1 onto G_1 such that $\sum_{x \in G_1} d(x, \pi(x)) + d(x, \eta o\pi(x))$ is maximized, then we can extend it to G by reflection to obtain the worst-case permutation.

Since we are interested in the coefficient of the n^3 term in A only, we need only consider continuous transformations from G_1 onto G_1 with Jacobians equal to ± 1. (An area-preserving continuous map is roughly the limit of one-one permutations.)

Divide G_1 into 10 regions as in Figure 2.5.5, where $e = (\frac{1}{2}, \frac{1}{2})$, $t = \left(\frac{3-\sqrt{6}}{2}, 1 - \frac{3-\sqrt{6}}{2} \right)$ such that area $B_1 =$ area B_3, area $B_2 =$ area B_4, area $A =$ areas C, area $D_1 =$ area D_3, area $D_2 =$ area D_4.

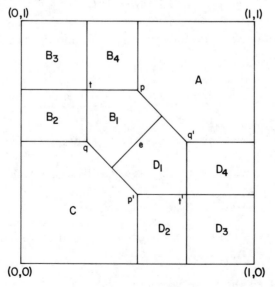

Figure 2.5.5

Next we define a real-valued function f on G_1 as follows, where d is again the L_1 metric:

$$
f(x) = \begin{cases}
2d(x,e), & \text{for } x \in A,C \\
d(x,e) + d(x,t), & \text{for } x \in B_2,B_3,B_4 \\
d(x,e) + d(x,t'), & \text{for } x \in D_2,D_3,D_4 \\
d(e,t), & \text{for } x \in B_1,D_1
\end{cases}
$$

By direct verification, we have for the L_1 metric

(i) $d(x,y) + d(x,\eta(y)) = f(x) + f(y)$; for $x \in A$, $y \in C$; $x \in B_1$, $y \in B_3$; $x \in B_2$, $y \in B_4$; $x \in D_1$, $y \in D_3$; $x \in D_2$, $y \in D_4$.

(ii) $d(x,y) + d(x,\eta(y)) \leq f(x) + f(y)$, for $x,y \in G_1$.

Inequality (ii) implies that for any transformation π

$$d(x,\pi(x)) + d(x,\eta\pi(x)) \leq f(x) + f(\pi(x)).$$

On the other hand, for any transformation π_0 such that it maps A onto C, B_1 onto B_3, B_2 onto B_4, D_1 onto D_3 and D_2 onto D_4, by (i)

$$d(x,\pi_0(x)) + d(x,\eta\pi_0(x)) = f(x) + f(\pi_0(x)).$$

It follows that π_0 maximizes $\sum_{x \in G_1} d(x,\pi(x)) + d(x,\eta\pi(x))$.

Direct calculation of Average $[\text{Cost}(\sigma \circ \pi_0)]$ yields the result $\sigma \in S$
stated in the theorem.

To achieve the worst case for the L_∞ metric, we recall that the mapping $g(x,y) = ((y+x)/2, (y-x)/2)$ (equation (2.2.13)) is an isometry between the plane with the L_∞ metric and that with the L_1 metric. Thus, instead of working with G_1 (with the L_∞ metric), it suffices to consider the triangle T_1 with vertices $(0,0)$, $(\sqrt{2},0)$, $(0,\sqrt{2})$ (with the L_1 metric). In other words, we have to construct a transformation form T_1 onto T_1 such that $\sum_{x \epsilon T_1} d(x,\pi(x)) + d(x,\eta\pi(x))$ is maximized, where d corresponds to the L_1 metric.

For convenience, we normalize T_1 to a triangle with vertices $(0,0)$, $(1,0)$, $(0,1)$. As before, we divide T_1 into 10 regions, such that area B_1 = area B_3, area B_2 = area B_4, area A = area C, area D_1 = area D_3, area D_2 = area D_4. (See Figure 2.5.6.) To do this, X, Y, Z must satisfy the equations:

$$2X^2 - 2XY - 2XZ - Y^2 - 3Z^2 + 4Z = 0$$

$$X^2 - 2X + 2XY - 2XZ - Z^2 + 2Z = 0$$

$$2X^2 - 4X + 2XY - 2XZ - Y^2 + Z^2 + 1 = 0,$$

which means $X = 0.27677$, $Y = 0.531439$ and $Z = 0.139882$. Again, any transformation mapping A onto C, B_1 onto B_3, B_2 onto B_4, D_1 onto D_3 and D_2 onto D_4 will maximize the desired sum and will be our solution. We compute, as before, that the mean distance is

$$\frac{2}{3} - X + 3X^2 - \frac{4}{3}X^3 + \frac{1}{6}Y^3 + Z^2 - \frac{1}{2}Z^3$$

$$- X^2Y + 3XY^2 - 2XY + 2X^2Z - 5XZ^2$$

$$- \frac{9}{2}Y^2Z + \frac{9}{2}YZ^2 + 2XYZ = 0.43878265158$$

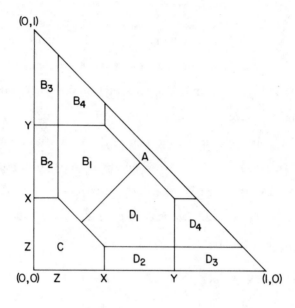

Figure 2.5.6

The case of the L_2 metric seems to be much more difficult and we are unable to obtain the coefficient of n^3 exactly. Only some simple bounds are presented here.

Consider the triangle T with vertices (0,0), (1,0), (1,1). Let w be an arbitrary but fixed point in T. Then, assuming that π maps all triangles in the grid onto themselves,

$$\frac{1}{8} \sum_{\sigma \in S} \sum_{x \in T} d(x, \sigma \circ \pi(x))$$

$$\leq \frac{1}{8} \sum_{\sigma} \sum_{x} [d(x, \sigma(w)) + d(\sigma(w), \sigma \circ \pi(x))]$$

$$= \frac{1}{8} \sum_{\sigma} \sum_{x} d(x, \sigma(w)) + \frac{1}{8} \sum_{\sigma} \sum_{x} d(w, \pi(x))$$

$$= \frac{1}{8} \sum_{\sigma} \sum_{x} d(x,\sigma(w)) + \sum_{x} d(w,x).$$

Let $T' = \sigma'(T)$ denote the translate of T by $\sigma' \epsilon$ S and $w' = \sigma'(w)$. Then we have exactly the same inequality:

$$\frac{1}{8} \sum_{\sigma \epsilon S} \sum_{x \epsilon T'} d(x,\sigma o \pi(x))$$

$$\leq \frac{1}{8} \sum_{\sigma} \sum_{x \epsilon T'} [d(x,\sigma(w')) + d(\sigma(w'),\sigma o \pi(x))]$$

$$= \frac{1}{8} \sum_{\sigma} \sum_{x \epsilon T} d(x,\sigma(w)) + \sum_{x \epsilon T} d(w,x).$$

Thus,

$$\frac{1}{8} \sum_{\sigma \epsilon S} \sum_{x \epsilon G} d(x,\sigma o \pi(x))$$

$$\leq \min_{w \epsilon T} \left\{ \sum_{\sigma \epsilon S} \sum_{x \epsilon T} d(x,\sigma(w)) + 8 \sum_{x \epsilon T} d(w,x) \right\}$$

For the L_1 metric, the minimization point turns out to be $w_o = \left(\frac{1}{2}, \frac{5-\sqrt{17}}{4} \right)$. While we are unable to determine the minimization point for either the L_∞ or L_2 metric, we can use w_o to obtain an upper bound:

$$\frac{1}{8} \sum_{\sigma \in S} \sum_{x \in G} d(x, \sigma \circ \pi(x)) \leq 0.6202 n^3.$$

To obtain a lower bound, let G_1, G_2, G_3, G_4 be the four quadrants of G and define a permutation π_0 mapping G_i onto itself, for $i=1,2,3,4$:

$$\pi_0 = \begin{cases} \rho^3 \tau \text{ in } G_1 \\ \rho \tau \text{ in } G_2 \\ \\ \rho^3 \tau \text{ in } G_3 \\ \rho \tau \text{ in } G_4, \end{cases}$$

where by ρ, τ we mean the symmetry operations on the appropriate quadrants. Direct computation shows that

$$\text{SCost}(\pi_0) = 0.53956 \, n^3.$$

Therefore, α is between 0.53956 and 0.6202.

□

To summarize, when a user gives us a permutation μ while the memory is in state σ, we form $\mu \circ \sigma^{-1}$, determine SCost $(\mu \circ \sigma^{-1}) =$ Cost $(\sigma' \circ \mu \circ \sigma^{-1})$ and realize the permutation $\sigma' \circ \mu \circ \sigma^{-1}$ using "cycle algorithm" or some other similar algorithm. Theorems 2.5.4 and 2.5.1 give the average cost and Theorem 2.5.5 gives the worst-case cost.

2.5.4. **The case $b=n^2$** In the case $b = n^2$, the read/write head contains enough memory to save the entire contents of the mass storage device. This possibility could arise, for example, if some large random-access device were available during the offline permuting period. The value $b = n^2$ is perhaps exorbitant, but it serves as a useful limiting value with which performance for smaller values of b may be compared.

Below we produce a straightforward algorithm for generating any permutation $\pi \epsilon P$, always taking time $2n^2$. Although this algorithm is very suboptimal for some permutations, it is not bad in the general case. As before, π is viewed here as an "absolute" permutation, and symmetry operations of the grid are ignored. In fact, no benefit whatsoever is gained by considering symmetry translates of a permutation if the final permutation is to be realized with the following algorithm.

Two-Pass Algorithm

Given $b = n^2$, permutation π to be realized, head initially in any location x on the grid.

Step 1 Read in entire contents of grid in a single pass across all n^2 cells.

Step 2 Write out the cell contents in their target locations in a second pass across the grid.

It is obvious that this algorithm always takes $2n^2$ steps, which is suboptimal for most permutations. However, we claim the algorithm is within a factor of optimal for almost all permutations.

Note first of all that *any* algorithm for realizing permutations with $b = n^2$ will usually take at least n^2 steps. To see this, note that

$$\Pr[\text{random } \pi \text{ has at least k unit cycles}] \leq \binom{n^2}{k} (n^2 - k)!/(n^2)!$$

$$= 1/k!.$$

(This probability may be evaluated precisely using the principle of inclusion and exclusion; see [23].) Now the algorithm must visit every point x on the grid for which $\pi(x) \neq x$, i.e., for which π is not a unit cycle. However, as the above inequality shows, the number of permutations having many unit cycles is a very small percentage of the total set (asymptotically negligible). So n^2 steps are necessary almost all the time, and the Two-Pass algorithm is at worst a factor of two away from optimal.

The Two-Pass algorithm *can* be improved upon somewhat. Observe that if we can devise a schedule for the read/write head which reads in many cells' contents *before* the head moves to the permutation targets for these contents during the initial read-in pass, then these contents can be dropped off when the target contents are read in. If enough contents can be dropped off in this manner, then the write-out pass will require the read/write head to visit only some fraction p ($0 < p < 1$) of the grid locations. The whole process might take only time $(1+p) n^2$.

In fact, we can guarantee $p \leq 1/2$. Consider *any* pass over the grid. Then either (1) at least half the points x in the pass are visited before $\pi(x)$ is visited in the pass, or else (2) this statement is true if the pass is reversed (done backwards). This observation leads to the following algorithm:

More Intelligent Two-Pass Algorithm

Step 1   Make a read-in pass over the grid, which has the property that at least half of the points x on the grid are passed over and before $\pi(x)$ is passed over. For each such point x, drop off its contents when $\pi(x)$ is passed over and the $\pi(x)$ contents are read in.

Step 2   Make a write-out pass over the grid which visits those points where contents must still be dropped off, and as few other points as possible.

This algorithm requires at most as much time as its predecessor, and has the additional benefit that it only uses $n^2/2$ registers at any given time. Hence, $b = n^2/2$ *is the most registers we could ever need,* and $b = n^2$ is wasteful.

We leave the precise analysis of this latter algorithm as an interesting open question. Is it always possible to choose a read-in pass schedule that guarantees p *smaller* than $1/2$, thereby improving Step 1? What algorithms may be used to generate efficient schedules for Step 2? etc.

2.5.5.   The case $1 <b<n^2$ We have now established that, when $b=1$, $0(n^3)$ time is necessary to realize the average permutation, while when $b = n^2$, only $0(n^2)$ time is necessary. It is interesting to ask what sort of behavior we get if we choose some intermediate value of b. It is obvious that

$$(\text{Time required}(b = 1)) \le k \ (\text{Time required } (b = k))$$

for any k between 1 and n^2, but it is not obvious whether the inequality can be replaced by equality. We show that, modulo constant factors, it can. That is, for $1<b\le n$, only $0(n^3/b)$ time is

necessary. This suggests that having a large number of registers may not be cost-effective.

We give an algorithm for b=n which uses time $6n^2$ (in any metric) to realize any permutation. The algorithm is based on the operation of the three-stage rearrangable switching network studied by Benes [2] and others. It comprises three passes, each taking time $2n^2$ and modeling one stage of the three-stage network.

Permutation Algorithm for b=n

Step 1   For each of the n rows of the grid,

(a) read the row in;

(b) write the row back out so that, at the end of Step 1, each column contains n items whose destinations are all in different rows.

Step 2   For each of the n columns of the grid,

(a) read the column in;

(b) write the column back out so that, at the end of Step 2, every item in the grid is in the same row as its destination.

Step 3   For each of the n rows of the grid,

(a) read the row in;

(b) write the row back out in permuted order.

It is obvious that the algorithm works if Step 1 can be made to do what it says it does. That it *can* is a consequence of the Slepian-Duguid theorem ([2], p. 86), the details of which are omitted here. An example is given in Figure 2.5.7. The algorithm makes

(3 steps)×(n rows/cols per step)

×(2n head movements per row/col)

$= 6n^2$ head movements,

as claimed.

11	7	19	23	24
6	1	10	12	25
16	4	18	15	17
22	2	5	9	21
14	13	20	3	8

(a) INITIAL CONFIGURATION
(NUMBERS INDICATE ROW-
MAJOR ORDERED
DESTINATIONS)

11	7	19	23	24
6	1	25	12	10
18	15	4	17	16
22	21	9	2	5
3	20	14	8	13

(b) AFTER FIRST STEP: EACH
COLUMN NOW CONTAINS 5
ITEMS WHOSE DESTINATIONS
ARE IN DIFFERENT ROWS.

3	1	4	2	5
6	7	9	8	10
11	15	14	12	13
18	20	19	17	16
22	21	25	23	20

(c) AFTER SECOND STEP:
COLUMNS HAVE BEEN
PERMUTED SO EACH
ITEM IS IN CORRECT
ROW.

1	2	3	4	5
6	7	8	9	10
11	12	13	14	15
16	17	18	19	20
21	22	23	24	25

(d) AFTER THIRD STEP:
GRID IS IN SORTED
ORDER.

Figure 2.5.7

This algorithm may be used recurisvely to derive interesting algorithms for $b < n$. Note that permuting a *row* (or column) of n cells using $b = \sqrt{n}$ registers using the same basic algorithm can be done by breaking the row (column) into $\sqrt{n}$ pieces of length $\sqrt{n}$. These pieces are then thought of as forming a $\sqrt{n} \times \sqrt{n}$ grid, except that here moving from one piece to the next takes time $\sqrt{n}$ instead of 1. Permuting one row of the grid using the algorithm then requires essentially

$$(2\sqrt{n} + \sqrt{n}) \times \sqrt{n} + 2(n - \sqrt{n}) \times n + (2\sqrt{n} + \sqrt{n}) \times \sqrt{n}$$

Step 1 (subrows)   Step 2 ("cols")   Step 3 (subrows)

$$= 2n^{3/2} + 4n \text{ head movements.}$$

Therefore, to permute the entire grid with $b = \sqrt{n}$ we make

$(3 \text{ steps}) \times (n \text{ rows/cols per step})$

$\times (2n^{3/2} + 4n \text{ head movements/row or col})$

$= 6n^{5/2} + 0(n^2) \text{ head movements.}$

In general, recursive application of this algorithm with $b = n^{1/2^j}$ for integral j produces an algorithm requiring on the order of

$6n^3/b \text{ head movements,}$

so for at least the values $k = n^{1/2^j}$ the inequality at the beginning of this section can be replaced by equality (within a constant factor near 6).

For very small values of b this approach will be inefficient. It would seem better in this situation to develop heuristics extending the basic cycle algorithm of Subsection 2.5.3. One possible extension is a "greedy" heuristic which reads in the contents of b cells and then proceeds to drop off the item whose destination is closest. A new item is read in when the old item is dropped off, again the head moves to drop off the item whose destination is closest, and so forth. However, we do not elaborate any further on this subject, leaving the development of algorithms for very small b as an interesting open problem.

One final comment should be made on the $b=n$ algorithm - namely, it may be generalized immediately to an algorithm for a system with *n read/write heads, which takes only 0(n) time.* Assuming each head has $b=n$ registers, each pass over a row or column in each of the three steps may be handled by a single head.

Obviously, the heads can be coordinated so that they do not conflict with one another's movement. This approach may be used when the grid may be read both horizontally and vertically (a mild generalization of the scheme in [4]): in effect, the grid becomes a "torus" with a 2n read/write head permanently fixed on the torus axes.

A more complete list of references for this chapter is given in Section 2.7.

2.6. Appendix 2.1. Proof of Lemma 2.2.1 Suppose the lemma is not true. Without loss of generality, we can assume that there exists a straight line L such that one of the following cases would occur:

$$I(A \cap \omega_1^*) \not\supset (B \cap \omega_1^*), \quad I(A \cap \omega_0^*) \not\supset (B \cap \omega_0^*), \qquad (A2.1.1)$$

$$I(A \cap \omega_1^*) \not\supset (B \cap \omega_1^*), \quad I(A \cap \omega_0^*) \supset (B \cap \omega_0^*), \qquad (A2.1.2)$$

and

$$I(A \cap \omega_1^*) \supset (B \cap \omega_1^*), \quad I(A \cap \omega_0^*) \not\supset (B \cap \omega_0^*), \qquad (A2.1.3)$$

where $\not\supset$ means "does not contain." We will show that (A2.1.1) leads to a contradiction. The other two cases can be similarly treated. Note that case (A2.1.1) does not rule out $I(B \cap \omega_1^*) \supset (A \cap \omega_1^*)$, $I(B \cap \omega_0^*) \supset (A \cap \omega_0^*)$. But the assumption that the lemma is not true takes care of the objection.

Figure A2.1.1 is an illustration of (A2.1.1).

Denote the region HAF by $\mathcal{G}$, AKGF by $\mathcal{A}$, KMG by $\mathcal{C}$, GNF by $\mathcal{C}'$, BJCE by $\mathcal{D}$, JDC by $\mathcal{B}$, CPE by $\mathcal{B}'$, IQR by $\mathcal{F}$ and QBER by $\mathcal{E}$. We will show that

$$\int_{\omega_1^*} \int_{\omega_0^*} > \int_{\mathcal{G}\mathcal{A}\mathcal{C}'} \int_{\mathcal{F}\mathcal{E}\mathcal{D}\mathcal{B}'},$$

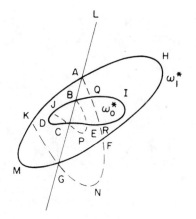

Figure A2.1.1

hence a contradiction.

$$\int_{\omega_1^*}\int_{\omega_0^*} - \int_{\mathcal{GAC}'}\int_{\mathcal{FEDB}'}$$

$$= \int_{\mathcal{GAC}}\int_{\mathcal{FEDB}} - \int_{\mathcal{GAC}'}\int_{\mathcal{FEDB}'}$$

$$= \int_{\mathcal{G}}\int_{\mathcal{F}} - \int_{\mathcal{G}}\int_{\mathcal{F}} + \int_{\mathcal{G}}\int_{\mathcal{EDB}}$$

$$\quad - \int_{\mathcal{G}}\int_{\mathcal{EDB}'} + \int_{\mathcal{AC}}\int_{\mathcal{F}} - \int_{\mathcal{AC}'}\int_{\mathcal{F}}$$

$$\quad + \int_{\mathcal{AC}}\int_{\mathcal{EDB}} - \int_{\mathcal{AC}'}\int_{\mathcal{EDB}'}$$

$$= \int_{\mathcal{G}}\int_{\mathcal{B}} - \int_{\mathcal{G}}\int_{\mathcal{B}'} + \int_{\mathcal{C}}\int_{\mathcal{F}}$$

$$\quad - \int_{\mathcal{C}'}\int_{\mathcal{F}} + \int_{\mathcal{A}}\int_{\mathcal{B}} - \int_{\mathcal{A}}\int_{\mathcal{B}'}$$

$$+ \int_{\mathscr{C}} \int_{\mathscr{B}} - \int_{\mathscr{C}'} \int_{\mathscr{B}'} + \int_{\mathscr{C}} \int_{\mathscr{E}}$$

$$- \int_{\mathscr{C}'} \int_{\mathscr{E}} + \int_{\mathscr{C}} \int_{\mathscr{D}} - \int_{\mathscr{C}'} \int_{\mathscr{D}}$$

$$= \int_{\mathscr{G}} \int_{\mathscr{B}} - \int_{\mathscr{G}} \int_{\mathscr{B}'} + \int_{\mathscr{C}} \int_{\mathscr{F}} - \int_{\mathscr{C}'} \int_{\mathscr{F}} + \int_{\mathscr{C}} \int_{\mathscr{E}} - \int_{\mathscr{C}'} \int_{\mathscr{E}}.$$

For each point y in $\mathscr{B}$, let y' in $\mathscr{B}'$ be its image with respect to L. Let x be a point of $\mathscr{G}$. By properties of the Euclidean metric, $d(x,y) > d(x,y')$, for x, y not on L. Therefore, it follows that

$$\int_{\mathscr{G}} \int_{\mathscr{B}} - \int_{\mathscr{G}} \int_{\mathscr{B}'} > 0,$$

and similarly for other pairs of integrals. Thus, the result follows.

□

2.7. References

[1]   Aho, A.V., Hopcroft, J.E. and Ullman, J.D., *The Design and Analysis of Computer Algorithms,* Addison-Wesley, Reading, Ma., 1974.

[2]   Benes, V., *Mathematical Theory of Connecting Networks and Telephone Traffic,* Academic Press, New York, 1965.

[3]   Bergmans, P.P., "Minimizing expected travel time on geometrical patterns by optimal probability rearrangements," Information and Control **20** (1972), 331-350.

[4]   Chandra, A.K., Chang, H. and Wong, C.K., "Two-dimensional magnetic bubble memory," U.S. Patent No. 4,174,538 (1979).

[5]   Coppersmith, D., Lee, D.T. and Wong, C.K., "An elementary proof of non-existence of isometries between L_p^k and L_q^k," IBM J. Res. Dev. **23**, 6 (1979), 696-699.

[6]   Coppersmith, D., Parker, D.S. and Wong, C.K., "Analysis of a general mass storage system," SIAM J. Comput. **11**, 1 (1982), 94-116.

[7]   Garey, M.R., Graham, R.L. and Johnson, D.S., "Some NP-complete geometric problems," in Proc. 8th Annual ACM Symposium on Theory of Computing, May 1976, 10-22.

[8]   Garey, M.R., and Johnson, D.S., *Computers and Intractability: A Guide to the Theory of NP-completeness,* W. H. Freeman and Company, San Francisco, 1979.

[9]   Gilmore, P.C., "Optimal and suboptimal algorithms for the quadratic assignment problem," J. Soc. Ind. Appl. Math. **10** (1962), 305-313.

[10]   Hanan, M., and Kurtzberg, J.M., "A review of the placement and quadratic assignment problems," SIAM Rev. **14** (1972), 324-342.

[11]   Hardy, G.H., Littlewood, J.E. and Pólya, G., *Inequalities*, Cambridge University Press, Cambridge, England, 1952.

[12]   Hempy, H., "IBM 3850 mass storage systems, performance evaluation using a channel monitor," in *Computer Performance*, K. M. Chandy and M. Reiser, Eds., North-Holland, Amsterdam, 1977, 177-196.

[13]   Hoagland, A.S., "Mass storage: past, present and future," Computer, 1973 (September), 29-33.

[14]   Hwang, F.K., "An O(n log n) algorithm for rectilinear minimal spanning trees," J. ACM **26** (1979), 177-182.

[15]   Johnson, C., "IBM 3850-Mass storage system" in *Memory and Storage Technology*, S. W. Miller, Ed., AFIPS Press, Arlington, Va., 1977, 93-98.

[16]   Johnson, D.S., private communication.

[17]   Karp, R.M., "Reducibility among combinatorial problems," in *Complexity of Computer Computations*, R.E. Miller and J.W. Thatcher, Eds., Plenum Press, New York, 1972, 85-104.

[18]   Karp, R.M., McKellar, A.C. and Wong, C.K., "Near-optimal solutions to a 2-dimensional placement problem," SIAM J. Comput. **4**, 3 (1975), 271-286.

[19]   Knuth, D.E., *The Art of Computer Programming*, Vol. III, Addison-Wesley, Reading, Ma., 1973.

[20]   Lee, D.T., "On finding K-nearest neighbors in the plane," Coordinated Science Laboratory Report R-728, University of Illinois, Urbana, Il., May 1976.

[21]   Lee, D.T., "Two-dimensional Voronoi diagrams in the

L_p – metric," J. ACM **27** (1980), 604-618.

[22] Lee, D.T., and Wong, C.K., "Voronoi diagrams in $L_1(L_\infty)$ metrics with 2-dimensional storage applications," SIAM J. Comput. **9**, 1 (1980), 200-211.

[23] Liu, C.L., *Introduction to Combinatorial Mathematics,* McGraw-Hill, New York, 1968, 106-107.

[24] Papadimitriou, C.H., and Steiglitz, K., "Some complexity results for the traveling salesman problem," in Proc. 8th ACM Symp. on Theory of Computing, Hershey, Pa., May 3-5, 1976, 1-9.

[25] Riordan, J., *An Introduction to Combinatorial Analysis,* John Wiley, New York, 1958.

[26] Rogers, C.A., *Packing and Covering,* Cambridge University Press, London, 1964.

[27] Rosenkrantz, D.J., Stearns, R.E. and Lewis II, P.M., "An analysis of several heuristics for the traveling salesman problem," SIAM J. Comput. **6** (1977), 563-581.

[28] Shamos, M.I., *Problems in Computational Geometry,* Springer-Verlag, New York, to be published.

[29] Shamos, M.I., and Hoey, D., "Closest-point problems," in Proc. 16th Annual Symposium on Foundations of Computer Science, Oct. 1975, 151-162.

[30] Wong, C.K., and Chu, K.C., "Average distances in L_p disks," SIAM Rev. **19** (1977), 320-324.

[31] Wong, C.K., Liu, C.L. and Apter, J., "A drum scheduling algorithm," in *Lecture Notes in Computer Science,* **2,** Springer-Verlag, New York, 1973, 267-275.

[32]   Yao, A., "An $O(|E| \log \log |V|)$ algorithm for finding minimum spanning trees," Information Processing Lett. **4** (1975), 21-23.

[33]   Yue, P.C., and Wong, C.K., "Near-optimal heuristics for an assignment problem in mass storage," Int. J. Comput. Inf. Sci. **4**, 4 (1975), 281-294.

3. MAGNETIC BUBBLE MEMORY

3.1. Introduction and basic models

3.1.1. **Introduction** Another recent development in mass storage technology is the introduction of magnetic bubble devices. Due to its high density, low cost and nonvolatility, magnetic bubble memory is expected to replace a majority of applications where conventional devices (such as disks and tapes) are used. Of course it can be used to simulate magnetic disks, so that the change to the existing software as well as hardware would be minimal. Early design indeed reflected such use [16]. But to do so would not fully utilize the power of bubble memory. By arranging the bubbles into loops, and by using special switches that permit control of the passage of bubbles, the memory is capable of a lot more intelligence than conventional storage devices have. It is now possible to perform in the bubble memory operations that are conventionally done by the CPU. Routine operations, such as data rearrangement, data sorting, etc. can now be done in the bubble memory, thus relieving the CPU for other, more useful processing.

In Section 2.6 of the last chapter, we studied the problem of rearranging records in a two-dimensional storage system. Here we develop the same theme in several directions in the new setting of bubble memories. New bubble memory structures are explored and corresponding algorithms designed and analyzed. Three aspects of the management of data are studied in detail: data rearrangement (permutation), sorting, and information retrieval and update. The algorithms related to these operations in conventional memories have been studied extensively in the existing literature. However, since the

225

data access and routing mechanisms in bubble memories differ
considerably from the way data are fetched and stored in conventional
memories, these algorithms cannot be applied directly to bubble
memories. Moreover, conventional algorithms usually use the number
of comparisons as a measure of complexity, whereas in a bubble
memory, a more appropriate measure would be the time it takes to
move the bubbles around.

Clearly, in designing bubble structures and their corresponding
data manipulation algorithms, the time complexity is not the only
important factor. There are physical constraints that must also be
considered. We distinguish three important parameters that should be
taken into consideration:

(1) number of switches in the bubble memory;

(2) number of control states needed to carry out the operations;

(3) time taken by the operations.

It is desirable to limit the number of switches in the bubble
memory, since they take up space, and too many of them would
decrease the amount of usable space for storing information. It is also
desirable to limit the number of control lines (and hence the number
of control states) required, since physically there is a limit to the
number of pins one can put on a chip. The performance is naturally
affected by the choice of these two numbers. Thus, there is a
trade-off among these three parameters.

All the results discussed in this chapter are equally applicable
to other shift register memories. The physical constraints imposed on
bubble memories are usually more stringent than any other shift
register memories. For instance, bubble memories usually require that
all bubbles be circulating at the same speed and that loops be

physically realizable in a two-dimensional plane. Such physical constraints make the design of efficient algorithms more difficult.

In Section 3.2, an optimal algorithm for permuting data in a bubble memory using only one switch is described and analyzed in detail. Section 3.3 discusses a bubble sorter where the sorting time is completely overlapped by the input/output time. In-place merging is also studied. The following section investigates the problem of performing tree search in a more conventional bubble memory, namely, the major/minor loop structure. While these three sections deal with data manipulation algorithms in specific memory structures, the next three sections are devoted to the study of trade-offs among the three parameters, number of switches, number of control states and time, for the permutation, sorting and searching problems in a variety of memory structures.

3.1.2. Basic model We now present a basic model for magnetic bubble memories. It is not our intention to describe the hardware of the magnetic bubble devices in detail. We will only give a conceptual model of a bubble memory relevant to our discussion. For readers interested in more implementation details, we refer to [16,20].

First, thin films of certain magnetic materials (i.e., a layer of magnetic garnet artificially grown on a nonmagnetic garnet substrate) contain randomly shaped domains (Figure 3.1.1). When a magnetic bias field is applied by two permanent magnets placed on either side of the device in a direction perpendicular to the thin film, these randomly shaped domains shrink into "bubbles" (actually cylindrical magnetic domains of fixed volume), the polarization of which is opposite to that of the thin film. Magnetic bubbles can be moved from point to point at very high speeds. To guide and control the movement of the

BUBBLE MEMORY

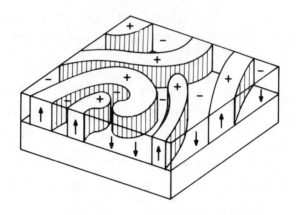

Figure 3.1.1

bubbles, a permalloy pattern of chevrons, for example, is applied to the surface of the film to form "paths" (Figure 3.1.2). When, in addition to the bias magnetic field, a rotating magnetic drive field in the plane of the film is applied by two coils, the bubbles can move at extremely high speed along these paths.

The permalloy paths are formed as loops. The presence of a bubble in a certain position on the loop corresponds to a "ONE bit"; the absence of a bubble, to a "ZERO bit."

In general, we may have either a single long loop, or several short loops. In the latter case, a record then may consist of bubbles in the same relative position in each loop.

Thus, the most primitive bubble memory can be visualized as bubbles circulating around a loop (Figure 3.1.3 (a)). Depending upon the permalloy patterns that are used to guide the bubbles, bubbles can be made to circulate in a clockwise or counterclockwise direction. In

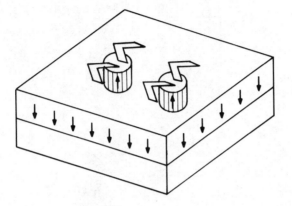

Figure 3.1.2

some bubble memories, the bubbles can change direction from one to the other by reversing the rotating field.

Bubbles can be created, annihilated and deleted by the use of special gates. Bubbles can be introduced into the loop by the use of a generator; they can be destroyed or duplicated by the use of a replicator/annihilator and can be detected by a detector. In general, the input operation involves the use of the generator, while the nondestructive read operation involves the replicator/annihilator and the detector. Since usually these gates are physically close to one another, we will group them together into what we shall call "access port" or "read/write port" (Figure 3.1.3(b)). It is through these ports that data can be read or written into the bubble memories.

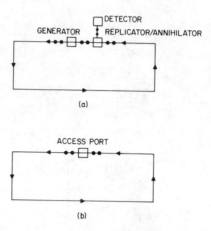

Figure 3.1.3

A bubble memory with a single loop is essentially a shift register memory. The average time to access a bit in a memory of n bits is n/2 propagation steps (the time to move a bubble from one place to the other). It can be reduced to n/4 if one allows bidirectional circulation of bubbles in the loop.

To reduce the access time, a major/minor loop organization of the bubble memory was introduced [11,12]. In this scheme (Figure 3.1.4), a set of minor loops of equal size are connected to a major loop that is used for communication. Through the action of transfer gates, bits of information, one from each minor loop, can be transferred from the minor loops to the major loop in parallel and then be shifted serially to the access port. The average bit access time for an n bit memory is then improved to $\sqrt{n}$.

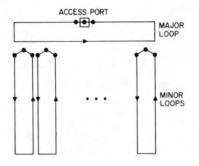

Figure 3.1.4

Beausoleil, Brown and Phelps [3] and Bonyhard and Nelson [13] independently propose a new bubble structure that allows two modes of operation, as shown in Figure 3.1.5 (Model 3.1.1). Here a node in the graph denotes a record. Operation (a) is the usual bubble propagation operation that cyclically moves the bubbles forward. In operation (c), the direction of propagation is reversed, and the bubble at the access port is also bypassed.

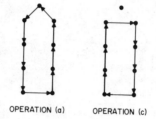

OPERATION (a)   OPERATION (c)

Figure 3.1.5

With the added second mode of operation, the average access time can be improved by implementing dynamic ordering in the bubble memory. The dynamic ordering of a file of items is the reordering of the items in the file such that the more recently referenced items are placed closer to the access port. Figure 3.1.6 shows such an ordering for 9 items before and after item 3 is accessed. Such an ordering can be achieved by the following algorithm:

Algorithm 3.1.1 To access an item k distance from the access port, maintaining the dynamic ordering, for Model 3.1.1:

    (1) Apply operation (a) k times.

    (2) Apply operation (c) k times.

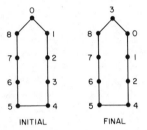

Figure 3.1.6

Notice that these two modes of operation of the bubble memory can be thought of as caused by the action of a 2-input, 2-output switch, placed between two loops of sizes 1 and (n-1) respectively. Such a switch has two modes of operation, as described schematically in Figure 3.1.7. Figure 3.1.8 shows a memory of 9 records for Model 3.1.1, now using the switch. Operation (a) is achieved by setting the switch to mode (a); operation (c) is achieved by setting the switch to mode (c) while reversing the direction of propagation.

This kind of switch forms the basis of our subsequent discussion of permutation and searching problems. Another kind of switch which can compare and steer two incoming bubble strings in a bubble memory will be used for our sorting problem.

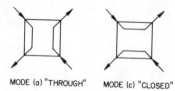

MODE (a) "THROUGH"   MODE (c) "CLOSED"

SCHEMATICALLY REPRESENTED AS ⊠

Figure 3.1.7

Figure 3.1.8

There are quite a few other bubble memory structures in the literature which we do not intend to cover here. For example, uniform ladders [18-23,48] will be described only briefly in Section 5.3 and bubble logic [20] and lattice files [15,52] will not be discussed at all. The interested reader may consult the reference list at the end of this chapter.

3.2. Optimal permutation algorithm in a simple model of bubble memory

3.2.1. Introduction In Section 3.1, we mentioned dynamic ordering as a means of decreasing the average time of access to a bubble memory. The basic assumption was that in general records were not equally likely to be accessed. Keeping the last requested record close to the access port and shifting all the records in front one position down would tend to make the records converge to an "ideal" arrangement, namely, an arrangement in descending order of access frequencies.

Another way to improve the average access time is to accumulate enough statistics about the access frequencies of the records and then rearrange them accordingly from time to time. This is the permutation problem, we want to address both here and in Section 3.5, namely, how to rearrange the records in a bubble memory to any required permutation in the shortest possible time. In this section, we consider a very simple model of bubble memory and propose an optimal algorithm for the permutation problem, whereas in Section 3.5, we shall consider a family of more sophisticated models and their associated permutation algorithms and shall study their trade-offs.

Two models are used in this section. The second one is Model 3.1.1 exactly. The first one is a slightly modified version.

3.2.2. The memory models In the first model (Model 3.2.1), the memory consists of two loops and a switch placed between them. The loops are of sizes 1 and n-1 respectively, where n is the number of records that can be stored in the memory. The positions of the records are labeled 0,1,...,n-1, with the loop of size 1 taking the position 0. (See Figure 3.2.1 for a memory of 7 records.) There are two modes of operation for the movement of records. If the switch is set to mode a ('through'), then we have the usual circular shift of records along the combined loop. If the switch is set to mode b ('closed'), then the record at position 0 is held fixed, while the other records circulate along the loop of size n-1. We will refer to the first operation as operation a and to the second as operation b. Figure

3.2.1 describes these operations for n=7.

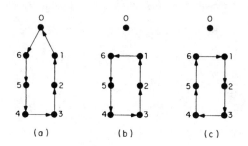

Figure 3.2.1

On the other hand, Model 3.2.2 allows operations a and c instead of a and b, where c is the opposite of b, (see Figure 3.2.1). Thus, it is identical to Model 3.1.1.

We shall study Model 3.2.1 in detail in the next subsection and shall discuss Model 3.2.2 briefly later.

3.2.3. Model 3.2.1 Assume initially that records 0,1,...,n-1 are at positions 0,1,...,n-1 respectively. A permutation

$$\begin{pmatrix} 0 & 1 & \dots & n-1 \\ p_0 & p_1 & \dots & p_{n-1} \end{pmatrix}$$

is therefore to be realized by taking record i to position p_i for all i. It is well known that a permutation P can be decomposed into cycles

$$P = C_1 C_2 \dots C_k,$$

where C_i can be written as

$$C_i = (f_1^i f_2^i ... f_{h_i}^i),$$

denoting a cycle of length h_i, and equivalent to the permutation

$$\begin{pmatrix} f_1^i & f_2^i & \cdots & f_{h-1}^i & f_h^i \\ f_2^i & f_3^i & \cdots & f_h^i & f_1^i \end{pmatrix}.$$

For example,

$$\begin{pmatrix} 0 & 1 & 2 & 3 & 4 & 5 & 6 \\ 2 & 6 & 0 & 4 & 1 & 5 & 3 \end{pmatrix} = (02)(1634)(5).$$

Without loss of generality, we assume that f_1^i is the smallest item in the cycle C_i and that

$$f_1^1 < f_1^2 < ... < f_1^k,$$

i.e., cycles are arranged according to their smallest items.

The algorithm to generate the permutation $P = C_1 C_2 ... C_k$ is given in Algorithm 3.2.1, (in which f[i,j] is used to denote f_j^i, the elements in the cycle C_i). The permutation P is realized by realizing the cycles C_i, one at a time, using the procedure 'cycle.' To realize the cycle C_i, f_1^i is first brought to position 0 (by successive applications of operation a). By applying operation b $(f_2^i - f_1^i - 1)$ times, it is held at position 0 while record f_2^i is brought to position 1. Operation a is then applied once, so that f_1^i takes up the position (i.e., relative position) of f_2^i, and f_2^i is now at position 0. The process is repeated for all items of the cycle until the realization of the cycle permutation is completed.

The permutation algorithm can be better understood by considering an alternate interpretation of the record movement. In this view, records 0, 1, ..., n-1 are initially arranged in a circle.

Instead of moving the records in a counterclockwise direction, we consider the equivalent view of keeping the records at positions 1, 2, ..., n-1 stationary while moving the record at position 0 in a clockwise direction. For ease of discussion, let us assume that there is a bus that can hold exactly one passenger (record); the bus is initially at station 0 (position 0); and it travels in a clockwise direction. It stops at each of the stations, where several things can happen:

(1) the bus goes on to the next station;

(2) if the bus is empty, the passenger gets on it and is carried to the next station,

(3) if the station is empty, the passenger gets off the bus and the empty bus goes to the next station;

(4) if the bus is not empty, the passenger gets off the bus, the passenger in the station gets on the bus and the bus goes to the next station.

It can be seen that operation (a) corresponds to moving the empty bus from one station to the next; operation (b) corresponds to moving the bus from one station to the next with a passenger.

To realize the cycle $C_i = (f_1^i f_2^i ... f_{h_i}^i)$, the empty bus is first brought to station f_1^i (statement D in Algorithm 3.2.1), where the passenger f_1^i gets on the bus. The bus then goes to station f_2^i, where passenger f_1^i gets off the bus and passenger f_2^i gets on the bus (statements A and B). The bus then goes to station f_3^i, and so on. At the last step, passenger $f_{h_i}^i$ is brought to f_1^i, where he gets off the bus (statement C). The empty bus then goes to f_1^{i+1} to start the next cycle C_{i+1}. At the end of the last cycle, the empty bus goes to station 0 (statement E), returning to its initial position.

Algorithm 3.2.1 To generate an arbitrary permutation of records in Model 3.2.1,

procedure permute; (* the permutation to be performed can be decomposed into k cycles, where the i-th cycle = (f[i,1],...,f[i,h[i]]*)

procedure cycle (i);

(* realize the i-th cycle of the permutation *)
(* f[i,1] is assumed to be at position 0 initially *)

begin if h[i] > 1 **then** (*skip cycles of length 1 *)
      begin for j←1 to h[i]-1 **do**
            begin if f[i,j+1]>f[i,j]
                  then r←f[i,j+1]-f[i,j]-1
                  else r←n+f[i,j+1]-f[i,j]-2;
                  b(r);(* apply operation b r times *)
                        (* statement A *)
                  a(1); (* apply operation a once *)
                        (* statement B *)
            end;
            b(n+f[i,1]-f[i,h[i]]-1);(* statement C *)
      end (* if *);
end (* cycle *);

begin (* permute *)
for i←1 to k **do**
      begin if i=1 **then** a(f[1,1])
                else a(f[i,1]-f[i-1,1]);(* statement D *)
            (* f[i,1] is now at position 0*)

        cycle (i);

    end;

if f[k,1]>0 **then** a(n-f[k,1]);(* statement E *)

end (* permute *);

To count the number of steps taken by Algorithm 3.2.1, we need to determine the *number of excedence* (or excedence for short) in a permutation.   The excedence e(C) of a cycle C is defined as the number of increasing sequences in C if the cycle length of C is greater than one, and is defined as 0 otherwise. (Remember that the first item in C is the smallest.) For instance, the cycle C=(14523) has 2 increasing sequences 145,23 in it. Each such increasing sequence will be referred to as a run in C.   The excedence of a permutation is defined as the sum of the excedences of its cycles.

For example, e((02)(1 6 3 4)(5)) = e((02)) + e((1 6 3 4)) + e((5)) = 1+2+0=3.

In the procedure 'cycle,' if the length of the cycle is one, then the procedure is skipped. On the other hand, if the cycle consists of only one run, one complete pass through all the records is needed to realize it.   In general, a cycle C of excedence e(C) would require a total of e(C)(n-1) operations.

The procedure 'permute' calls the procedure 'cycle' k times. (Remember, k is the number of cycles in the permutation.) In addition, a total of n operations is needed to bring the beginnings of the cycles to position 0.   Let T1(n) denote the maximum number of steps necessary to generate an arbitrary permutation for n records; then

$$T1(n) = \max_{P} \{n + (n - 1)e(P)\}.$$

In the worst case, $e(P)$ can be $(n-1)$, thus giving us an $n^2 + O(n)$ algorithm. The following argument shows that by minor modification of Algorithm 3.2.1 (which will be referred to as Algorithm 3.2.1*), $T1(n)$ can be reduced to $\frac{1}{2}n^2 + O(n)$. Let P be the permutation desired, and let $P.a^r$ be the permutation obtained from P by r successive execution of operation a. Algorithm 3.2.1 is used to generate $P.a^r$ instead of P. P can then be obtained by $(n-r)$ mod n additional executions of operation a. Therefore,

$$T1(n) = \max_{P} \min_{r} \{n + (n - 1)e(P.a^r) + (n - r) \bmod n\}.$$

$$(3.2.1)$$

We show that

Lemma 3.2.1 For any given permutation P, there exists an r such that

$$e(P.a^r) \leq \frac{1}{2}(n - 1) .$$

Proof We first note that an excedence occurs in a permutation

$$\begin{pmatrix} 0 & 1 & \dots & n-1 \\ p_0 & p_1 & \dots & p_{n-1} \end{pmatrix}$$

for any i such that $i > p_i$. Now consider all the permutations $p.a^r, r = 0,1,...,n - 1$. Record i, originally at position i, would be permuted to position $(p_i - r) \bmod n$ in $p.a^r$. For a given i, an excedence occurs in all permutations such that $i > (p_i - r) \bmod n$, that is, in i cases. Hence, we have

$$\sum_{r=0}^{n-1} e(P.a^r) = \sum_{i=0}^{n-1} i = \frac{1}{2}n(n-1).$$

Since there are n permutations $P.a^r$, we conclude that there exists an r such that

$$e(P.a^r) = \frac{1}{2}(n-1) .$$

Therefore, we have

Theorem 3.2.1 The worst-case running time for Algorithm 3.2.1* is

$$T1(n) \leq n + (n-1)\frac{1}{2}(n-1) + n - 1 \leq \frac{1}{2}n^2 + n - \frac{1}{2}.$$

$$(3.2.2)$$

For example, the permutation

$$P = \begin{pmatrix} 0 \ 1 \ 2 \ 3 \ 4 \ 5 \ 6 \\ 2 \ 6 \ 0 \ 4 \ 1 \ 5 \ 3 \end{pmatrix}$$

has excedence 3. But

$$P.a^4 = \begin{pmatrix} 0 \ 1 \ 2 \ 3 \ 4 \ 5 \ 6 \\ 5 \ 2 \ 3 \ 0 \ 4 \ 1 \ 6 \end{pmatrix}.$$

has excedence 2, while all other permutations $P.a^r$ have excedences 3 or 4.

Note that a straightforward algorithm to compute the value of r which minimizes $e(P.a^r)$ would run in time $O(n^2)$. Like all other control operations for the functioning of a bubble memory, however, this computation is executed in central store and does not affect the timing of the permutation algorithm.

To compute the average running time of the algorithm, we should compute the value $\min\limits_{0 \le r \le n-1} e(P.a^r)$ for each possible P and then average over all such values in relation (3.2.1). Although this computation is not easy, there is a somewhat surprising argument which shows that the asymptotic value of such an average is $\sim\frac{1}{2}n$. Therefore, the algorithm has the same asymptotic behavior both in the worst case and on average. Let $\left\langle\!\left\langle{n \atop s}\right\rangle\!\right\rangle$ be the number of permutations of n elements having exactly excedence s, i.e., e(P)=s; and let $\left\langle{n \atop s}\right\rangle$ be the Eulerian numbers (i.e., the numbers of permutations of n elements having exactly s runs (see [35, p. 34 sq.])). The following fact is a subcase of a theorem proved by Foata in 1965 (see [35, p. 27, Theorem B]).

Lemma 3.2.2 $\left\langle\!\left\langle{n \atop s}\right\rangle\!\right\rangle = \left\langle{n \atop s+1}\right\rangle$

Thus, it suffices to consider the distribution of the Eulerian numbers. However, it has been proved in [4, p. 97], that this distribution is asymptotically normal, with mean $\mu_n = \frac{1}{2}n$ and variance $\sigma_n^2 = \frac{1}{12}n$, i.e.,

$$\lim_{n \to \infty} \sup_y \left| \sum_{z \le \sigma_n y + \mu_n} \frac{\left\langle{n \atop z}\right\rangle}{n!} - \frac{1}{\sqrt{2\pi}} \int_{-\infty}^{y} e^{-t^2/2} dt \right| = 0.$$

If we choose $y = -\sqrt{c \lg n}$, we have

$$\int_{-\infty}^{y} e^{-t^2/2} dt = \int_{|y|}^{\infty} e^{-t^2/2} dt$$

$$\le \int_{|y|}^{\infty} e^{-t|y|/2} dt = \frac{2}{|y|} e^{-y^2/2}$$

$$= \frac{2}{\sqrt{c\lg n}\, n^{c/2}} \le \frac{1}{n^{c/2}} \tag{3.2.3}$$

for large c and n. In short, if we let $\beta(c) = \frac{1}{2}n - \sqrt{c\lg n} - 1$, then

$$\sum_{x \le \beta(c)+1} \left\langle {n \atop x} \right\rangle /n! \le 1/n^{c'},$$

where c' is a monotonically increasing function of c. In particular, one can choose c large enough such that $c' > 1$. By Lemma 3.2.2,

$$\sum_{s \le \beta(c)} \left\langle\!\!\left\langle {n \atop s} \right\rangle\!\!\right\rangle /n! \le 1/n^{c'}.$$

That is, the total number of permutations P with $e(P) \le \beta(c)$ is at most $n!/n^{c'}$.

Letting $e(P)_m = \min_{0 \le r \le n-1} e(P.a^r)$, we have that the total number of permutations with $e(P)_m \le \beta(c)$ is at most $n \cdot n!/n^{c'} = n!/n^{c'-1}, c' - 1 > 0$. That is, the fraction of all the n! permutations with $e(P)_m \le \beta(c)$ is at most $1/n^{c'-1} = o(1)$. By noting that the average value of $e(P)$ for all P is $\frac{1}{2}(n-1)$ (see the argument in the proof of Lemma 3.2.1), we can write

$$\frac{1}{2}(n-1) \ge \underset{P}{\text{average}} \ (e(P)_m) \ge \beta(c)(1 - 1/n^{c'-1})$$

$$= (\frac{1}{2}n - \sqrt{c\lg n} - 1)(1 - 1/n^{c'-1}),$$

that is,

$$\text{average}_{P} \; (e(P)_m) = \frac{1}{2}n + o(n). \qquad (3.2.4)$$

Thus, we have

Theorem 3.2.2 The asymptotic average running time $T2(n)$ of Algorithm 3.2.1* is

$$T2(n) = \text{average}_{P} \; \min_{r} \{n + (n - 1)e(P.a^r)$$

$$+ (n - r) \bmod n\} \cong \frac{1}{2}n^2. \qquad (3.2.5)$$

Note that if we had directly applied the procedure 'permute' to obtain P (i.e., if we had not obtained $P.a^r$ with minimum $e(P.a^r)$), we should have obtained the same asymptotic average value $\frac{1}{2}n^2$. In this case, however, the worst case value would have increased to n^2.

3.2.4. A lower bound In this subsection, we derive a lower bound of $n^2/2 - 5n/2 + 3$ for any permutation algorithm in Model 3.2.1, thus proving that Algorithm 3.2.1* is optimal (asymptotically) in the worst case. In fact, a stronger statement can be made - namely, in all cases where Algorithm 3.2.1* requires more than linear time, it is optimal within a linear additive term. In other words, the algorithm is optimal in all cases, except possibly for the trivial cases when it runs in linear time.

Let a^r (or b^r) denote a sequence of r consecutive applications of operation a (or b), and let $\sigma = a^{r_1}b^{s_1} a^{r_2}b^{s_2}...a^{r_t}b^{s_t}$ be any sequence of operations $(r_1,s_1,...,r_t,s_t \geq 0)$. Also, let $|\sigma| = \sum_{i=1}^{t} (r_i + s_i)$ be the *length* of σ, and let $P \cdot \sigma$ be the permutation obtained from permutation P after the application of σ.

We always assume that 0, 1, ..., n-1 are the initial positions of records 0, 1, ..., n-1, respectively. Let I denote the identity permutation. For any permutation P to be constructed, a permutation algorithm must produce a sequence σ such that $I \cdot \sigma = P$. We will derive a worst-case lower bound for $|\sigma|$.

As mentioned in the proof of Lemma 3.2.1, for any permutation

$$P = \begin{pmatrix} 0 & 1 & ... & n-1 \\ p_0 & p_1 & \cdots & p_{n-1} \end{pmatrix},$$

where p_i is the position of record i,

$e(P)$ = number of i's such that $i > p_i$.

Lemma 3.2.3 Let $P \cdot \sigma = Q$, where $|\sigma| = n - 1$. Then $e(Q) \leq e(P) + 1$.

Before proving this lemma, we use the following example as illustration.

Example:

$$P = \begin{pmatrix} 0 & 1 & 2 & 3 & 4 & 5 & 6 & 7 \\ 4 & 1 & 0 & 2 & 5 & 6 & 7 & 3 \end{pmatrix}, e(P) = 3$$

$\sigma = ab^2a^3b$, (from left to right)

$|\sigma| = 7 = n - 1$

$$Q = \begin{pmatrix} 0 & 1 & 2 & 3 & 4 & 5 & 6 & 7 \\ 5 & 4 & 1 & 2 & 6 & 0 & 7 & 3 \end{pmatrix}, \ e(Q) = 4$$

Proof During the execution of σ, each record i of P falls in one of three situations:

(1)   i never occupies position 0 (i.e., whenever i is in position 1, operation b occurs in σ, taking i to position n-1). Thus, i is shifted along a loop of (n-1) positions. Since $|\sigma| = n - 1$, i appears in Q at position p_i again.

(2)   i occupies position 0 at some point (e.g., i initially occupies position 0, or when i is at position 1 operation a occurs, taking i to position 0), and is later removed from 0 (i.e., operation a occurs again before the end of σ). Then i appears in Q in a position $p_i' > p_i$.

(3)   i occupies position 0 at the end of σ, i.e., position 0 in Q.

We conclude that any i of (1) or (2) occupies a position $p_i' \geq p_i$. Thus if $i \leq p_i$, then clearly $i \leq p_i'$. In other words, if i did not contribute to e(P) before, it will not contribute to e(Q). Only record i of (3) may contribute to e(Q). Thus, $e(Q) \leq e(P) + 1$.

□

The following corollary applies to the identity permutation I:

Corollary 3.2.1 Let $I \cdot \sigma = Q$, and let $|\sigma| = h(n - 1)$, where h is a non-negative integer. Then $e(Q) \leq h$.

Proof Since $e(I) = 0$, it follows from Lemma 3.2.3.

□

Although the excedence of a permutation cannot be increased by more than one every n-1 steps (Lemma 3.2.3), such a number is widely variable during the execution of a sequence σ of arbitrary length. There are permutations, however, whose excedences are almost constant under any sequence of applications of operation a. In fact, we have

Lemma 3.2.4 There exists a permutation S such that $e(S \cdot a^r) \geq \lfloor \dfrac{n-1}{2} \rfloor$ for all r=0, 1, 2, ..., n-1.

Proof Take

$$S = \begin{pmatrix} 0 & 1 & \dots & n-2 & n-1 \\ n-1 & n-2 & \dots & 1 & 0 \end{pmatrix}.$$

It has the desired property. For example, when n=5, we have $e(S)=2$, $e(S \cdot a)=2$, $e(S \cdot a^2)=2$, $e(S \cdot a^3)=2$ and $e(S \cdot a^4)=2$.

□

Theorem 3.2.3 Any permutation algorithm in Model 3.2.1 takes

$$|\sigma| \geq \lfloor \frac{n-1}{2} \rfloor (n-1)-(n-2) \geq \frac{n^2}{2} - \frac{5n}{2} + 3 \tag{3.2.6}$$

operations in the worst case.

Proof It suffices to show that realizing the permutation S requires at least $\dfrac{n^2}{2} - \dfrac{5n}{2} + 3$ operations for any algorithm.

Let $I \cdot \sigma = S$ for some σ. Let $\sigma' = \sigma a^r$, where r is the smallest non-negative integer such that

$$|\sigma'| = |\sigma| + r = h(n - 1),$$

with h non-negative integer. $(0 \leq r \leq n - 2.)$

Now, $I \cdot \sigma' = I \cdot \sigma a^r = S \cdot a^r$.

By Corollary 3.2.1, $e(S \cdot a^r) = e(I \cdot \sigma') \leq h$.

By Lemma 3.2.4, $\lfloor \dfrac{n-1}{2} \rfloor \leq h$, or

$$|\sigma| = h(n - 1) - r$$

$$\geq \lfloor \frac{n-1}{2} \rfloor (n - 1) - (n - 2) \geq \frac{n^2}{2} - \frac{5n}{2} + 3,$$

Since $\lfloor \dfrac{n-1}{2} \rfloor \geq \dfrac{n}{2} - 1$.

$\square$

3.2.5. Optimality of Algorithm 3.2.1* Let σ^* be the sequence of operations performed by Algorithm 3.2.1*. By Theorem 3.2.1, we have

$$|\sigma^*| \leq \lfloor \frac{n-1}{2} \rfloor (n - 1) + 2n - 1 \qquad (3.2.7)$$

Comparing this with the lower bound

$$|\sigma| \geq \lfloor \frac{n-1}{2} \rfloor (n - 1) - (n - 2) \qquad (3.2.8)$$

in Theorem 3.2.3, we immediately conclude that, in the worst case, Algorithm 3.2.1* is optimal within an additive term of 3n-3.

As may be expected, the permutation S in Lemma 3.2.4 is also a worst-case permutation for Algorithm 3.2.1*, i.e., it achieves the upper bound (3.2.7). However, the argument developed above to derive the lower bound (3.2.8) will now be extended to prove that Algorithm 3.2.1* is optimal whenever it requires a superlinear number of steps.

Let P be a permutation produced from I by a sequence σ, that is, $I \cdot \sigma = P$; and let r be the smallest non-negative integer such that $|\sigma| + r = h(n - 1)$, with h non-negative integer. By Corollary 3.2.1, we have:

$$h \geq e(I \cdot \sigma a^r) = e(P \cdot a^r), \ 0 \leq r \leq n - 2.$$

From this we derive

$$|\sigma| = h(n - 1) - r \geq e(P \cdot a^r)(n - 1) - (n - 2)$$

$$\geq \min_{0 \leq t \leq n-1} \{e(P \cdot a^t)\}(n - 1) - (n - 2), \tag{3.2.9}$$

which gives a lower bound to the number of steps of any permutation algorithm to produce P, as a function of the minimum excedence in all the cyclic shifts of P.

On the other hand, equation (3.2.1) implies that the number of steps required by Algorithm 3.2.1* to produce P satisfies the relation

$$|\sigma^*| \leq \min_{0 \leq t \leq n-1} \{e(P \cdot a^t)\}(n - 1) + 2n - 1. \tag{3.2.10}$$

By comparing relations (3.2.9) and (3.2.10), we conclude that, for all the permutations T such that $\min_{0 \leq t \leq n-1} \{e(P \cdot a^t)\}$ is an increasing function of n (i.e., the running time $|\sigma^*|$ is superlinear), the running time meets the lower bound of (3.2.9) within a linear additive term of 3n-3. That is, Algorithm 3.2.1* is optimal in all cases, except possibly for the trivial cases when it runs in linear time.

3.2.6.   Model 3.2.2 To generate a permutation using operations (a) and (c) instead of (a) and (b), we have only to replace the procedure 'cycle' in Algorithm 3.2.1 by the following procedure 'cycle__two' to obtain Algorithm 3.2.2; everything else remains the same.

procedure cycle__two (i);
begin if h[i] $\geq$ 1 **then**
       begin for j$\leftarrow$1 to h[i]-1 **do**
              begin if f[i,j+1] > f[i,j]
                     then r$\leftarrow$n-f[i,j+1]+f[i,j]
                     else r$\leftarrow$f[i,j]-f[i,j+1]+1;
                     c(r);
                     a(l);
              end;
              c(f[i,h[i]]-f[i,1]);
       end;
end;

      Note that procedure 'cycle__two' is obtained from procedure 'cycle' by replacing b(r) with c(n-1-r). It can be shown again that the worst-case running time for this algorithm is $\frac{1}{2}n^2 + O(n)$ and the asymptotic average running time is $\frac{1}{2}n^2$. Similar optimality results as in Model 3.2.1 also apply here, showing that this algorithm is asymptotically optimal.

3.3.   Up–down bubble sorter

3.3.1.   Introduction The permutation problem discussed in Section 3.2 assumed that the destination locations of the records were known before the permutation algorithm began. Thus, it was only a matter of moving the records to their designated locations. However, the sorting problem we discuss here does not make such an assumption. In other words, given a set of records, we will compare their keys and rearrange the records in ascending or descending order. In general, the first part of a record is its key. But for sorting purposes, we may assume without loss of generality that the key is the whole record, and use the terms key and record interchangeably. This compare and steer operation is performed by a switch known as a *bubble string comparator* [1], which compares two input data strings, sets a switch with memory, and guides the larger and smaller data strings respectively to designated max and min outputs. The device not only compares and steers data strings, but also performs these functions without external control lines. The main advantages of having comparators inside a magnetic bubble memory are: (1) it frees the CPU from such simple operations as comparisons so that it can take on more complicated tasks, and (2) it makes the magnetic bubble memory a self-contained unit.

In this section we shall propose a sorting device composed of bubble string comparators and evolve efficient sorting algorithms for the new sorter. This sorter, called the up-down sorter, will begin sorting as soon as keys enter the device. Once the sorter is full, output begins, and the keys will come out from the device in sorted order. Thus, the actual sorting time will be completely overlapped by the input/output time.

3.3.2. The up-down sorter The basic component of the up-down sorter to be described in this section is the compare/steer unit shown in Figure 3.3.1.

The unit consists of four interconnected cells. Cells A and B are the input ports of a comparator. The unit holds two keys at C and D initially. During each cycle of operation, it takes a new key into A, transfers the key in C to B, and delivers the key in D to the output. Then the keys in A and B are compared, and the results are delivered to C = min(A,B) and to D=max(A,B).

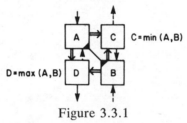

Figure 3.3.1

To accommodate the actions in the up-down sorter, the compare/steer unit can function in downward or upward mode. See the solid and dotted arrows in Figure 3.3.2. In the downward (upward) mode, an outside key is loaded from the top (bottom) into cell A(B) of the unit, and an inside key previously at C(D) is loaded into B(A). After loading, the comparison is executed, and the minimum is delivered to C and the maximum to D, following the transition paths as indicated by the double arrows.

Loading and comparison can be executed almost simultaneously. For convenience, we shall take the execution duration as a unit of time. All compare/steer units operate synchronously and take the same amount of time to operate. The notation $[t_i,t_{i+1})$ denotes the time interval from time instant t_i to time instant t_{i+1}, but not including t_{i+1}.

The up-down sorter consists of a stack of compare/steer units and operates in two phases. During the downward input phase, 2n keys are loaded into n units in 2n periods, with each unit delivering the larger key to its lower unit in every period. During the upward output phase, each unit delivers the smaller key to its upper unit in every period, outputting one item per period from the sorted keys. (See Figure 3.3.2.)

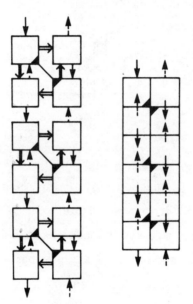

Figure 3.3.2

3.3.3. Sorter complexity The following claims about the hardware and timing complexity of the sorter are made:

1) To sort n numbers, only $\lceil n/2 \rceil$ units (comparators) are needed.

2) The sorting time is completely absorbed in the input/output time. Moreover, we shall show in Subsection 3.3.4 that the output operation of a sorted sequence can be made to overlap with the input

operation of the subsequent sequence if the sequences are properly tagged.

Before we prove our claims, let us explain how the up-down sorter performs sorting in ascending order. In Figure 3.3.3 we show a complete histogram of the sorter during the sorting of an input of six numbers, 4, 3, 1, 6, 2 and 5 (4 leading).

Initially, at time t_0, the contents of the buffer cells in each compare/steer unit are all set to $+\infty$ or to any number larger than all possible input data. This initial state can be realized by continuously feeding $+\infty$ into the bottom unit before t_0. During the first cycle, the first number 4 is compared to $+\infty$ and routed to the upper right cell. During the second cycle, the number 3 is loaded and compared to 4; then the number 3 is routed to the upper right cell and 4 is routed to the lower left cell of the first unit. During the third cycle, as the third number is being loaded into the first unit, the number 4 is loaded into the second unit. In other words, the larger of the two numbers will be "pushed" out of the compare/steer unit in which it resides. At the end of time t_3, the upper right cell of the first unit contains 1 and the lower left cell contains 3; and the upper right cell of the second unit contains 4 and the lower left cell contains $+\infty$. In this fashion the sorter continues to work. At the end of time t_5, all the six numbers have been loaded into the sorter, thus completing the input (downward) phase.

From time t_6 on, the output (upward) phase begins. Note that in the input phase the $+\infty$'s are pushed out of the bottom of the sorter; in the output phase the $+\infty$'s are pushed back into the sorter from the bottom. At the end of time t_6, the smallest number 1 is out and the second smallest 2 is in the upper right cell of the first unit awaiting to be output. In this output phase, the smaller of the two

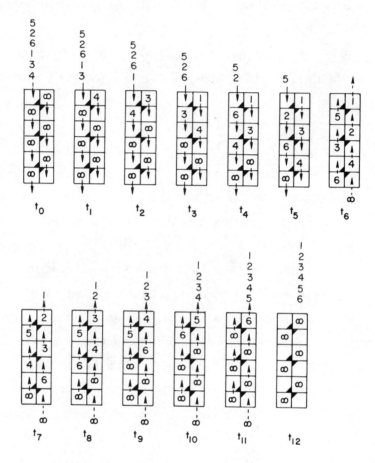

Figure 3.3.3

numbers within each compare/steer unit is "popped" up, leaving the
unit it resides in and entering the unit on top of it. In the case of the
top unit, the smaller number is delivered as output. Thus, the sorter
continues to put out the numbers in order. At the end of time t_{11}, all
data in the sorter will have been output in ascending order as desired.
At the same time, the sorter is automatically reset to its initial state
(all $+ \infty$) and is ready to accept the next input sequence.

To sum up, in input phase the larger of the two numbers in each compare/steer unit is pushed down, and in output phase the smaller of the two numbers is popped up. In general, the time interval $[t_0, t_n)$ corresponds to input phase and $[t_n, t_{2n})$ to output phase, where n is the number of keys to be sorted. While spending 2n units of time (or periods) to do input and output, we have automatically obtained a sorted sequence. The sorting is performed in a stack of n/2 compare/steer units.

Now let us show that the sorter indeed works correctly. Assume that the compare/steer units are numbered from top down as 1, 2, ..., n/2 .

Lemma 3.3.1 Let C_i and D_i denote the contents (keys) stored in the buffer cells of the i-th compare/steer unit. Then we have

$$\min (C_{i+1}, D_{i+1}) \geq \min (C_i, D_i) \text{ for } i = 1, 2, ..., n/2 - 1.$$

Proof It is the function of the compare/steer unit to push down the larger of its two keys in input phase, and to pop up the smaller of the two keys in output phase. In input phase the keys C_{i+1} and D_{i+1} are obtained via steering unit i. Hence, C_{i+1} (or D_{i+1}) must be greater than or equal to the key in compare/steer unit i, against which it was compared. So

$$\min (C_i, D_i) \leq \min (C_{i+1}, D_{i+1}).$$

Similarly, in output phase the popped-up key, C_i or D_i, is obtained from compare/steer unit i+1; hence, it must be smaller than or equal to the key in compare/steer unit i+1 against which it was compared.

Therefore

$$\min (C_i, D_i) \leq \min (C_{i+1}, D_{i+1}).$$ □

Lemma 3.3.2 Suppose that there are i keys in the top i/2 compare/steer units, $0 \leq i \leq n$. Then the j-th smallest key, $1 \leq j \leq$ i/2 of these keys is in some compare/steer unit k such that $k \leq j$.

Proof By Lemma 3.3.1, we have

$$\min (C_1, D_1) \leq \min (C_2, D_2) \leq ... \leq \min (C_m, D_m),$$

where m = i/2 . If the j-th smallest key X were in compare/steer unit k', such that $k' > j$, then we could find in each compare/steer unit s, $1 \leq s < k'$, a key which is smaller than X - that is, we could find $k' - 1 \geq j$ keys smaller than X, which is a contradiction to the assumption that X is the j-th smallest.

□

By the previous lemma, it is immediately obvious that after n keys have been read into the sorter, the smallest key must be in the first compare/steer unit, the second smallest must be in either compare/steer unit 1 or compare/steer unit 2, and so on. Therefore, the very first key output must be the smallest. After the first key has been output, the smallest key among the remaining n-1 is on the top of the sorter again and is ready to be output. Thus, the output sequence is indeed in ascending order and the total time for the sorting process is just the time for input/output of the data to and from the sorter. Therefore, we have the following theorem:

Theorem 3.3.1 The up-down sorter with m compare/steer units can sort $k(\leq 2m)$ records in 2k periods.

3.3.4. Enhancements – reversing, overlapping, and merging In this subsection we shall describe methods of enhancing the operation described in the previous subsection.

Descending-order sorting

In the previous subsection we described sorting to be done in ascending order. It is natural to ask whether or not the sorter can output a sequence in descending order. The answer is yes, but the input/output process must be somewhat modified. We propose two possibilities. The first approach is that we still use the same sorting mechanism except that on top of the sorter we add a multiplier which multiplies each input/output datum by -1. Actually, we perform a complement operation, changing 1 to 0 and 0 to 1. (See also Subsection 3.3.5.)

The second approach is to exchange the input and output ports. That is, let the input data enter the sorter from the lower right end (i.e., where the number $+ \infty$ enters), and output data come out from the lower left end (i.e., where $+ \infty$ comes out). In addition to the I/O port exchange, the sorter must be initialized to contain a number known to be smaller than the input data. As we shall see later, since initialization is not much of a problem and we also need to input the number $+ \infty$ from the bottom of the sorter in output phase using the first approach, we may just as well take the second approach and make the sorter capable of taking input and output from both ends, so as to function symmetrically and thus eliminate the multiplier.

Overlapping consecutive sorting sequences

Now we have made the up-down sorter sort numbers in both ascending and descending orders. The next attempt to make it more powerful is to see if it is possible to overlap the input of the next sequence with the output of the current sequence.

Again, the answer is in the affirmative if the following conditions can be satisfied. First, the next sequence is to be sorted in the opposite order - namely, if the current output is in ascending order, the next output will be in descending order and vice versa. Second, the data entered from the top are to be prefixed with a tag bit 0 and the data entered from the bottom, prefixed with a 1. As the comparator compares the tag bits together with the keys themselves, those keys with tag bit 1 will be judged larger than those with tag bit 0. Thus, the two sequences will be kept distinct before, during, and after sorting.

Let us illustrate this idea through an example (see Figure 3.3.4). Assume that the contents of the sorter are initialized as 1;0, where the first bit (tag bit) is 1 and the remaining bits are 0's. Each time we use the same sorter to sort 6 numbers. The time interval $[t_0, t_6)$ is the time for the input of the first sequence in which each datum is affixed with a bit 0. At time t_6 the first sequence is ready to be output and the second sequence can be read in at the same time. Each datum in the second sequence is affixed a tag bit 1. In the time interval $[t_6, t_{12})$, the output of the first sequence and the input of the second sequence are overlapped (i.e., performed simultaneously).

At time t_{12}, the first sequence has been sorted in ascending order and the sorter is now filled with the second sequence, which at the same time is about to be output. The third sequence, in which every datum is affixed with 0, can in the meantime be read in from the

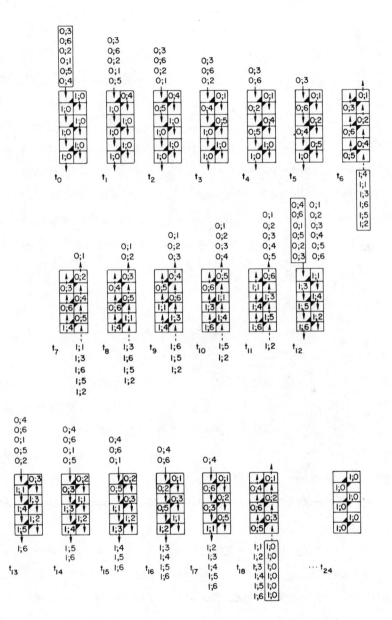

Figure 3.3.4

top. At time t_{18}, the second sequence has been sorted in descending

order and the third sequence is about to be output. If there is no more sequence to sort, we shall feed from the bottom a sequence of 0's, each affixed with a 1. If there is an even number of sequences to sort, the last sequence will be all 0's, each affixed with a 0, entering the sorter from the top.

As can be seen easily, since input and output can be overlapped, the number of periods needed to sort m sequences of n numbers is $(m+1)n$, instead of $2mn$. Moreover, initialization is done only once in the very beginning and is never needed afterward. If the sorter contains all 0's in the beginning, it needs no initialization when the sorter is to receive the first sequence from the bottom and sort it in descending order.

Sorting and merging

Then the next question arises. What if we have a sequence of numbers whose length (m) is greater than the up-down sorter (size n) can handle? A straightforward method is to divide the sequence into k $(k = \lceil m/n \rceil)$ subsequences, each of size n (with the possible exception of the last one), and feed them into the sorter. After we have obtained k sorted subsequences, we shall use the sorter to do a k-way merge if $k \le n$. If $k > n$, then we perform n-way merge as many passes as necessary. (See [35].) With no loss of generality, let us assume $k \le n$.

We have two cases to consider. First, suppose that we have buffer space large enough to hold the merged output. In this case the standard k-way merge technique applies. That is, we feed the k smallest numbers, one from each subsequence, into the sorter. Output the smallest one. Then feed in the next number from the subsequence to which the previous output number belongs. The detection of the originating subsequence is by tag which is affixed as the least significant bits on each number. Obviously, the total number of periods for sorting these m numbers is $(k+1)n+2m$, where $k= m/n$, and the first term is for sorting k subsequences and the second term, for merging.

Second, suppose that we do not have extra storage besides the space for the input data. In this case we need to do an "in-place" merging. Imagine that we have k data chips (numbered 1 through k). It is desired to arrange the output sequence after sorting such that the first chip holds the n smallest numbers and the second chip the next n smallest numbers, and so on.

We shall adapt the idea of odd-even merge used in Batcher's sorting network [2,35] to perform the in-place merging. First, let us describe the odd-even merge.

1) Given two sorted sequences in ascending order, $a_1,a_2,...,a_{2p}$ and $b_1,b_2,...,b_{2p}$, $p \geq 1$.

2) Merge odd sequences $a_1,a_3,...,a_{2p-1}$ and $b_1,b_3,...,b_{2p-1}$ to form a sorted sequence $v_1,v_2,...,v_{2p}$. Similarly, merge even sequences $a_2,a_4,...,a_{2p}$ and $b_2,b_4,...,b_{2p}$ to form a sorted sequence $w_1,w_2,...,w_{2p}$. Note that v_1 and w_{2p} are the smallest and largest number respectively.

3) Compare w_i and v_{i+1} for $i = 1,2,...,2p-1$. Let $c_i = \min(w_i,v_{i+1})$ and $d_i = \max(w_i,v_{i+1})$. Then the sequence $v_1,c_1,d_1,c_2,d_2,...,d_{2p-1},w_{2p}$ is the final sorted sequence resulting from the merging.

The odd-even merge algorithm can be generalized to merge two sequences where elements a_i and b_i are replaced by two sorted subsequences [35]. The algorithm to merge sequences follows.

1) Given two ascending-order sorted sequences, each composed of subsequences with the same number of keys, $A_1,A_2,...,A_{2p}$ and $B_1,B_2,...,B_{2p}$, $p \geq 1$.

2) Merge odd sequences $A_1, A_3, ..., A_{2p-1}$ and $B_1, B_3, ..., B_{2p-1}$ to form a sorted sequence $V_1, V_2, ..., V_{2p}$. Similarly, merge even sequences $A_2, A_4, ..., A_{2p}$ and $B_2, B_4, ..., B_{2p}$ to form a sorted sequence $W_1, W_2, ..., W_{2p}$.

3) Instead of comparison, merge W_i and V_{i+1} for $i = 1, 2, ..., 2p-1$. The smaller and larger halves of the merged sequence are denoted by C_i and D_i. Then the sequence

$$V_1, C_1, D_1, C_2, D_2, ..., C_{2p-1}, D_{2p-1}, W_{2p}$$

is the final sorted sequence resulting from the merging.

Now we are ready to apply the generalized odd-even merge. Consider the case of two data chips, each with a storage capacity equal to that of the sorter, and each storing a sorted sequence of n numbers. Let A and B denote the two sequences on the chips respectively. We divide A into two halves A_1 and A_2 such that A_1 has the smaller $n/2$ numbers and A_2 has the larger. Similarly, B is divided into B_1 and B_2. The data movement to execute the generalized odd-even merge is illustrated by Table 3.3.1.

Initially, the sorter is assumed to have n 0's, each with a tag bit 1, as indicated in the last column, in which each bit 0 or 1 stands for $n/2$ tag bits of 0's or 1's. Steps 1 and 2 feed A_1 and B_1 into the sorter from the top, with each number being tagged with a 0. In step 2, i.e., at the end of the input of B_1, the sorter is ready to begin delivery of the sequence $V_1 V_2$ (still being sorted). In step 3, while the sorter is delivering V_1 to Chip 1 from the top, the sequence B_2 of Chip 2 is read into the sorter from the bottom, with each number being tagged with a 1. Step 4 feeds A_2 into the sorter and obtains V_2 from the sorter. In step 5, W_2 is output to Chip 2, but only 0's are

Table 3.3.1

Merging of two chips

Step	Chip 1	Chip 2	Sorter	Tag Bits
0	A_1A_2	B_1B_2	00(initially)	11
1	A_2	B_1B_2	A_10	01
2	A_2	B_2	$B_1A_1 \rightarrow V_1V_2$	00
3	A_2V_1	---	V_2B_2	01
4	V_1	V_2	$B_2A_2 \rightarrow W_1W_2$	11
5	V_1	V_2W_2	$0W_1$	01
6	V_1	W_2	$W_1V_2 \rightarrow C_1D_1$	11
7	V_1	D_1W_2	$0C_1$	01
8	V_1C_1	D_1W_2	00	00

fed into the sorter. Now V_2 can be fed into the sorter from the bottom, with each number being tagged with a 1. Notice that the sequence V_2 is fed into the sorter from the bottom. The reason is that V_2 is to be merged with W_1 and W_1 is tagged with 1. Steps 7 and 8 output D_1 and C_1 into Chip 2 and Chip 1 respectively, thereby completing the merge process. Note that the sorter is in a different "state," in which the tag bits are 0's instead of 1's.

As can be seen from the table, each step is an I/O operation involving n/2 numbers. Thus, the total time for merging 2n numbers is 8*n/2 = 4n periods. The performance of the scheme would become worse were the number of sorted sequences to be merged to become larger. To illustrate the idea, let us consider the case when there are 4 data chips. We shall perform a binary merge, i.e., we merge the 2n numbers in Chips 1 and 2, and the 2n numbers in Chips 3 and 4, using the merge algorithm just described. This initial merge operation takes $2*(4n) = 8n$ periods.

Now we have two sorted sequences, each of $2n$ numbers. We then merge them by first dividing them into 4 subsequences each, i.e., A_1, A_2, A_3 and A_4 and B_1, B_2, B_3 and B_4 such that each subsequence has $n/2$ numbers, and performing the generalized odd-even merge operation as shown in Table 3.3.2. The first 8 steps (steps 1-8) merge A_1, A_3, B_1 and B_3 (odd-merge). Steps 9-16 merge B_4, B_2, A_4 and A_2 (even merge). Steps 17-24 perform the last phase of merging. Note that in steps 9-16 the ordering of the 4 subsequences to be merged is in reverse order as compared to the ordering of the 4 subsequences in odd-merge phase because the sorter is in different states at the beginning of odd- and even-merge phases. A total of $24*(n/2)+8n = 20n$ periods is consumed. As a remark, note that the total time may be reduced by a more careful implementation. For instance, in step 7, the sorter performs only output operations, and it can be fed a new subsequence A_2 simultaneously, instead of 0's, so as to save $n/2$ periods of time. We choose not to use such a sophisticated algorithm to simplify the analysis of the running time of the algorithm.

In general, suppose we have $k = 2^p$ chips of data to be merged, where p is an integer greater than 1. We can use a divide-and-conquer technique to merge the first $k/2$ chips and the second $k/2$ chips of data recursively to obtain two sorted sequences A and B, each with $n*k/2$ numbers, and then use the generalized odd-even merge algorithm to merge these 2 sequences by dividing them into k subsequences each, i.e., $A_1, A_2, ..., A_k$ and $B_1, B_2, ..., B_k$ such that each subsequence has $n/2$ numbers and performing the odd-even merge operations. If $T(k)$ denotes the time required to merge k data

Table 3.3.2

Merging of four chips

Step	Chip 1	Chip 2	Chip 3	Chip 4	Sorter	Tag Bits
0	A_1A_2	A_3A_4	B_1B_2	B_3B_4	00(initially)	11
1	A_2	A_3A_4	B_1B_2	B_3B_4	A_10	01
2	A_2	A_3A_4	B_2	B_3B_4	$B_1A_1 \rightarrow V_1V_2'$	00
3	A_2V_1	A_3A_4	B_2	B_4	$V_2'B_3$	01
4	A_2V_1	A_4	B_2V_2'	B_4	$B_3A_3 \rightarrow V_3'V_4$	11
5	A_2V_1	A_4	B_2V_2'	B_4V_4	$0V_3'$	01
6	A_2V_1	A_4	B_2	B_4V_4	$V_3'V_2' \rightarrow V_2V_3$	11
7	A_2V_1	A_4	B_2V_3	B_4V_4	$0V_2$	01
8	A_2V_1	A_4V_2	B_2V_3	B_4V_4	00	00
9	A_2V_1	A_4V_2	B_2V_3	V_4	$0B_4$	01
10	A_2V_1	V_2	B_2V_3	V_4	$B_4A_4 \rightarrow W_3'W_4$	11
11	V_1	V_2	B_2V_3	V_4W_4	A_2W_3'	01
12	V_1	V_2	V_3W_3'	V_4W_4	$B_2A_2 \rightarrow W_1W_2'$	00
13	V_1W_1	V_2	V_3W_3'	V_4W_4	$W_2'0$	01
14	V_1W_1	V_2	V_3	V_4W_4	$W_3'W_2' \rightarrow W_2W_3$	00
15	V_1W_1	V_2W_2	V_3	V_4W_4	W_30	01
16	V_1W_1	V_2W_2	V_3W_3	V_4W_4	00	11
17	V_1	V_2W_2	V_3W_3	V_4W_4	W_10	01
18	V_1	W_2	V_3W_3	V_4W_4	$V_2W_1 \rightarrow C_1D_1$	00
19	V_1C_1	---	V_3W_3	V_4W_4	D_1W_2	01
20	V_1C_1	D_1	W_3	V_4W_4	$W_2V_3 \rightarrow C_2D_2$	11
21	V_1C_1	D_1	D_2	V_4W_4	W_3C_2	01
22	V_1C_1	D_1C_2	D_2	W_4	$V_4W_3 \rightarrow C_3D_3$	00
23	V_1C_1	D_1C_2	D_2C_3	W_4	D_30	01
24	V_1C_1	D_1C_2	D_2C_3	D_3W_4	00	11

chips, then we have the following recurrence relation:

$$T(k) = 2*T(k/2) + M(k,k)$$

$$T(2) = 8,$$

where $M(k,k)$ denotes the time to merge $A_1,A_2,...,A_k$ and $B_1,B_2,...,B_k$. Since $M(k,k)$ can be expressed as

$$M(k,k) = 2*M(k/2,k/2) + 2*k$$

$$M(4,4) = 24,$$

we can solve for $M(k,k)$ and $T(k)$. In fact, $M(k,k) = 2(\lg k + 1)k$ and $T(k) = (\lg k)(\lg k + 3)k$. Therefore, the time for merging k chips of data is $(\lg k)*(\lg k + 3)*k*n/2$ periods.

3.3.5. Remarks Although we use numbers as sorted data to illustrate the function of the sorter, they are not restricted to numeric keys as long as the collating sequence of a character set is properly chosen. Furthermore, the numbers used need not be all of the same sign as long as an appropriate representation of numbers is chosen. For example, for the BSC to work, all positive numbers have a bit 1 as the most significant bit (sign bit), and the remaining bits represent their magnitudes; and all negative numbers, on the other hand, have a bit 0 as the most significant bit, and the remaining bits represent the one's complements of their magnitudes. (A very simple bubble device specifically designed to perform this number representation conversion is reported in [9].) In adopting this "unconventional" representation we ensure by comparing the sign bits, that positive numbers are greater than negative numbers and that between two negative numbers the one with smaller absolute value is indeed greater than the other when the bit-pair-by-bit-pair comparison is carried out by the BSC. We may also point out that the design of up-down sorter is not only suitable in magnetic bubble domain, but also applicable in other technologies, e.g., in very large-scale integrated (VLSI) circuit design. The configuration is similar to the linearly connected systolic array, as proposed by Kung and Leiserson [37], and is also capable of being utilized as a systolic priority queue, as discussed in Leiserson [39].

3.4. Tree searching in a major/minor loop bubble memory

3.4.1. Introduction In the preceding sections we were concerned with the problem of data rearrangement and sorting in a bubble memory. Specific models and associated algorithms were designed to speed up the time for such operations. In this section we turn to the problem of searching in magnetic bubble memories. The specific model we use is the basic major/minor loop structure. Several tree search schemes are investigated, namely, the balanced tree search the one-sided height-balanced (OSHB) tree search, and the one-sided k-height-balanced (OSk-HB) tree search schemes. (Note that a balanced tree can be regarded as an OSk-HB tree with $k=0$ and an OSHB tree, as an OSk-HB tree with $k=1$.) Two quantities are of interest here: the amount of record movement and the number of comparisons. After detailed analysis, we shall conclude that the OSHB tree search scheme provides the best trade-off.

3.4.2. Basic major/minor loop structure We assume that the basic major/minor loop structure under consideration (Figure 3.4.1) has M minor loops, each consisting of N bits. A record has M bits and is stored across the M minor loops, occupying the same bit in each minor loop. For example, record 3 in Figure 3.4.1 occupies all the top bits of the minor loops. The minor loops are rotating (in counterclockwise direction) synchronously. To access a record, we have to first bring it to the top bit position. By activating the transfer line, all the bits in the record are transferred to the major loop simultaneously. This transfer can be either destructive or nondestructive. For searching, we shall assume nondestructive transfers. The major loop is also rotating (in counterclockwise direction). The record is read one bit at a time at the read/write port. Thus, we have bit-parallel propagation of records but bit-serial read/write. We also assume that comparison of records is done at the read/write port.

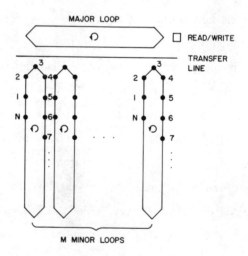

Figure 3.4.1

Thus, in this model a search consists of a series of comparisons of records in the minor loops until the desired record is found or is determined not in the memory. To perform a comparison, we have first to bring the record to be compared to the top position and second to transfer it to the read/write port and compare. We assume that the second part of the operation always takes constant time, i.e., to transfer and compare a record requires constant time, say, the time to rotate the minor loops for K bit positions. The first part, however, depends on the position of the record to be compared in the minor loops, i.e., how far it is from the top position. Thus, the cost for searching a record consists of two parts: total number of comparisons and total amount of record movement.

We assume that the N records in the minor loops are stored in sorted order, say, records 1, 2, ..., N are in ascending order and are stored in clockwise directions, and that the minor loops are held still during the time when a record is transferred to the read/write port and compared. We are interested only in the first part of the cost, namely, the total amount of record movement, and we shall study those search schemes where the total number of comparisons is bounded above by O(lg N). The objective is to minimize the total record movement.

Later on, we shall consider another way of storing the records in minor loops, i.e., not necessarily in sorted order, and we shall discuss the corresponding search schemes.

For our purpose, we can now assume that we have a loop with N locations, with each location containing one record (Figure 3.4.2). Each record can be accessed only at the read/write port.

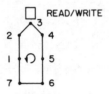

Figure 3.4.2

In a later subsection we shall discuss the case where the loop is not completely full.

It should be pointed out that in the case of a static file we need not physically stop the minor loops. Instead, we store the N records in ascending order and in clockwise direction, but with a distance of K-1 between consecutive records, where K is defined above. Specifically, if we label the locations in the minor loops as 0, 1, 2, ..., N-1, and assume K and N are relatively prime, then record i, $1 \leq i \leq N$, will occupy position (i-1)K mod N. For example, if K=3, N=7, then the records are arranged in the sequence 1,6,4,2,7,5,3. This will be equivalent to arranging the records in the sequence 1,2,3,4,5,6,7 and being able to stop the minor loops during transfer and compare.

3.4.3. General formula for total path length To satisfy the constraint that the number of comparisons be no more than O(lg N), it is reasonable to investigate tree search schemes. In this case, as usual, the height of the tree will correspond to the worst-case total number of comparisons for a search. On the other hand, if we weight the tree edges properly, the (weighted) path length will give us the total amount of record movement. Specifically, the average path length will correspond to the average total amount of record movement, while the maximum path length will correspond to the worst-case total amount of record movement. For example, assume $N=7$ and assume that the search is performed according to the balanced tree in Figure 3.4.3, where the nodes are records, i.e., after comparing with record 4, we compare with either 2 or 6, depending on the outcome, and so on. To go from record 4 to record 6, for example, the loop has to travel a distance of 2 (i.e., 2 record movements are needed), and we thus assign weight 2 to the edge from node 4 to node 6. In general, to the edge from node i to node j, we assign a weight the distance from i to j measured along the loop in clockwise direction, which is defined as the amount of record movement from record i to record j. Figure 3.4.3 is the resulting tree.

To compute the average path length of a weighted tree, it suffices to calculate its total path length and to divide it by the total number of paths, i.e., the number of nodes in the tree. We shall next derive a general formula for the total path length of such weighted trees. While the weights are defined as above, the trees are not fixed. For specific search strategies we end up with specific trees. The specific formulas for their total path lengths will be given in the following subsections.

Let nodes n_ℓ and n_r be the left and right children of node n. Let the edge weights be β and α respectively, and let N, N_A and N_B be the number of nodes of the entire tree, the right subtree of n_ℓ, and the left subtree of n_r respectively (Figure 3.4.4). Then we have

$$\alpha = N_B + 1 \tag{3.4.1}$$

since to go from n to n_r we must pass through all the records of B. Similarly,

$$\beta = N - N_A - 1 \tag{3.4.2}$$

since to go from n to n_ℓ we must pass through all the records of the entire tree except those of A.

We shall next calculate the total path length of such a weighted tree recursively (see Figure 3.4.5). Suppose that T(A) and T(B) are the total path lengths of A and B respectively, and that α and β are the weights of the right and left edges respectively, starting from the root of C. Furthermore, as before let N_A, N_B be the numbers of nodes in A and B. We then have the following recurrence relation:

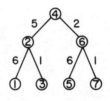

Figure 3.4.3

$$T(C) = T(A) + T(B) + \beta N_A + \alpha N_B + f(C). \qquad (3.4.3)$$

The function $f(C)$ is needed for the following reason (see Figure 3.4.6). Any left edge in A (or B) has a weight of the form $N_A - N^* - 1$ (or $N_B - N_1^* - 1$) according to (3.4.2), where N^* (or N_1^*) depends on which levels the edge is between. But when we construct C from A and B, this edge will have a new weight of the form $N_C - N^* - 1$ (or $N_C - N_1^* - 1$). Thus, the weights of all left edges in A (or B) are augmented by a quantity $N_C - N_A$ (or $N_C - N_B$). Of course, each of these new weights affects the weight of any path to which it belongs. For example, a left edge going to node n' in A (or B) adds $N_C - N_A$

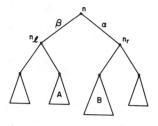

Figure 3.4.4.

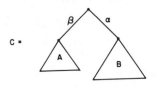

Figure 3.4.5

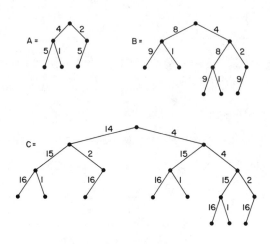

Figure 3.4.6

(or $N_C - N_B$) to the weights of all paths going to all nodes in the subtree rooted at n'. Since this is true for any left edge in A and B, we have

$$f(C) = (N_C - N_A)F(A) + (N_C - N_B)F(B), \qquad (3.4.4)$$

where $F(t)$, for a tree t, is defined as the sum of the number of nodes of each subtree of t whose root is a left child, i.e., the number of nodes of all left subtrees in t. For example, in Figure 3.4.7, there are four left subtrees in t, namely, the one rooted at a, and the nodes b, c, d (as left subtrees with single nodes). Thus, $F(t)=6$. Substituting (3.4.4) into (3.4.3), we obtain the following general formula for the total path length:

$$T(C) = T(A) + T(B) + \beta N_A + \alpha N_B$$

$$+ (N_C - N_A)F(A) + (N_C - N_B)F(B). \qquad (3.4.5)$$

Of course, for different kinds of search trees, different functions N,F will result and consequently, a different T will appear.

We will see, in the following, what kind of total path lengths will emerge for balanced trees, OSHB trees and OSk-HB trees.

3.4.4. Completely balanced trees In this subsection we consider the most obvious search tree, namely, a completely balanced tree. That is, the left and right subtrees of any node have exactly the same height (see Figure 3.4.8). (For simplicity, we shall refer to this as a balanced tree from now on.) Specifically, if we let t_i denote a balanced tree of height i, then t_i has t_{i-1} as both its left and right subtrees, with initial condition that t_0 consists of a single node. If H_i denotes the number of nodes in t_i, then

$$H_i = 2H_{i-1} + 1, \qquad (3.4.6a)$$

with initial condition that $H_0 = 1$. Thus,

$$H_i = 2^{i+1} - 1. \qquad (3.4.6b)$$

Clearly, the maximum number of comparisons required for a search is lg N. Thus, the constraint on the number of comparisons is satisfied. (We reiterate the well-known definitions and properties of balanced trees here solely to motivate later discussions on OSHB and OSk-HB trees.)

Let T_n denote the total path length as defined in (3.4.5) for a balanced tree of height n, i.e., t_n. Then we can rewrite (3.4.5) as

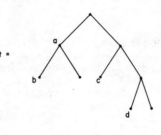

Figure 3.4.7

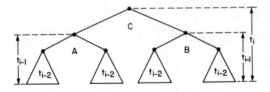

Figure 3.4.8

follows:

$$T_n = 2T_{n-1} + (H_n - H_{n-2} - 1)H_{n-1} + (H_{n-2} + 1)H_{n-1}$$

$$+ 2(H_n - H_{n-1})F_{n-2}, \qquad (3.4.7)$$

where $\beta = H_n - H_{n-2} - 1$ $\alpha = H_{n-2} + 1$ and F_i stands for $F(t_{i+1})$. The reason for writing it this way is that in (3.4.5), $F(A)$, A being t_{n-1}, is the sum of the number of nodes of all left subtrees in A. But the maximum height of such subtree is $n-2$. Thus, we define $F(A) = F(t_{n-1}) = F_{n-2}$ to make the counting easier and more consistent.

Relation (3.4.7) can now be rewritten as

$$T_n = 2T_{n-1} + H_n H_{n-1} + 2(H_n - H_{n-1})F_{n-2}, \qquad (3.4.8)$$

and the initial condition is $T_0 = 0$ (a tree with a single node has total path length equal to zero).

To solve the recurrence relation (3.4.8), we must first find the actual value of F_{n-1}. It can be easily seen that F_n satisfies the following recurrence relation:

$$F_n = 2F_{n-1} + 2^{n+1} - 1,$$

with initial condition $F_0 = 1$. This recurrence relation has the solution

$$F_n = n2^{n+1} + 1. \qquad (3.4.9)$$

Substituting (3.4.9) and (3.4.6b) into (3.4.8) and simplifying, we have

$$T_n = 2T_{n-1} + n2^{2n} - 2^n + 1, \qquad (3.4.10)$$

which has the solution

$$T_n = (n - 1)2^{2n+1} - n2^n + 3 \cdot 2^n - 1. \qquad (3.4.11)$$

To compute the average path length, just recall that the total number of nodes in a balanced tree of height n is given by

$N = H_n = 2^{n+1}-1$. Thus, the average path length for a tree of height n is

$$\overline{T}_n = \frac{T_n}{N} = \frac{T_n}{2^{n+1}-1}$$

$$= 0.5N\lg(N + 1)-0.5N-1.5\lg(N + 1) + 1 + \varepsilon, \qquad (3.4.12)$$

where $\varepsilon = (\lg(N + 1)-(3/2))/N$. Since ε tends to zero as N tends to infinity, we have

$$\overline{T}_n = 0.5N\lg N-O(N). \qquad (3.4.13)$$

For the worst case, we have to study the maximum path length in the tree, i.e., the path with the largest weight. But this is exactly the path having the maximum number of left edges, that is, the path going from the root to the leftmost node of the tree (Figure 3.4.9). Such a path has a total weight

$$T_W = \sum_{i=0}^{n-1} (N - 2^i) = N\lg\left(\frac{N + 1}{2}\right)-\left(\frac{N + 1}{2}\right) + 1. \qquad (3.4.14)$$

That is,

$$T_W = N\lg N - O(N). \qquad (3.4.15)$$

3.4.5. One-sided height-balanced trees From the structure of edge weight discussed above, it is clear that to minimize the average path length as well as the maximum path length, we prefer a tree with as few left edges as possible. For this reason, we study a class of trees known as one-sided height-balanced (OSHB) trees, which is a special case of the well-known AVL trees [30-32, 35, 36, 40-46, 53, 54]. Specifically, we consider trees where the left subtree of any node has height exactly one less than that of the right subtree. If we let t_i denote an OSHB tree of height i, then t_i has t_{i-2} as its left subtree and t_{i-1} as its right subtree with initial conditions that t_0 consists of a single node and t_1 consists of two nodes and a right edge (see Figure 3.4.10). If H_i denotes the number of nodes in t_i, then

$$H_i = H_{i-1} + H_{i-2} + 1, \tag{3.4.16a}$$

with initial conditions $H_0 = 1$, $H_1 = 2$. It has the solution [46, Sec. 6.42]

$$H_i = a_1 b_1^i + a_2 b_2^i - 1, \tag{3.4.16b}$$

where $a_1 = 1 + \dfrac{2}{\sqrt{5}}$, $b_1 = \dfrac{1+\sqrt{5}}{2}$, $a_2 = 1 - \dfrac{2}{\sqrt{5}}$, $b_2 = \dfrac{1-\sqrt{5}}{2}$, and also $i \approx 1.44 \lg H_i$. In other words, the height of the tree is 1.44 lg N, where N is the number of nodes in the tree. In terms of our problem, it means that the worst-case number of comparisons for a search is 1.44 lg N, thus satisfying the constraint.

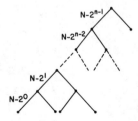

Figure 3.4.9

To derive the total path length for such a tree, we rewrite relation (3.4.5) as follows (see Figure 3.4.10):

$$T_n = T_{n-1} + T_{n-2} + (H_n - H_{n-3} - 1)H_{n-2}$$

$$+ (H_{n-3} + 1)H_{n-1} + F_{n-4}(H_n - H_{n-2})$$

$$+ F_{n-3}(H_n - H_{n-1}) \tag{3.4.17}$$

with initial conditions $T_0 = 0$, $T_1 = 1$, and F_i standing for $F(t_{i+2})$. F_i

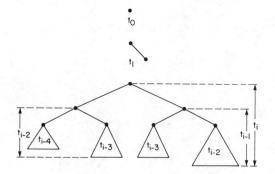

Figure 3.4.10

satisfies the following recurrence relation:

$$F_n = F_{n-1} + F_{n-2} + H_n$$

with initial conditions $F_0 = 1$ and $F_1 = 3$. This has the solution (see Appendix 3.1)

$$F_n = c_1 b_1^n + c_2 b_2^n + d_1 n b_1^n + d_2 n b_2^n + 1, \qquad (3.4.18)$$

where $c_1 = -c_2 = -0.0894$, $d_1 = \dfrac{a_1 b_1^2}{2 + b_1}$ and $d_2 = \dfrac{a_2 b_2^2}{2 + b_2}$. Substituting (3.4.18) into (3.4.17), we have the solution (see Appendix 3.2)

$$T_n = 1.3944272 a_1 b_1^n - 0.2763932 n a_1 b_1^n - 0.4527864 a_1^2 b_1^{2n}$$

$$+ 0.2763932 n a_1 b_1^{2n} - 0.1600001(-1)^n$$

$$+ 0.2n(-1)^n - 1. \qquad (3.4.19a)$$

Since the second term in (3.4.16b) approaches zero very rapidly as i tends to infinity, the number of nodes of a tree of height n is asymptotically $N \approx a_1 b_1^n - 1$. Also, as noted above, the height of a tree of N nodes is asymptotically $n \approx 1.44 \lg N$. Therefore, the total and average path lengths are asymptotically

$$T_n \approx 0.398 N^2 \lg N - 0.452 N^2 - 0.398 N \lg N + O(N) \qquad (3.4.19b)$$

and

$$\overline{T}_n \approx 0.398 N \lg N - 0.452 N - 0.398 \lg N + O(1). \qquad (3.4.20)$$

That is,

$$\overline{T}_n = 0.398 N \lg N - O(N). \tag{3.4.21}$$

To calculate the maximum path length, we have only to look at paths with the largest number of left edges. To do so we have to distinguish two cases: n even and n odd (see Figure 3.4.11).

If n is even, it is easy to see that there is a single path having n/2 left edges, namely, the path from the root to the leftmost node of the tree. Any other path in the tree has at most $\left(\dfrac{n}{2}-1\right)$ left edges. For this leftmost path, we have the path length

$$T_{w,e} = H_n - 1 + \sum_{i=0}^{\frac{n}{2}-1} (N - H_{2i+1} - 1).$$

Since

$$\sum_{i=0}^{\frac{n}{2}-1} (N - H_{2i+1} - 1) = N \cdot \frac{n}{2} - \frac{H_{n+1} - 2}{(b_1^2 - 1)} - \frac{n}{2}$$

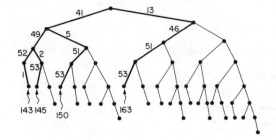

Example for $n = 7$

Figure 3.4.11

and $b_1^2 - 1 = b_1$ and using the asymptotic value $H_n = a_1 b_1^n$, we have

$$\sum_{i=0}^{\frac{n}{2}-1} (N - H_{2i+1} - 1) = N \cdot \frac{n}{2} - H_n + \frac{2}{b_1} - \frac{n}{2}.$$

Substituting $n = 1.44 \lg N$, we have

$$T_{w,e} = 0.72 N \lg N - N - 0.72 \lg N - 2.23.$$

That is,

$$T_{w,e} = 0.72 N \lg N - O(N). \tag{3.4.22}$$

If n is odd, then there are several paths having the maximum possible number of left edges, namely, $\lfloor \frac{n}{2} \rfloor$ left edges. However, these left edges may locate in different parts of the path. Since left edges become heavier if they are farther down the tree, we thus choose the path whose left edges are as far away from the root as possible. This means the path from the root to the leftmost node of the right subtree of the root. In fact, this is the only path with $\lfloor \frac{n}{2} \rfloor$ left edges existing on the right side of the root. All these left edges are under the right child of the root. On the other hand, all paths with $\lfloor \frac{n}{2} \rfloor$ left edges on the left side of the root have one left edge starting from the root. In Figure 3.4.11, we have an example for $n=7$; the numbers following arrows are the respective path lengths.

In this case, we have

$$T_{w,o} = H_n - 1 + \sum_{i=0}^{\lfloor \frac{n}{2} \rfloor - 2} (N - H_{2i+1} - 1) + H_{n-3} + 1.$$

By the same calculation as in the case of n even,

$$\sum_{i=0}^{\lfloor \frac{n}{2} \rfloor -2} (N - H_{2i+1} - 1) = \frac{n}{2}N - \frac{3}{2}N - H_{n-3} - \frac{n}{2} + 1.73.$$

Again substituting n=1.44 lg N, we have

$$T_{w,o} = 0.72NlgN - 0.5N - 0.72lgN + 1.73$$

or

$$T_{w,o} = 0.72Nlg\,N - O(N). \tag{3.4.23}$$

3.4.6. One-sided k-height-balanced trees In the previous subsection we considered OSHB trees because their number of left edges was less than that of the balanced trees (at the expense of more comparisons). Continuing with this approach, we are naturally led to one-sided k-height-balanced (OSk-HB) trees [40, 41, 43]. (Note that the trees considered here are specific kinds of OSk-HB trees; they are analogous to Fibonacci trees.) These are trees where the left subtree of any node has height exactly k less than that of the right subtree. Specifically, if t_i^k denotes an OSk-HB tree of height i, then t_i^k has a left subtree t_{i-k-1}^k and a right subtree t_{i-1}^k with initial conditions that t_i^k, $0 \le i \le k$, has (i+1) nodes connected by i right edges (see Figure 3.4.12).

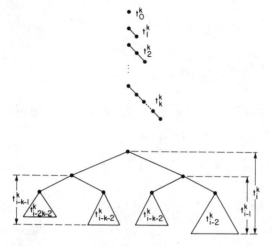

Figure 3.4.12

Again, if we let H_i^k denote the number of nodes in t_i^k, then

$$H_n^k = H_{n-1}^k + H_{n-k-1}^k + 1 \qquad (3.4.24a)$$

with initial conditions $H_i^k = i + 1$, $0 \le i \le k$.

In [40] it is shown that for all fixed k, $i = \alpha_k \lg H_i^k + O(1)$, where the coefficient α_k is a monotonically increasing function of k - for example, $\alpha_2 = 1.814$, $\alpha_3 = 2.151$, $\alpha_4 = 2.464$, $\alpha_5 = 2.762,\ldots$. Thus, for all fixed k, the height of the tree is of order $O(\lg N)$, where N is the number of nodes in the tree, hence satisfying our constraint on the number of comparisons for a search.

To derive the total path length for this family of trees, we rewrite relation (3.4.5) as follows (see Figure 3.4.12):

$$T_n^k = T_{n-1}^k + T_{n-k-1}^k + (H_{n-k-2}^k + 1)H_{n-1}^k$$

$$+ (H_n^k - H_{n-k-2}^k - 1)H_{n-k-1}^k + (H_n^k - H_{n-1}^k)F_{n-k-2}^k$$

$$+ (H_n^k - H_{n-k-1}^k)F_{n-2k-2}^k \qquad (3.4.24b)$$

with initial conditions $T_i^k = \sum_{j=0}^{i} j$, $0 \le i \le k$. F_i^k now stands for $F(t_{i+k+1}^k)$. It satisfies the recurrence relation

$$F_n^k = F_{n-1}^k + F_{n-k-1}^k + H_n^k \qquad (3.4.24c)$$

with initial conditions $F_i^k = \sum_{j=0}^{i} (j + 1)$, $0 \le i \le k$.

Unfortunately, all these recurrence relations have a degree which is a function of the parameter k and cannot be solved in closed form. However, we have numerically computed the values of T_n^k, H_n^k, and $\overline{T}_n^k (= T_n^k/H_n^k)$ for several values of k and n, where T_n^k is, as usual, the total path length of t_n^k and $\overline{T}_n^k$ is the average path length. We tabulate the quantities $C_N^k = \overline{T}_n^k/N\lg N$ in Table 3.4.1 for several values of k and N.

It can be seen that for fixed k, C_N^k is an increasing function of N, but the increment is decreasing. In fact, based on numerical evidence we believe that for fixed k, C_N^k tends to a finite limit as N tends to infinity, which is very close to the k-th entry of the last row in Table 3.4.1. On the other hand, for fixed N, C_N^k is a decreasing function of k, as expected. That is, the more skewed the tree is (i.e., the larger the value of k is), the smaller the average path length is.

To calculate the maximum path length for an OSk-HB tree, we have the following observation. For a given k, all trees of height i(k+1), i=0,1,..., have i left edges in the path from the root to the leftmost node, and at most (i-1) left edges in any other path. Figure 3.4.13 demonstrates the case when k=2, i=1,2,3. Therefore, for these trees we have, by relation (3.4.2),

$$T_w^k = N - 1 + \sum_{i=1}^{\frac{n}{k+1}-1} (N - H_{i(k+1)-1} - 1)$$

$$= \frac{n}{k+1}N - O(N) - O(n) - 1.$$

As before, for fixed k, we can express the height in terms of the number of nodes

$$n = \alpha_k \lg N + O(1).$$

Table 3.4.1

Values of C_N^k

k \ N	2	3	4	5	6	7	8	9	10
10^8	0.3251	0.2994	0.2813	0.2681	0.2575	0.2489	0.2416	0.2355	0.2301
10^9	0.3281	0.3022	0.2842	0.2705	0.2599	0.2512	0.2438	0.2377	0.2323
10^{10}	0.3305	0.3043	0.2862	0.2725	0.2618	0.2531	0.2457	0.2394	0.2339
10^{11}	0.3324	0.3061	0.2879	0.2741	0.2633	0.2546	0.2472	0.2408	0.2354
10^{12}	0.3341	0.3076	0.2893	0.2756	0.2646	0.2558	0.2484	0.2421	0.2365
10^{13}	0.3354	0.3089	0.2904	0.2767	0.2658	0.2569	0.2495	0.2431	0.2375
10^{14}	0.3366	0.3100	0.2916	0.2777	0.2668	0.2578	0.2504	0.2439	0.2384
10^{15}	0.3377	0.3110	0.2925	0.2786	0.2676	0.2586	0.2511	0.2447	0.2391

Thus,

$$T_w^k = \frac{\alpha_k}{k+1} N \lg N - O(N), \hspace{3em} (3.4.25)$$

where $\alpha_2 = 1.814$, $\alpha_3 = 2.151$, $\alpha_4 = 2.464$, $\alpha_5 = 2.762$,....

3.4.7. Linearized trees If we relax the requirement that the records be stored in sorted order in the loop, we can form a one-sided balanced (OSB) tree of all the records, and then store it level by level. (By an OSB tree, we mean that the leaves of the tree are on either level ℓ or $\ell + 1$, for some ℓ, and those on level $\ell + 1$ are located to the left of those on level ℓ.) Specifically, if a node is in position i, $1 \leq i \leq N$, in the stored sequence, then its left and right children (if any) will occupy positions 2i and (2i+1) respectively. An example of N=8 is given in Figure 3.4.14.

In this case, since we always go forward for a search, the average record movement (i.e., the average distance traveled by the

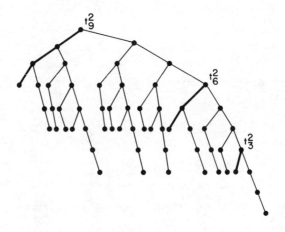

Figure 3.4.13

loop) is

$$\left(\sum_{i=0}^{N-1} i \right) /N = \frac{N-1}{2},$$

and the maximum record movement is obviously N-1. The average and maximum numbers of comparison are both lg N +O(1). However, to output the records in sorted order will require a total record movement of N lg N +O(N) since one has always to return to a standard position to output the next record.

3.4.8. Summary and comparison of results We summarize our results of previous subsections in the Table 3.4.2. For comparison, we also include sequential search. It can be seen from Table 3.4.2 that while there is a substantial reduction in record movement from balanced trees to OSHB trees, i.e., OSk-HB with k=1, (about 20 percent), the gains for increasing k become smaller and smaller. This means that it

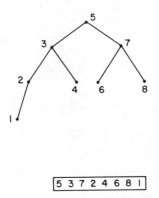

Figure 3.4.14

is probably not worthwhile to choose k greater than 1 since the
increase in number of comparisons is quite large.

Table 3.4.2

Summary of Results

	Record Movement		Number of Comparisons		Record Movement
	Average	Maximum	Average	Maximum	for Sorted Output
Balanced tree	0.5 N lgN	N lg N	lg N	lg N	N-1
OSk-HB					
k=1	0.39N lg N	0.72N lg N	1.04 lg N*	1.44 lg N*	N-1
k=2	~0.34N lg N	0.60N lg N		1.81 lg N+	N-1
k=3	~0.31N lg N	0.53N lg N		2.15 lg N+	N-1
k=4	~0.29N lg N	0.49N lg N		2.46 lg N+	N-1
k=5	~0.28N lg N	0.46N lg N		2.72 lg N+	N-1
Sequential search	(N-1)/2	N-1	(N-1)/2	N-1	N-1
Linearized tree**	(N-1)/2	N-1	lg N	lg N	N lg N

** Records are not stored in sorted order.

* See [46, Sec. 6.42].

+ See [40].

3.4.9. Generalization to incompletely full memory loops So far, we have assumed that the loop is full of records. However, previous results can be easily generalized to incompletely full loops. Assume that N records are stored contiguously in a loop of P positions. Furthermore, the records are stored in sorted order. We shall look at the various tree search schemes studied before. Notice only that to reach a preceding record in the ordering, we do not travel a distance $N-n_i$, but rather $P-n_i$. This means that to compute the total path lengths, any left-edge weight must be augmented by a quantity $Q = P-N$.

Following the same reasoning for defining f(C) in relation (3.4.3), we can see that for balanced trees the new total path length T'_n is given by

$$T'_n = T_n + QF_{n-1}, \tag{3.4.26}$$

where T_n and F_n are given in (3.4.11) and (3.4.9). Thus,

$$T' = T + 0.5QN\lg N - O(QN),$$

and the new average path length is

$$\overline{T'} = \overline{T} + 0.5Q\lg N - O(Q)$$

$$= 0.5P\lg N - O(P - N). \tag{3.4.27}$$

For OSHB trees, we have

$$T'_n = T_n + QF_{n-2},$$

where T_n and F_n are given in (3.4.19a) and (3.4.18). Thus, the new total path length is

$$T' = T + 0.39QN\lg N - O(QN),$$

and the new average path length is

$$\overline{T'} = \overline{T} + 0.39Q\lg N - O(Q)$$

$$= 0.39P\lg N - O(N - P). \tag{3.4.28}$$

By comparing (3.4.27) and (3.4.28), we see the gain from using OSHB trees rather than balanced trees is the same as before. Similar results can be obtained for general OSk-HB for $k>1$.

3.4.10 Other considerations If an extra feature can be added to the major/minor loop memory, then we can insert or delete records easily. Namely, we allow the loop to be in one of two possible states: (1) normal state and (2) detach state, at any time (see Figure 3.4.15). In the normal state the loop functions as before. In the detach state the record in position X is detached from the main loop. The implementation of this feature has been reported in the literature (see [50]). Clearly, to insert a new record R between records R_i and R_{i+1}, we first move an empty location to X and write R in it. Then we detach X and rotate the main loop so that R_i, R_{i+1} occupy positions Y, Z respectively. Returning the loop to the normal state completes the insertion. Obviously, deletion can be done in a similar fashion.

Now if we store the records in sorted order, as discussed in Subsections 3.4.2-3.4.6, then insertion and deletion can be done very easily since all we have to do is first to find out a record's proper position in the loop, and then insert or delete it. Furthermore, the remaining records are again in contiguous sorted order. Of course, the various search tree schemes have to be updated (i.e., the trees have to be rebalanced), but updating needs to be done only in external control structure, not in the bubble memory. There is a large amount of literature on efficient ways of rebalancing the trees discussed in this section; we refer the interested reader to [30-32, 35, 36, 40-46, 53, 54]. On the other hand, to do insertion and deletion in a linearized tree structure as discussed in Subsection 3.4.7 is no easy task if we want to keep the remaining records again in a linearized tree since a large number of records in the loop may have to be reshuffled.

Finally, if we can allow the loop to rotate in both directions and physically to stop at will, then the balanced tree search scheme is, of course, the best choice. In this case the maximum number of comparisons is lg N and the maximum amount of record movement is N. Insertion and deletion can be done in the same manner as above if the required extra hardware feature is available.

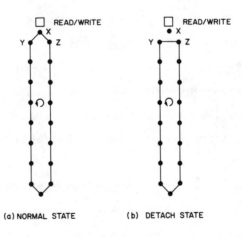

Figure 3.4.15

3.5. Permutation algorithms in different models of bubble memories

3.5.1. Introduction The last three sections dealt with the problems of permutation, sorting and searching in various models. The main objective was to find simple memory structures and associated algorithms so that these operations could be performed efficiently. In other words, we did not pay specific attention to the hardware complexity of the models, even though they were in fact quite simple. This and the two following sections will take a more comprehensive approach to these problems, namely, as mentioned in Section 3.1, three important parameters will be taken into consideration in designing the memory structures and their corresponding algorithms:

(1) the number of steps (to be defined) to perform the algorithms,

(2) the number of switches used and

(3) the number of control states necessary to carry out the algorithm.

The last two parameters deal with hardware complexity, explicitly since switches occupy physical space and increase manufacturing complexity, while the number of control states directly reflects the number of control lines and hence the number of pins.

Naturally, it is desirable to minimize all these parameters. But this is in general not possible. We are therefore interested mainly in their trade-offs.

In this section we are looking for bubble memory structures with corresponding algorithms that would enable us to perform arbitrary permutations of the records inside the memory. Records are restricted to move along certain physically predefined paths (i.e., loops), but we do have the freedom to choose the number of loops and their physical arrangements, the number of switches and their locations and the ordering of the records inside the loops. We will present several different bubble memory structures (models) with different number of loops and switches. In each model, an algorithm for permuting records is given and analyzed, in terms of time complexity and the required number of control states. We assume a switch has two states. Thus, in general, a model with x switches may have a total of 2^x possible states. However, in our proposed algorithms only a subset of them is required. The cardinality of this subset is the number of control states necessary.

3.5.2. Basic model We assume that a magnetic bubble memory consists of loops. A loop of size m is capable of holding m records. Under the control of a switch, a loop can circulate records in a counterclockwise direction or can hold the records in position. The time it takes to move one record from one position to an adjacent position (in a counterclockwise direction) is called a *step* and is assumed to be the basic unit of time. The "holding" action of the loops can be realized by one of the following two methods:

1. By placing over the loop an additional magnetic field, which, when turned on, cancels the original rotating magnetic field that drives the bubble domains around.

2. By using the model proposed in [7], which is an unconventional major/minor loop structure with specially designed switches (to be described in the next paragraph.)

We use one minor loop for a record, with a switch connecting each of the minor loops to a major loop. Thus, a loop of size m in our model actually consists of one major loop and m minor loops. (See

Figure 3.5.1.) All the switches connecting the major loop to its minor loops are under a single control and can be opened or closed simultaneously. If they are all closed, in one step the bubbles in one minor loop move to an adjacent minor loop. On the other hand, if they are all open, then in one step the bubbles complete a cycle within the minor loops and the holding action is achieved.

We now describe the function of a switch for all our models in this section. Two adjacent loops can exchange records by means of a switch. When the switch between them is open, the two loops remain separate (see Figure 3.5.2 (a)). But when it is closed, they form a single big loop. (See Figure 3.5.2(b)). These switches can also be used to implement the major/minor loop switches described in (2)

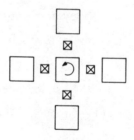

Figure 3.5.1

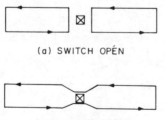

Figure 3.5.2

above.   Implementation of such switches in hardware has been
demonstrated in many previous studies; see, e.g., [1,48].

3.5.3. Separation algorithm In the models and algorithms to follow,
one basic algorithm is always used; it separates the data into two
adjacent loops connected by a switch.   More specifically, given two
loops of records with the destination loop of each record known, this
algorithm describes a sequence of switch settings which moves the
records to their destination loops.

Throughout this section, we use the notation "move (1, 2, ...,
$m;x$)" to mean "simultaneously shift loops 1, 2, ..., m by x steps." If
$x=1$, we simply write "move (1, 2, ..., m)."

procedure separate (i,j);

(Comment: Perform a separation of records in adjacent loops i and

j. Size [i] denotes the size of loop i, and destination [i,k] denotes

the loop to which the record at position k of loop i is to be

moved. Switch [i,j] designates the switch between loops i and j);

begin

C1 ← 1;

C2 ← 1;

(Comment Call the positions of the record of loop i and the record

of loop j at the switch both 1);

repeat

if destination $[i,1]=i$ **and** destination $[j,1]=i$ **then**

begin switch $[i,j]$←"open";

move (i);

C1←C1+1;

end

```
    else if destination [i,1]=i
        and destination [j,1]=j then
        begin switch [i,j]←"open";
        move (i,j);
        C1←C1+1;
        C2←C2+1;
        end
    else if destination [i,1]=j
        and destination [j,1]=i then
        begin switch [i,j]←"closed";
        move (i,j);
        C1←C1+1;
        C2←C2+1;
        end
    else if destination [i,1]=j
        and destination [j,1]=j then
        begin switch [i,j]←"open";
        move (j);
        C2←C2+1;
        end
    until C1>size [i] and C2>size[j];
end;
```

In the example of Figure 3.5.3, there are two loops, designated 1 and 2. The size of loop 1 is 4 and the size of loop 2 is 6. A total of 10 records reside in these two loops. All records numbered less than or equal to 4 have loop 1 as their destination, while the others have loop 2 as their destination. At the beginning, records 7 and 2 are at the switch. The sequence of switch settings for the separation of records is "closed," "open," "open," "open," and "closed."

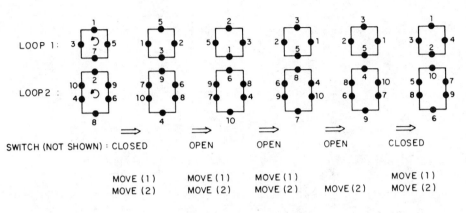

Figure 3.5.3

Note that, in general, the number of steps required by the separation algorithm is less than or equal to the sum of size [i] and size [j].

We next consider several models of magnetic bubble memories and propose corresponding permutation algorithms. All these algorithms have the previous separation algorithm as a basic building block. However, it is adapted to suit the specific models.

3.5.4. Model 3.5.1 In this model, the bubble memory system consists of loops of sizes 2, 2, 4, 8, ..., i.e.,

$$\text{size[i]} = \begin{cases} 2^{i-1} & \text{for } i \geq 2; \\ 2 & \text{for } i = 1. \end{cases}$$

Thus, the total capacity of a memory system consisting of k loops is $2+2+...+2^{k-1}=2^k$. Between loop i and loop i+1, for i=1,2,...,k-1, there is a switch s_i; thus, a total of k-1 switches is required. (See Figure 3.5.4.) Loops 1, 2, ..., k-1 are regarded as forming the first half of the memory system, while loop k is regarded as forming the second half.

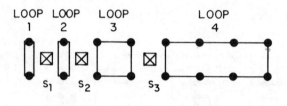

(a) A MEMORY SYSTEM OF CAPACITY 16

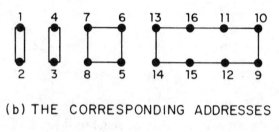

(b) THE CORRESPONDING ADDRESSES

Figure 3.5.4

We impose a special ordering on the memory locations and refer to it as the memory addresses (Figure 3.5.4(b)). The permutation problem means that, for a given set of records with relative ordering known beforehand, we want to place the records in the memory locations such that the i-th record goes to the i-th memory location. The relative order of a record is also referred to as the address of the record.

Before stating the permutation algorithm formally, we first describe it informally:

1.   The first step of the algorithm calls for the separation of records so that the ones with larger addresses go to the first half of the memory.

2.   Then perform the desired permutation of them, while holding the records in the second half of the memory. The

permutation of the records in the first half of the memory is done recursively.

3. Swap the first half with the second half by closing the appropriate switch (s_{k-1}) and cycling the records through 2^{k-1} record lengths.

4. Repeat step 2.

This algorithm calls for a special address scheme for the memory locations. Assume the memory capacity is $n(= 2^k)$ and regard the memory system as a $2 \times (n/2)$ array, with loop 1 occupying the first column, loop 2 the second column, loop 3 the third column, loop 4 the fourth column, and so on. (See Figure 3.5.4.) Thus, the first half of the memory occupies the first $n/4$ columns, while the second half of the memory occupies the remaining $n/4$ columns. Let (x,y), $1 \leq x \leq 2$, $1 \leq y \leq n/2$ be the coordinates of the memory locations and $d(x,y)$ the address to be assigned to (x,y). The address scheme is defined recursively as follows:

1. If $n=2$, assign $d(1,1)=1$, $d(2,1)=2$.

2. If $n= 2^i$ for $i>1$, then the address scheme for the first half of the memory is the same as when $n = 2^{i-1}$. For the second half of the memory, assign $d(x,y)=d(3-x,(n/2)+1-y)+(n/2)$ for $1 \leq x \leq 2$, $1 + (n/4) \leq y \leq n/2$.

An example of this address scheme for a memory of capacity 16 is given in Figure 3.5.4(b).

We can now describe the permutation algorithm formally.

procedure swap (n):

(Comment: Swap contents of the first (lg n−1) loops with the (lg n)-th loop by closing the switches and shifting the resulting big loop for half the total length);

begin

    for $i \leftarrow 1$ to (lg n−1) **do** $s_i \leftarrow$ "closed";

    (Comment: Set the first (lg n−1) switches to "closed");

    move (1,2,..., lg n;n/2);

    (Comment: Move first lg n loops n/2 steps);

end;

The following procedure is an adaptation of the separation algorithm described in Subsection 3.5.3 to the current model.

procedure separate__1 (n,n_0);

    (Comment: Given n records with destination addresses $n_0, n_0 + 1,...,n_0 + n - 1$ in the first lg n loops of the memory, the procedure performs a separation on the records such that the address of any record in the first (lg n−1) loops is larger than that of any record in the (lg n)-th loop. Denote by c(k) the destination address of the record currently at memory address k numbered as before);

begin

    for $i \leftarrow 1$ to (lg n) − 2 **do** $s_i \leftarrow$ "closed";

    (Comment: The first lg n−1 loops form a big loop);

$$x \leftarrow \left(\frac{n}{4} + 1 \right);$$

$$y \leftarrow \left(\frac{3n}{4} + 1 \right);$$

(Comment: x and y are the memory addresses at the inputs to
$s_{\lg n-1}$);
count $\leftarrow$ 0;

    for i $\leftarrow$ 1 to n/2 **do**

      if $c(i) < (n_0 + n/2)$ **then** count $\leftarrow$ count+1;

      (Comment: Count is the number of records that should be moved
      from the first (lg n−1) loops to the (lg n)-th loop);

  while count $>$ 0 **do**

    if $c(x) \geq n_0 + n/2$ **and** $c(y) \geq n_0 + n/2$ **then**

      begin $s_{\lg n-1} \leftarrow$ "open";

        move(1,2,...,lg n−1);

      end

    else if $c(x) \geq n_0 + n/2$ **and** $c(y) < n_0 + n/2$ **then**

      begin $s_{\lg n-1} \leftarrow$ "open";

        move(1,2,...,lg n);

      end

    else if $c(x) < n_0 + n/2$ **and** $c(y) \geq n_0 + n/2$ **then**

      begin $s_{\lg n-1} \leftarrow$ "closed";

        move(1,2,...,lg n);

        count $\leftarrow$ count−1;

      end

    else begin $s_{\lg n-1} \leftarrow$ "open";

      move(lg n);

    end

  end;

procedure permute__1(n,n_0);

(Comment: Given n records with destination addresses $n_0,n_0 + 1,...,n_0 + n - 1$ in the first lg n loops, let $c(i)$ denote the destination address of the record at memory address i. Given an initial set of $c(i)$, which is a permutation of the set $\{n_0,n_0 + 1,...,n_0 + n - 1\}$, the procedure performs a permutation of the records such that $c(i) = n_0 + i - 1$ for i=1,...,n);

begin

   if n=2 **then**

   if $c(1)>c(2)$ **then** move (1);

   (Comment: Put the records of loop 1 in order)

   else begin

     separate__1(n,n_0);

     (Comment: Separate n records so that records with larger destination addresses go to the first half);

     $s_{\lg n-1} \leftarrow$ "open";

     permute__1 $(n/2,n/2+n_0)$;

     (Comment: Apply recursion to the first (lg n−1) loops);

     swap (n);

     $s_{\lg n-1} \leftarrow$ "open";

     permute__1$(n/2,n_0)$;

     (Comment: Apply recursion to the first (lg n−1) loops while holding the (lg n)-th loop);

   end;

end;

     An example of permuting eight records is given in Figure

3.5.5.

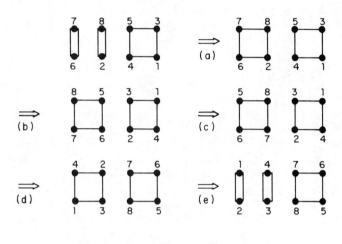

(a) FORM 2 BIG LOOPS
(b) SEPARATION
(c) PERMUTE FIRST HALF AND HOLD SECOND HALF
(d) SWAP
(e) PERMUTE FIRST HALF AND HOLD SECOND HALF

Figure 3.5.5

We next analyze this algorithm. Let $p_1(n)$ be the number of steps to achieve an arbitrary permutation of n records. To separate a set of n records, the worst case for our separation algorithm requires n steps. (Actually, the worst case requires only $(n-1)$ steps. This occurs when there are two loops of size $n/2$ each and the record destinations are as shown in Figure 3.5.6. However, to simplify the calculation, we assume that the worst case for the separation algorithms is n.) To swap two loops of size $n/2$ requires $n/2$ steps. Altogether we have

$$p_1(n) = n + p_1(n/2) + n/2 + p_1(n/2)$$

$$= \frac{3}{2}n + 2p_1(n/2)$$

$$= \frac{3}{2}n \lg n + c.$$

Since $p_1(2) = 1$, we have

$$p_1(n) = \frac{3}{2}n \lg n - 2.$$

LOOP 1

LOOP 2

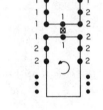

1 ≡ DESTINATION IS LOOP 1
2 ≡ DESTINATION IS LOOP 2

Figure 3.5.6

The number of switches in the memory system is clearly

$$s_2(n) = \lg n - 1.$$

To compute the number of control states, we consider the situation when permutation is being performed on the first k loops, while loops $k+1$, $k+2$, ..., $\lg n$ are all on "hold." Four states are used in the procedure separate__1:

1.   Move first (k-1) loops, hold loop k;

2.   Hold first (k-1) loops, move loop k;

3.   Move all k loops, with switch s_{k-1} "open";

4.   Move all k loops, with switch s_{k-1} "closed."

The procedure swap uses only the last state of the above. Therefore, for each step in the iteration, only four states are introduced. Thus, the total number of control states is

$$c_1(n) = 4(\lg n - 1) = 4 \lg n - 4.$$

3.5.5. Model 3.5.2 In this model, the memory system consists of loops of equal size. After the data have been separated in the loops, the contents of the loops can be permuted in parallel.

In general, let the size of each loop be h and let the number of loops in the memory system be w. Between loops i and i+1, there is a switch $s_i, i = 1,...,w - 1$, with a total of $w-1$ switches. (See Figure 3.5.7(a)). We also assume that $w = 2^k$. Thus, the total capacity of the memory system is $n = 2^k h$. The final result depends on the structure of individual loops, which is described later.

The addresses of the memory locations are assigned sequentially from loop 1 to loop w, i.e., loop 1 has memory addresses 1 to h, loop 2 has addresses h+1 to 2h, and so on. The memory addresses within the loops depend on the details of the loops and will become clear later. (See Figure 3.5.7(b) and Figure 3.5.7(c).)

The following procedure is an adaptation of the separation algorithm in Subsection 3.5.3 to the current model. Note that it differs from the adaptation for model 3.5.1 in that records with smaller addresses now go to the first half of the memory.

procedure separate__2 (t, t_0);

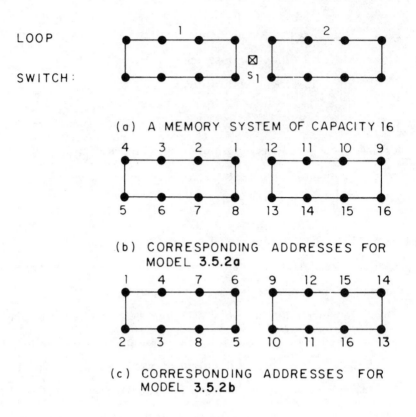

(a) A MEMORY SYSTEM OF CAPACITY 16

(b) CORRESPONDING ADDRESSES FOR
    MODEL **3.5.2a**

(c) CORRESPONDING ADDRESSES FOR
    MODEL **3.5.2b**

Figure 3.5.7

(Comment: Given t loops numbered $t_0, t_0 + 1, ..., t_0 + t - 1$, each of
size h, and letting $c(i)$ denote the destination address of the
record currently at memory address i, the procedure separates the
records of the t loops such that any record in the loops
$t_0, t_0 + 1, ..., t_0 + (t/2) - 1$ has a destination address smaller than
that of any record in the loops $t_0 + (t/2), ..., t_0 + t - 1$);

begin

    for $i \leftarrow t_0$ to $t_0 + t/2 - 2$ **do** $s_i \leftarrow$ "closed";

    for $i \leftarrow t_0 + t/2$ to $t_0 + t - 2$ **do** $s_i \leftarrow$ "closed";

    (Comment: Form two big loops);

    $x \leftarrow$ memory address at the input of switch $s_{t_0 + t/2 - 1}$ in loop t_0

$+t/2-1$;

$y \leftarrow$ memory address at the other input of switch $s_{t_0+t/2-1}$ in loop $t_0 + t/2$;

$a \leftarrow (t_0+t/2-1) \times h$;

for $i \leftarrow 1$ **to** $t \times h$ **do**

if $c(x) \leq a$ **and** $c(y) \leq a$ **then**

  begin $s_{t_0+t/2-1} \leftarrow$ "open";

    move $(t_0, t_0 + 1,..., t_0 + t/2 - 1)$;

  end

else if $c(x) \leq a$ **and** $c(y) > a$ **then**

  begin $s_{t_0+t/2-1} \leftarrow$ "open";

    move $(t_0, t_0 + 1,..., t_0 + t - 1)$;

  end

else if $c(x) > a$ **and** $c(y) \leq a$ **then**

  begin $s_{t_0+t/2-1} \leftarrow$ "closed";

    move $(t_0, t_0 + 1,..., t_0 + t - 1)$;

  end

else $s_{t_0+t/2-1} \leftarrow$ "open";

    move $(t_0 + t/2, t_0 + t/2 + 1,..., t_0 + t - 1)$;

end;

end;

procedure permute__$2(t, t_0)$;

  (Comment: Given t (assumed to be a power of 2) loops numbered $t_0, t_0 + 1,.., t_0 + t - 1$, each of size h, and letting $c(i)$ denote the destination address of the record currently at memory address i, the procedure performs a permutation on the records such that $c(i) = i$);

begin if $t = 1$ **then** permute__$x(h)$

(Comment: Procedure permute__x depends on the model used for a single loop)

    else begin

      separate__2(t,t_0);

      $s_{t_0+t/2-1} \leftarrow$ "open"

    simultaneously begin

      permute__2$(t/2,t_0)$;

      permute__2$(t/2,t_0+t/2)$;

    end;

  end;

end;

To analyze this algorithm, we let $p_2(n)$ be the number of steps to permute n records. Then

$$p_2(n) = n + p_2(n/2)$$

with initial condition

$$p_2(h) = p_x(h),$$

where $p_x(h)$ is the number of steps to permute the contents of a single loop and is dependent on the loop structure. Thus,

$$p_2(n) = 2n-2h + p_x(h). \tag{3.5.1}$$

To specify the details of the individual loops, we have the following two models:

Model 3.5.2a Each loop has only one switch. (See Figure 3.5.8.) When the switch is closed, the loop contents shift in a counterclockwise direction (Figure 3.5.8(a)). On the other hand, when the switch is open, the original loop is separated into two smaller loops (Figure 3.5.8(b)): one of size 1, the other of size $h-1$. The records in the latter loop can shift in a counterclockwise direction independently of the single record loop. The memory addresses are assigned in a sequential fashion, starting with 1 for the location which becomes the loop of size 1 when the switch is open and continuing in a clockwise direction. Note that this is exactly the Model 3.2.1 of Section 3.2. By Algorithm 3.2.1*, the number of steps to permute h records is at most $(1/2)h^2 + O(h)$. Thus, substituting in (3.5.1), we have

$$p_{2a}(n) = 2n + \frac{1}{2}h^2 + O(h). \qquad (3.5.2)$$

If we choose $h = \sqrt{n}$, then

$$p_{2a}(n) = \frac{5}{2}n + O(\sqrt{n}),$$

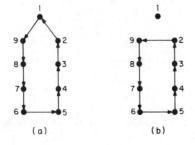

(a)   (b)

Figure 3.5.8

and the total number of switches in the system is

$$s_{2a}(n) = 2\sqrt{n} - 1.$$

Model 3.5.2b Each loop is now structured exactly as in Model 3.5.1 with the corresponding address scheme transplanted here as well. (See Figure 3.5.7(c)). Then

$$p_{2b}(n) = 2n - 2h + \frac{3}{2}h \lg h - 2.$$

If we choose $h = 2^w$ (recall that w is the total number of loops in the system), then $n = hw = h \lg h$ and

$$p_{2b}(n) = \frac{7}{2}n - 2h - 2.$$

The total number of switches is

$$s_{2b}(n) = (w - 1) + w(\lg h - 1)$$

$$= w \lg h - 1$$

$$= \lg^2 h - 1.$$

The fact that $n = h \lg n$ implies $h \sim (n/\lg n)$ for large n. Therefore,

$$p_{2b}(n) \sim \frac{7}{2}n - \frac{2n}{\lg n} - 2,$$

and

$$s_{2b}(n) \sim (\lg n - \lg \lg n)^2$$

for large n.

To count the number of control states, we note that the procedure separate_2 requires only four states, as in Model 3.5.1. With each iteration of the procedure permute_2, the operations in separate_2 are carried out in parallel, each independent of the other; hence, the total number of control states can be summed up as follows:

$$c_2(w) = 4 + 4^2 + 4^4 + \ldots + 4^{w/2} + c_x(h,w)$$

$$= \sum_{i=0}^{k-1} 4^{(2^i)} + c_x(h,w)$$

$$= \sum_{i=1}^{k} 2^{(2^i)} + c_x(h,w),$$

where $w = 2^k$, and $c_x(h,w)$ is the number of control states for the w individual loops and is included here to account for the control states used in the last recursion step. The value of $c_x(h,w)$ depends only on the model used. Note that

$$c_2(w) < 2^{w+1} + c_x(h,w).$$

For Model 3.5.2a, $w = \sqrt{n}$, $c_x(h,w) = 2^w$ since each loop has 2 control states; hence,

$$c_{2a}(n) < 3 \cdot 2^{\sqrt{n}}$$

For Model 3.5.2b, $w = \lg h$, to count the number of control states for the w individual loops, we note that each loop goes through (lg h−1) iterations and each iteration is synchronized for all loops; i.e., all loops go from one iteration to the other at exactly the same time. For any iteration, each loop requires 4 control states, with a total of 4^w control states. Thus, $c_x(h,w) = (lg\ h - 1)4^w$ and

$$c_{2b}(n) < 2^{lg\ h+1} + 4^{lg\ h}(lg\ h - 1)$$

$$= (lg\ h - 1)h^2 + 2h.$$

3.5.6. Model 3.5.3 In this model, we assume that the number of switches is arbitrary but fixed, say, k. Suppose there are k+1 loops of size $L_1, L_2, .., L_{k+1}$ respectively, where $L_1 = 1$. Also assume there is a switch s_i between loop i and loop i+1. Let $q_k(n; L_1, ..., L_{k+1})$ be the number of steps to achieve an arbitrary permutation of n records in this model.

For k=1, using Algorithm 3.2.1*, we have $q_1(n; 1, n - 1) = (1/2)n^2 + O(n)$.

For k=2, we have $n = L_1 + L_2 + L_3$. We next describe informally an algorithm which achieves an arbitrary permutation. This algorithm can then be recursively applied to larger k.

1.   We assign the addresses in the three loops as in Figure 3.5.9(a).

2.   Regard loops 1 and 2 as one loop, loop 3 as another loop. For ease of discussion, we call them A, B respectively. Separate the records into these two loops so that records with the smaller addresses are in loop A. (This part takes $L_1 + L_2 + L_3 = n$ steps.)

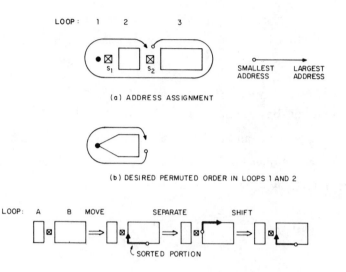

(a) ADDRESS ASSIGNMENT

(b) DESIRED PERMUTED ORDER IN LOOPS 1 AND 2

(c) PART (4) OF THE ALGORITHM IN MODEL 3.5.3

Figure 3.5.9

3. Permute the records in loop A so that the resulting order is as shown in Figure 3.5.9(b), while holding the records in loop B. (This part takes $(1/2)(L_1 + L_2)^2 + O(L_1 + L_2)$ steps.)

4. Now move the sorted records from loop A to loop B. Then separate the remaining L_3 records into loops A and B so that records with the smallest addresses are in loop A. Next, shift loop B further so that the sorted records are in the same position as when they were first moved into loop B at the beginning of this step. (See Figure 3.5.9(c).) (This part takes a total of n steps.)

5. Repeat parts 3 and 4 until all the addresses are in order. (This part is executed $\lceil L_3/(L_1 + L_2) \rceil$ times.)

The total number of steps required by this algorithm is therefore

$$q_2(n;L_1,L_2,L_3) = \left\lceil \frac{L_3}{L_1+L_2} \right\rceil [n + q_1(L_1 + L_2;L_1,L_2)].$$

Since $q_1(L_1 + L_2;L_1,L_2) = (1/2)(L_1 + L_2)^2 + O(L_1 + L_2)$, it is clear that the best choice for L_2 is such that $L_1 + L_2 = a\sqrt{n}$ (this makes both terms n and q_1 have the same order of magnitude). Under this choice and omitting L_1,L_2,L_3 in the notation, we have (neglecting the term $O(L_1 + L_2)$):

$$q_2(n) = \left\lceil \frac{n-a\sqrt{n}}{a\sqrt{n}} \right\rceil \left(n + \frac{1}{2}a^2n \right)$$

$$< \frac{n}{a\sqrt{n}} \left(n + \frac{1}{2}a^2n \right)$$

$$= \left(\frac{1}{a} + \frac{a}{2} \right)n^{3/2}$$

since $\lceil x \rceil < x+1$. The coefficient is minimum when $a = \sqrt{2}$. Thus we have

$$q_2(n) < \sqrt{2}\,n^{3/2}$$

and

$$L_2 = \sqrt{2n} - 1.$$

For $k>2$, the procedure can be applied recursively. Suppose we can permute records on the first k loops using $(k-1)$ switches. We let the first k loops form a single loop and loop $k+1$ another loop. We then apply the same procedure as before; therefore,

$$q_k(n) = \left\lceil \frac{L_{k+1}}{\sum\limits_{i=1}^{k} L_i} \right\rceil \left[n + q_{k-1}\left(\sum\limits_{i=1}^{k} L_i \right) \right] \qquad (3.5.3)$$

Claim $q_k(n) < 2^{-1/k}kn^{1+1/k}$, if we assume

$$\sum\limits_{i=1}^{k} L_i = 2^{1/k}n^{1-1/k}.$$

(Recall $\sum\limits_{i=1}^{k+1} L_i = n$.)

Proof We prove this claim by induction. The claim is true for $k=2$. From (3.5.3) and by the induction hypothesis, we have

$$q_k(n) < \frac{n}{2^{1/k}n^{1-1/k}}\left[n + 2^{-1/(k-1)}(k-1)(2^{1/k}n^{1-1/k})^{k/(k-1)} \right]$$

$$= 2^{-1/k}n^{1/k}[n + (k-1)n]$$

$$= 2^{-1/k}kn^{1+1/k}.$$

Note that the corresponding loop sizes $L_1,L_2,..,L_{k+1}$ are respectively

$$1,(2^{1/2}n^{1/2}-1),...,(2^{1/k}n^{1-1/k}-2^{1/(k-1)}n^{1-1/(k-1)}),$$

$$(n - 2^{1/k}n^{1-1/k}).$$

Remark When doing a permutation on two loops, our address assignment requires that the final configuration be as in Figure 3.5.10(a). However, the recursive application of the algorithm requires that the final configuration be as in Figure 3.5.10(b), so that it is ready to be moved out into the next bigger loop (the one on the right in Figure 3.5.10(b)). We can achieve this in the following way: As soon as the "head" of the record stream (i.e., the record with the smallest address; cf. Figure 3.5.9(c)) reaches the switch connecting the bigger loop (the rightmost switch in Figure 3.5.10(b)), the switch is closed so that the record stream moves directly into the bigger loop (Figure 3.5.10(c)) instead of circulating back. This modification in fact saves some running time.

To count the number of control states for Model 3.5.3, we note that the process of separating records requires four states, as before. Moreover, when the first p loops, say, are separating records, loops $p+1,...,k+1$ are all on "hold." Also, two control states are sufficient to permute records in the first two loops. Therefore, the total number of control states is

$$c_3(n) = 4(k - 1) + 2$$

$$= 4k - 2.$$

3.5.7. Summary We summarize our results in Table 3.5.1. We also give some numerical examples in Table 3.5.2 to illustrate the relative values of these three parameters for the various models. We assume $n = 10^6$. Note that as far as the number of control lines is concerned, Model 3.5.2a is practically not usable. Model 3.5.2b is of some theoretical interest since it gives a linear-time permutation algorithm with a small number of switches as well as control lines. It is also interesting to note that in Model 3.5.3 the minimum number of steps is achieved when $k=\ln(n/2)$. Thus, Model 3.5.3 performs well only when k is small. (Note the substantial increase in performance when

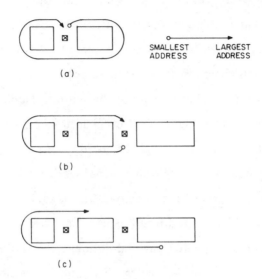

SMALLEST   LARGEST
ADDRESS   ADDRESS

(a)

(b)

(c)

Figure 3.5.10

$k=2$, $(O(n^{3/2}))$, as compared to the $O(n^2)$ performance of Model 3.2.1. In terms of its simplicity in the permutation algorithm as well as the favorable values of its three parameters, Model 3.5.1 seems to be a reasonable choice for a practical implementation of magnetic bubble memories.

Before closing this section, we want to mention briefly another structure in the literature for doing permutation, called a *uniform bubble ladder* [18,21]. Basically, there are n loops, each containing one record. Between two adjacent loops there is a switch as described in Subsection 3.5.2. Thus, there is a total of n−1 switches. By setting the switch to the "closed" mode (Figure 3.5.2(b)), two records can be interchanged. It is easy to see that such a memory structure is well-suited for the implementation of the odd-even transportation sort

[35, p. 241]. In this sorting algorithm, there are two alternating phases: the even sorting phase, where records at even switches are compared and exchanged (if necessary); and the odd sorting phase, where records at odd switches are compared. It is known that it takes at most n such phases to sort n items in order.

Adapting such a scheme to the uniform ladder, it is clear that records can be put in the desired order in n steps, where a step is the time to completely interchange 2 records. However, in the uniform ladder, two phases of operation can be overlapped (i.e., a new phase can be initiated when the previous one is only halfway through); therefore, $(n+1)/2$ steps are sufficient to sort n records in order.

It must be pointed out that although the sorting algorithm can be implemented in the bubble memory, sorting is not actually done there. Keys of the records are duplicated in the CPU and the odd-even transportation sort simulated there. Comparisons are done in the CPU and the modes of switches are set based on the results of the comparisons. Thus, it is more appropriate to view the adaptation of the odd-even transportation sort as a permutation algorithm rather than a sorting algorithm. In Section 3.6 we shall introduce a new kind of switch that can do comparisons inside a bubble memory, enabling records to be sorted internally. Model 3.6.2 in that section is based on exactly the odd-even transportation sort mentioned here.

Finally, we tabulate all the results in Tables 3.5.1 and Table 3.5.2.

The question still remains open as to the relationship of these three parameters in an optimal magnetic bubble memory designed for doing permutations of data, except for the obvious fact that in a linear memory structure, where $O(n)$ steps are necessary to move a

Table 3.5.1

Complexity of permuting records for different memory models

Model	Number of switches	Number of steps	Number of control states
3.5.1	$\lg n - 1$	$\frac{3}{2}n\lg n - 2$	$4 \lg n - 4$
3.5.2a	$2\sqrt{n} - 1$	$\frac{5}{2}n + O(\sqrt{n})$	$< 3 \times 2^{\sqrt{n}}$
3.5.2b	$\lg^2 h - 1$	$\frac{7}{2}n - 2h - 2$ $(n = h \lg h;$ hence $h \sim n/\lg n)$	$< (\lg h - 1)h^2 + 2h$
3.5.3	k	$< 2^{-1/k}kn^{1+1/k}$	$4k - 2$
3.2.1	1	$\frac{1}{2}n^2 + O(n)$	2
Uniform ladder	$n - 1$	$\frac{n}{2}$	2^{n-1}

Table 3.5.2

Numerical examples of complexity

Model	Number of switches	Number of steps	Number of control states	Number of control lines $(= \lceil \lg(\text{control states}) \rceil)$
3.5.1	19	2.99×10^7	76	7
3.5.2a	2×10^3	2.5×10^6	1.07×10^{301}	10^3
3.5.2b	$(h = 6.27 \times 10^4)$ 254	3.5×10^6	1.25×10^5	17
3.5.3	$k = 2$	1.41×10^9	6	3
	$k = 3$	2.38×10^8	10	4
	$k = 4$	1.06×10^8	14	4
	$k = 12$	3.58×10^7	46	6
	$k = 13$ $(\lg (n/2) = 13.1)$	3.57×10^7	48	6
	$k = 15$	3.60×10^7	58	6
3.2.1	1	5×10^{11}	2	1
Uniform ladder	10^6	5×10^5	2^{10^6}	10^6

record from one end of the memory to the other, we know of no other theoretical lower bounds.

All models considered so far are essentially one-dimensional. It would be interesting to see if any two-dimensional memory structures would give better performance.

3.6. Sorting algorithms in different models of bubble memories

3.6.1. Introduction Section 3.3 studied the problem of sorting with a switching device called the bit string comparator, which routed the data according to their contents. Also, the data are sequentially input to and output from the sorter. In this section, we study the sorting problem using the same approach as in Section 3.5, namely, we study the trade-offs among the number of steps, the number of switches and the number of control states. The switches are again the compare and steer switches described in Section 3.3. However, the input is assumed to be already in the memory before sorting begins and the sorted output remains in the memory, i.e., we discount the input/output time. We shall propose several simple models and show how sorting can be done in each of them. The first two models are straightforward implementations of the well-known "bubble" sort and odd-even transportation sort respectively. The last two models are built on the first two and use the concept of bitonic sort introduced by Batcher [2].

3.6.2. Basic model We assume that a magnetic bubble memory consists of loops of bubble domains. All the loops are continuously circulating at the same speed in a counter-clockwise direction. Each bubble domain represents one bit of information. The basic information unit we are interested in is a record, which consists of r bits. The records are to be sorted according to their keys. (We assume the first k bits of a record form the key of the record.) The number of bubble domains in each loop is assumed to be an integer multiple of the record size. Thus, when we say the size of the loop is m, we mean that the loop contains m records. The time required to move a bubble domain for the distance of r bubble positions is defined as one step, which is our basic time unit. A move (d) instruction will mean circulating the loop of bubble domains in question for d record lengths. When d=1, we shall simply say move. Records can pass from one loop to the other through "compare and steer" switches (switches for short) placed between two loops. Each switch has four modes of operation (see Figure 3.6.1)

1) $a \rightarrow c, b \rightarrow d$

2) $b \rightarrow c, a \rightarrow d$

3) If key (a) < key (b), then $a \rightarrow c, b \rightarrow d$

   else $b \rightarrow c, a \rightarrow d$

4) If key (a) > key (b), then $a \rightarrow c, b \rightarrow d$

   else $b \rightarrow c, a \rightarrow d$.

The first two modes indicate fixed routes for the records. We shall refer to mode 1 as the "closed" mode and mode 2 as the "through" mode. The third and fourth modes describe the routes of the records after a comparison. Thus, they will be referred to as "compare" nodes. Such comparisons can be done by comparing the bubbles pair by pair as they pass through the switch. There is no need for lookahead or memories. Such a switch is basically the bit-string comparator and is physically realizable by current bubble technology.

In general, a model with x switches may have a total of 4^x possible states. However, in our proposed sorting algorithms only a small subset of them will be required. The cardinality of this subset is

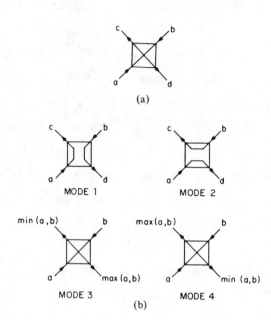

Figure 3.6.1

the number of control states necessary. We would assume in general that number of control lines = ⌈lg (number of control states)⌉, which would be true if some decoding circuit were available in the magnetic bubble memory. We shall concern ourselves only with the number of control states from now on.

Before closing, it should be pointed out that one of the difficulties in sorting in magnetic bubble memories is the synchronization problem, namely, we assume that all the loops in the memory are continuously circulating; none of them can be held still at any time. That is why we have to be very careful in maintaining proper orders of records in various loops, so that they are in the right position at the right time.

3.6.3. Model 3.6.1 The memory consists of two loops. One loop is of size 1; the other loop is of size $(n-1)$. In Figure 3.6.2(a), the loop of size 1 is labeled Z. The two records in the other loop, which are on the opposite side of the switch, are labeled X, Y. The loops are circulating in a counterclockwise direction. The records X, Y correspond to a, c respectively in Figure 3.6.1 and the record Z corresponds to both b and d. Suppose the switch is set to, say, mode 2; then after a "move" instruction, record X will move to the original position of Z and Z will move to that of Y, and the rest of the records will move for one record length in a counterclockwise direction. If the switch is set to, say, mode 3, then after a "move" instruction, the smaller of X, Z will move to the original position of Y and the larger will occupy the original position of Z. The sorting algorithm proposed here is a modified "bubble" sort.

```
procedure sort__1 (n,type);
(comment: sort n records in Model 3.6.1);
(comment: if type=1, then sort according to ascending order
(Figure 3.6.2(c)); if type=2, then sort according to descending order
(Figure 2(d)));
begin
  for i ← 1 to n−1 do
    begin switch ← type+2;
      (comment: set switch to "compare" mode 3 or 4);
      move (n−1);
      (comment: move the loop for (n−1) record lengths in
      counter-clockwise direction);
      switch←2;
      move;
```

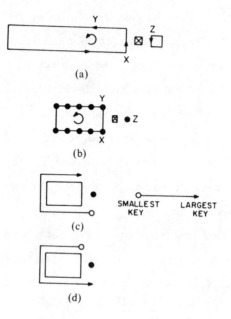

Figure 3.6.2

    end;

end;

Example: n=8, type=1. The input sequence is {4,3,6,2,1,7,5,8}, (see Figure 3.6.3.) The output sequence will be {1,2,3,4,5,6,7,8}. Some configurations after execution of certain steps of the algorithm are displayed in Figure 3.6.3.

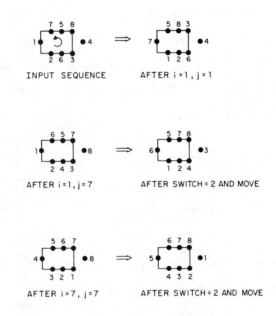

INPUT SEQUENCE

AFTER i = 1 , j = 1

AFTER i = 1 , j = 7

AFTER SWITCH = 2 AND MOVE

AFTER i = 7 , j = 7

AFTER SWITCH = 2 AND MOVE

Figure 3.6.3

Clearly, the total number of steps to sort n records is given by

$$S_1(n) = n(n - 1) = n^2 - n.$$

The number of switches in this model is

$$W_1(n) = 1,$$

and since the switch can only be in mode 2, 3 or 4, the number of control states is

$$C_1(n) = 3.$$

3.6.4.   Model 3.6.2 This model can be regarded as diametrically opposite to Model 3.6.1.   It consists of n loops, each of size 1. Between loop i and loop (i+1), there is a switch s_i, for i=1, 2, ..., n−1. Thus, there is a total of (n−1) switches (Figure 3.6.4(a)).

procedure sort__2 (n,type);

  (comment: type 1 means the sorted keys are in ascending order starting from loop 1; type 2 means the sorted keys are in descending order starting from loop 1);

variable switch: **array [1...n];**

begin

    (comment: initially the beginning of the records in loop i and in loop (i+1) are at switch i, for i odd);

    for i←1 to n **do**

      if odd (i) **then** switch [i] ← type + 2

                  else switch [i]←1;

    (comment: set odd switches to "compare" mode, even ones to "closed" mode);

    move (1/2);

    (comment: move the loops by half a record length. The beginnings of records are now at even-numbered switches);

    for i←1 to $\left\lfloor \dfrac{n-1}{2} \right\rfloor$ **do**

    switch [2*i] ←type+2;

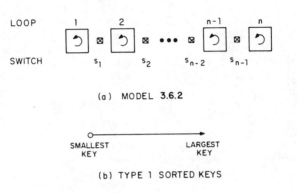

(a) MODEL **3.6.2**

(b) TYPE 1 SORTED KEYS

(c) TYPE 2 SORTED KEYS

Figure 3.6.4

(comment: all switches are now in "compare" mode);

$$\text{move}\left(\left\lfloor \frac{n-1}{2} \right\rfloor + \frac{1}{2} \right);$$

(comment: the memory system is doing comparisons simultaneously at even switches and at odd switches in an alternating fashion);

end;

In Figure 3.6.5, an example for n=6, type=1 is given, where the configurations after every instruction "move (1/2)" are shown. In general, we have the number of steps

$$S_2(n) = \lceil n/2 \rceil,$$

the number of switches

$$W_2(n) = n - 1$$

and the number of control states

$$C_2(n) = 2.$$

3.6.5.   Model 3.6.3 This model uses the concept of bitonic sorting. We first list some previous results by Batcher [2] here, which will be needed later.

Definition 3.6.1 Let $a_1 \le a_2 \le \ldots \le a_{k_1}$, $b_1 \le b_2 \le \ldots \le b_{k_2}$, $k_1 + k_2 = n$. Then the sequence (or any cyclic shift thereof)

$$a_1 a_2 \ldots a_{k_1} b_{k_2} b_{k_2-1} \ldots b_2 b_1$$

is called a *bitonic sequence.*

Definition 3.6.2 The process of sorting a bitonic sequence in order is called a *bitonic sort.*

Theorem 3.6.1 If $a_1 a_2 \ldots a_{n-1} a_n$ (n even) is a bitonic sequence, then the sequences

(1) $\min (a_1, a_{\frac{n}{2}+1})$, $\min (a_2, a_{\frac{n}{2}+2})$,..., $\min (a_{\frac{n}{2}}, a_n)$

(2) $\max (a_1, a_{\frac{n}{2}+1})$, $\max (a_2, a_{\frac{n}{2}+2})$,..., $\max (a_{\frac{n}{2}}, a_n)$

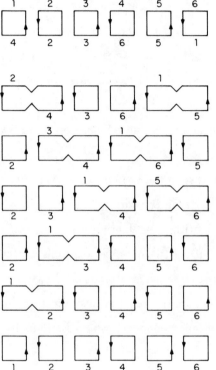

Figure 3.6.5

are also bitonic sequences, and all the numbers in (1) are no larger
than any number in (2).

Corollary 3.6.1 To sort a bitonic sequence, it suffices to sort the two
bitonic sequences formed in Theorem 3.6.1, and concatenate them:
bitonic sort $[a_1 a_2 ... a_{n-1} a_n]$

$$= \text{bitonic sort } [\min(a_1, a_{\frac{n}{2}+1}), ..., \min(a_{\frac{n}{2}}, a_n)],$$

bitonic sort $[\max(a_1, a_{\frac{n}{2}+1}), \ldots, \max(a_{\frac{n}{2}}, a_n)]$.

We are now ready to propose Model 3.6.3.

There are m loops each of size h (n=hm). The loops are numbered 1,2,...,m. We assume that m is a power of 2. There is a switch s_i between loop i and loop (i+1) for i=1 to n−1. Each loop is of the structure of Model 3.6.1, i.e., each loop consists of two smaller loops and a switch between them. One of these two loops is of size 1 and is called the "head" of the whole loop. The switch is called t_i if the loop is numbered i. For i = 1,2,...,n/2, the heads of loops (2i−1) and 2i are placed next to the switch s_{2i-1}. (See Figure 3.6.6(a).)

Before describing the sorting algorithm formally, we present an overview of the algorithm in Figure 3.6.7, where S(n) denotes a sorter to sort n records and B(n) denotes a bitonic sorter to sort a bitonic sequence of n records. S(n) is composed of two S(n/2)' s and a B(n). The two S(n/2)' s sort the records in opposite direction, so that their output forms a bitonic sequence, which is input to the B(n). In the

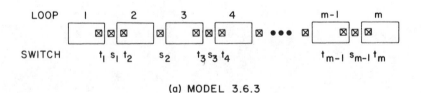

(a) MODEL 3.6.3

(b) A BIG LOOP IS FORMED
AFTER SWITCHES t_i, s_i, t_{i+1}
ARE SET TO MODE 2

Figure 3.6.6.

B(n), the splitter performs the function of Theorem 3.6.1. The two bitonic sequences thus generated are fed to the two B(n/2)'s. Because of the loop structure, their output must be shifted properly to form a single sorted loop.

In short, sorting of n records is accomplished by sorting two sequences of n/2 records followed by a bitonic sorting of n records, which in turn is accomplished by bitonically sorting two sequences of n/2 records. Recursively, it reduces to sorting of the m basic loops. For this, we apply the modified "bubble" sort as described in Model 3.6.1. The main difficulty lies in maintaining proper ascending or descending orders among the loops throughout the sorting procedure. A detailed example is given after the formal description of the sorting algorithm.

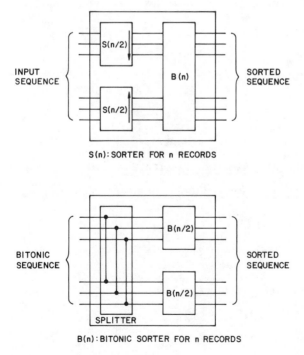

S(n): SORTER FOR n RECORDS

B(n): BITONIC SORTER FOR n RECORDS

Figure 3.6.7

We first define several procedures.

procedure shift (loop__number, size, number__steps);

(comment: suppose loop__number=p, size=q. Assume the switches
   have been set properly so that loop p, loop (p+1), ... , loop
   (p+(q/h)−1) form a large loop of size q. This procedure shifts
   the large loop for "number__steps" record lengths);

begin

   for i←loop__number to (loop__number + (size)/h−2)

   do

   begin

      s[i]←2;

      t[i]←2;

      (comment: set s and t switches to "through" model);

   end;

   t [loop__number+(size)/h−1]←2;

   move(number__steps);

end;

procedure sort__1a (loop__number, type);

   (comment: this is exactly procedure sort__1 in Model 3.6.1 and
      sorts the loop "loop__number" according to the type
      required);

begin

   for i←1 to (h−1)**do**

   begin t[loop__number]←type+2;

   move(h−1);

   t[loop__number]←2;

   move;

end;

end;

procedure bitonic__split (loop__number, size, type: integer);

(comment: as in procedure shift, assume we have a large loop of
size "size," starting from loop "loop__number." Furthermore,
we assume the records in this loop form a bitonic sequence.
This procedure splits the sequence into two halves according to
Theorem 3.6.1. Thus, they are both bitonic. If type =1, we

TYPE 1   TYPE 2

(a) BITONIC SPLIT: [b] MEANS BITONIC SEQUENCE

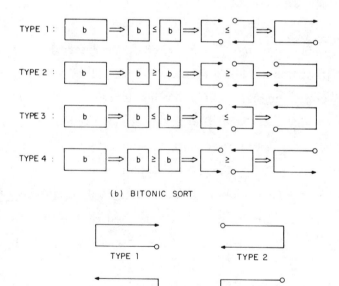

(b) BITONIC SORT

TYPE 1   TYPE 2

TYPE 3   TYPE 4

(c) SORTED ORDER IN MODEL 3.6.3

Figure 3.6.8

require that records in the first half be smaller than or equal to those in the second half. If type=2, otherwise. (See Figure 3.6.8(a), where b inside a square means a bitonic sequence));

begin

    for i← loop__number to (loop__number+size/h−2)**do**

      begin

        s[i]←2;

        t[i]←2;

      end;

    t[loop__number+size/h−1]←2;

    s[loop__number+size/(2*h)−1]←type+2;

    (comment: set the middle switch to "compare" mode);

    move (size/2);

end;

procedure bitonic__sort (loop__number, size, type: integer);

    (comment: given a bitonic sequence of size "size" starting from loop "loop__number," sort according to type 1, 2, 3 or 4, as shown in Figure 3.6.8(b). For example, if the required type is 1, then the given bitonic sequence is split into two halves, with records in the first half smaller than or equal to those in the second half. Then they are recursively sorted by bitonic__sort. Finally, they are pieced together and are shifted 1/4 the length of the input bitonic sequence to obtain a final sorted sequence);

begin

    If size=h **then**

      if type=1 or type=2 **then** sort__1a (loop__number, 1)

                          else sort__1a (loop__number, 2);

      else begin

      if type=1 or type=3 **then** bitonic__split (loop__number, size, 1)

            else bitonic__split (loop__number, size,2);

s[loop__number+size/(2*h)−1]←1;

(comment: set middle switch to "closed" mode);

if type=1 or type=2 **then**

  simultaneously begin

      bitonic__sort (loop__number, size/2, 1);

      bitonic__sort (loop__number + size/(2*h), size/2,2);

  end;

else simultaneously begin

      bitonic__sort(loop__number, size/2,4);

      bitonic__sort (loop__number + size/(2*h),size/2,3);

  end;

shift (loop__number, size, size/4);

(comment: shift to correct position);

      end;

end;

Finally, we have the following sorting algorithm for Model 3.6.3:

procedure Sort__3 (loop__number, size, type:integer);

  (comment: sort a sequence of size "size," starting at loop "loop__number." There are four possible types of sorted sequences for output, which are shown in Figure 3.6.8(c));

begin

If size=h **then if** type=1 **then** sort__1a(loop__number,1)

                    else sort__1a(loop__number,2);

  else begin

    s[loop__number + size/(2*h)−2]←1;

    (comment: set the middle switch to "closed" mode);

  simultaneously begin

    sort__3 (loop__number,size/2,1);

sort__3 (loop__number+size/(2*h),size/2,3);

(comment: the first half of the input sequence is sorted according to type 1, the second according to type 3.   As a whole, they form a bitonic sequence);

   end;

   bitonic__sort (loop__number, size, type);

   end;

end;

In Figure 3.6.9, an example of sorting in Model 3.6.3 is given, where n=8h, type=2.   Line 1 is the input sequence, which is distributed among 8 loops.   Line 2 shows the result of sorting individual loops (sort__1a).   Note that odd-numbered loops are sorted

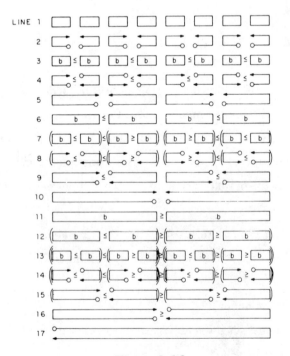

Figure 3.6.9

according to type 1, while even-numbered loops are sorted according to type 2. As a result, loops i and (i+1), form a bitonic sequence for i=1,3,5,7. Line 3 shows the result of applying bitonic_split of type 1 to these four bitonic sequences. Individual loops are sorted again in line 4. The types are 1,1,2,2,1,1,2,2. Now each pair of loops forms a sorted sequence. Line 5 shows the result of shifting the four sorted sequences for 1/4 of their lengths. Thus, the first two sequences now form a bitonic sequence. And we are in the same situation as line 1 except that we have four sorted sequences now instead of 2. Applying bitonic_splits (lines 6 and 7), sort_1a (line 8) and shifts (lines 9 and 10), we end up with two sorted sequences in line 10. 3 more bitonic_splits (lines 11, 12, 13) and 1 sort_1a (line 14) and 3 shifts produce the final results in line 17.

We now study the complexity of sorting in Model 3.6.3. Let $B(n)$ be the number of steps to bitonic sort n records (i.e., procedure bitonic_sort). Then

$$B(n) = \frac{1}{2}n + B\left(\frac{n}{2}\right) + \frac{n}{4}$$

$$= \frac{3}{4}n + B\left(\frac{n}{2}\right),$$

with $B(h) = h^2 - h$. In the first expression of $B(n)$, the term $\frac{1}{2}n$ comes from the bitonic split and the term $\frac{n}{4}$ is the result of shifting the whole sequence for one quarter of the length. The initial condition $B(h)$ comes from Model 3.6.1. Solving the recurrence relation, we have

$$B(n) = \frac{3}{2}n + h^2 - \frac{5}{2}h.$$

Let $S_3(n)$ be the number of steps to sort n records in Model

3.6.3 (i.e., procedure sort__3).

$$S_3(n) = S_3\left(\frac{n}{2}\right) + B(n)$$

$$= S_3\left(\frac{n}{2}\right) + \frac{3}{2}n + h^2 - \frac{5}{2}h$$

with initial condition $S_3(h) = h^2 - h$. Thus,

$$S_3(n) = 3n + \left(h^2 - \frac{5}{2}h\right)\lg\left(\frac{n}{h}\right) + h^2 - 4h.$$

If $h = \sqrt{n}$, then the number of steps is

$$S_3(n) = \frac{1}{2}n \lg n + O(n).$$

If $h = \sqrt{n/\lg n}$, then

$$S_3(n) = \frac{7}{2}n + O\left(\frac{n \lg \lg n}{\lg n}\right).$$

We can now count the number of switches and control states. Recall that m is the number of loops (n=mh). We note that the total number of control states depends on m only. Moreover, whenever the t-switches are set to modes 3 or 4, i.e., sorting in the individual loops, the s-switches are set to mode 1 (the "closed" mode). On the other hand, if the s-switches are not in mode 1, then the t-switches are in mode 2. Therefore, t-switches are in modes 3 or 4 if and only if s-switches are in mode 1. Let $C_s(m), C_t(m)$ be the numbers of control states of s-switches and t-switches respectively for sorting m loops. Then the total number of control states $C_3(m)$ is given by $C_3(m) = C_s(m) + C_t(m) - 1$. It is easy to see that during the sorting process only a total of $\lg m+2$ distinct control states for the t-switches is needed, i.e., $C_t(m) = \lg m + 2$. In fact, these control states can be explicitly enumerated as in Table 3.6.1.

In the example of Figure 3.6.9, in all lines where no sorting is involved, the control state of the t-switches is number 1. This is the case in lines 1, 3, 5, 6, 7, 9, 10, 11, 12, 13, 15, 16, 17. However, sorting is required before reaching lines 2, 4, 8, 14. During those sorting phases, the control states of the t-switches are 2, 3, 4, 5 respectively.

To compute $C_s(m)$, we look at the process of bitonic sorting more carefully. Given a bitonic sequence, this process splits the sequence up into two halves, each being a bitonic sequence, such that the first and the second satisfy the inequality $\leq$ or $\geq$. Two kinds of operations are involved, namely, bitonic split and shift. Furthermore, at any time only one of the two is in operation. There are exactly $\lg m$ kinds of shifts, namely, 1) all m loops form a big loop and shift; 2) the first $m/2$ loops form a big loop, and the second $m/2$ loops form another big loop, and they shift simultaneously; 3) every $m/4$ loops form a big loop and shift; and so on. The corresponding control states for the s-switches are described in Table 3.6.2.

Let the number of occurrences of bitonic splits in a bitonic sorting of m loops be $B'(m)$. Then

$$B'(m) = 1 + B'(m/2)$$

with initial condition $B'(1) = 0$, where the "1" in the above equality

Table 3.6.1

Control states for t-switches

Control State	t_1	t_2	t_3	t_4	.	.	.		t_m
1	2	2	2	2	.	.	.		2
2	3	4	3	4	3	4	.	.	.	3	4
3	3	3	4	4	3	3	.	.	.	4	4
4	3	3	3	3	4	4	4	4	3	...	4	4
.									
.									
.									
lg m+2	3	3	3	3	.	.	.		3	3

Table 3.6.2

Control states for s-switches

Control States for Shifts	s_1 $\cdots\cdot s_{\frac{m}{4}}$ $\cdots\cdot$ $s_{\frac{m}{2}}$ $\cdots\cdot s_{\frac{3}{4}m}$ $\cdots$ s_{m-1}
1	2 . . . . 2 . . . . 2 . . . . 2 . . . 2
2	2 . . . . 2 . . . . 2 1 2 . . . 2 . . . 2
3	2 . . . 2 1 2 . . . 2 1 2 . . .2 1 2 . . . 2
.	
.	
.	
lg m	2 1 . . 2 1 2 1 . . 2 1 2 1 . .2 1 2 1 . .2

denotes one occurrence of bitonic split. Thus,

$$B'(m) = \lg m.$$

Let the number of occurrences of bitonic splits in the sorting procedure be $B_s(m)$. Then

$$B_s(m) = B_s(m/2) + B'(m)$$

with $B_s(1) = 0$. Thus,

$$B_s(m) = \frac{1}{2}\lg^2 m + \frac{1}{2}\lg m.$$

Since each such occurrence in our sorting procedure requires a distinct control state, the corresponding number of control states is also $B_s(m)$. Thus, the total number of control states for the s-switches is

$$C_s(m) = \frac{1}{2}\lg^2 m + \frac{3}{2}\lg m.$$

Finally,

$$C_3(m) = \frac{1}{2}\lg^2 m + \frac{5}{2}\lg m + 1.$$

The total number of switches is

$$W_3(m) = 2m - 1.$$

When $h = m = \sqrt{n}$, we have the total number of control states and switches for sorting n records given as follows:

$$C_3(n) = \frac{1}{8}\lg^2 n + \frac{5}{4}\lg n + 1$$

and

$$W_3(n) = 2\sqrt{n} - 1.$$

When $h = \sqrt{n/\lg n}, m = \sqrt{n \lg n}$, we have

$$C_3(n) = \frac{1}{8}\lg^2 n + \frac{1}{4}\lg n \lg \lg n + \frac{1}{8}(\lg \lg n)^2$$

$$+ \frac{5}{4}\lg n + \frac{5}{4}\lg \lg n + 1,$$

$$W_3(n) = 2\sqrt{n \lg n} - 1.$$

3.6.6 Model 3.6.4 The memory system consists of k loops of size 1, 1, 2, 4, ..., 2^{k-2}; thus, $n = 2^{k-1}$. There is a switch between adjacent loops with a total of (k-1) switches designated $s_1, s_2, ..., s_{k-1}$ (Figure 3.6.10).

We also sort the records in this model by implementing the bitonic sorting scheme. It differs from Model 3.6.3 in that during the sorting process the larger loops are used mainly as temporary storage, while the smaller loops do the actual sorting. It is therefore a basically sequential process. To sort data, the algorithm recursively sorts the first half in its leftmost bubble memories; it then exchanges left and right halves, sorting the second half in the leftmost cells. A bitonic sorting is then applied.

This model has the advantage of reducing the amount of hardware required at the expense of time.

We redefine some of the procedures in Model 3.6.3 for Model 3.6.4.

procedure shift__2 (size, number__steps);

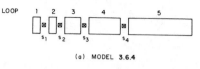

(a) MODEL 3.6.4

(b) SORTED ORDER IN SORT_2a

(c) AN EXAMPLE OF SORT_2a

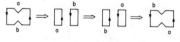

(d) BITONIC SORT

Figure 3.6.10

(comment: assume switches have been properly set so that the first lg (size)+1 loops form a large loop. This procedure shifts it for "number__steps" record lengths);

begin

    for i←1 to lg (size) **do**

    s[i]←2;

      (comment: set switches to "through" mode);

      move(number__steps);

end;

procedure sort__2a (delay, type);

  (comment: sort 2 records in the first two loops and then keep them there so that the total number of steps=delay and at the end of the process the sorted sequence must be of the required type. (See Figure 3.6.10(b)). We assume delay is always an even number);

begin

    $s[1] \leftarrow 2$;

    (comment: set switch s_1 to "through" mode);

    move $(1/2)$;

    (comment: move the loop for $1/2$ record length);

    if type$=1$ **then** $s[1] \leftarrow 4$;

            else $s[1] \leftarrow 3$;

    move;

    $s[1] \leftarrow 2$;

    move (delay$-3/2$);

    (comment: move the loop for (delay $- 3/2$) record lengths);

end;

An example of sorting two records a,b,a$<$b, according to type$=1$ and delay$=4$ is shown in Figure 3.6.10(c), where the arrowheads represent the beginnings of records. The first configuration is the input, the second configuration is the result of setting switch to mode 2 and shifting the loop for half a record length. Then the switch is set to mode 4 and the loop runs through one record length arriving at configuration 3. Finally, set the switch to mode 2 and let the loop move for $1\frac{1}{2}$ record lengths. We thus have configuration 4, which is type 1.

procedure bitonic__split__2 (size,type);

    (comment: assume the first lg (size)$+1$ loops form a large loop. Assume the records in this loop form a bitonic sequence. This procedure splits it into two halves, each a bitonic sequence. If type$=1$, we require that records in the first half be smaller than or

equal to those in the second half.   If type=2, the reverse is
required. (See Figure 3.6.8(a)));

begin

for i←1 to lg (size) − 1 **do**

s[i]←2;

(comment: set the first lg (size) −1 switches to "through"
mode. Thus, the first lg (size) loops form a large loop);

s [lg (size)]←type+2;

(comment: set the switch between the two large loops to
"compare" mode);

move(size/2);

end;

procedure bitonic__sort__2 (size, type:integer);

(comment: assume the first lg (size) + 1 loops form a large loop and
records there form a bitonic sequence. This procedure sorts them
according to type 1 or type 2. See Figure 3.6.10(d). In type 1, a
bitonic sequence is split into two halves, each a bitonic sequence
such that records in the first half are larger than or equal to those
in the second half.   Then the first half is bitonically sorted
according to the same type. A shift brings the second half to the
first half. It is then bitonically sorted according to the same type.
A final shift completes the procedure (Figure 3.6.7). Steps for
type 2 are similar);

begin

if size=2 **then** sort__2a(4);

(comment: sort 2 records with delay=4);

else

begin

move(3*(size)/4);

(comment: move the bitonic sequence for 3*(size)/4 record lengths before bitonic sort);

bitonic__split__2 (size, 3−type);

bitonic__sort__2 (size/2,type);

shift__2 (size,size/2);

bitonic__sort__2 (size/2,type);

shift__2 (size,size/4);

    end;

end;

Remark For this procedure to work, the relative positions of records in the loops must be maintained carefully. In the procedure, the first lg (size) loops form a large loop called L_1, which has the same size as loop (lg (size)+1), which we call L_2. The procedure sorts L_1, then interchanges it with L_2. While L_2 is being sorted, L_1 is circulating. When the sorting of L_2 is done, the beginning of L_1 should be at the switch separating L_1 and L_2 so that a shift will produce a sorted sequence of the original sequence. To achieve this, we introduce the delay 3*(size)/4 in the procedure before the actual bitonic sort begins. This will become clearer after the following calculation. Let B(n) be the number of steps to sort a bitonic sequence of size n. Then

$$B(n) = \frac{3n}{4} + \frac{n}{2} + B\left(\frac{n}{2}\right) + \frac{n}{2} + B\left(\frac{n}{2}\right) + \frac{n}{4}$$

$$= 2n + 2B\left(\frac{n}{2}\right)$$

$$= 2n \lg n + c,$$

where c is a constant depending on the initial condition. In particular, if we choose the delay of sort__2a to be 4, then $B(2)=4$ and $c=0$. Thus,

$$B(n) = 2n \lg n.$$

Now since n is a power of 2, $B(n)$ is always a multiple of n.

procedure sort__4 (size, type: integer);
(comment: sort first lg (size)+1 loops according to types 1 or 2 as specified in Figure 3.6.10(b));
begin
    if size=2 **then** sort__2a(6);
    else
      begin
      move((size)/2);
      (comment: move the input sequence for (size)/2 record lengths before sorting);
      sort__4 (size/2,2);
      shift (size, size/2);
      sort__4 (size/2,1);
      bitonic__sort__2 (size,type);
    end;
end;

Let $S_4(n)$ be the number of steps to sort n records in this model. Then

$$S_4(n) = \frac{n}{2} + S_4\left(\frac{n}{2}\right) + \frac{n}{2} + S_4\left(\frac{n}{2}\right) + B(n)$$

$$= 2S_4\left(\frac{n}{2}\right) + 2n \lg n + n.$$

With initial condition $S_4(2) = 6$, we have

$$S_4(n) = n \lg^2 n + 2n \lg n.$$

Again, a delay of size/2 is introduced so that $S_4(n)$ is a multiple of n. The number of switches in this model is

$$W_4(n) = k-1 = \lg n.$$

(Recall $n = 2^{k-1}$.)

To count the number of control states, we first note that when the first two loops (of size 1 each) are doing sorting, all the other switches are set in "closed" mode. During this sorting process, the switch s_1 can be in states 2, 3 or 4. Thus, we have the following three control states first:

2	1	1	...	1
3	1	1	...	1
4	1	1	...	1.

In sort__4, two basic operations are in execution, namely, shifts and bitonic splits. To count the maximum number of control states possible when a shift is in execution, we first note that switch s_1 is always in mode 2. When the shift is done for the first three loops, i.e., they form a single loop of size 4 and shift, then $s_2 = 2$ also. By the same reasoning, all the possible control states for shifts of various sizes are as follows:

2	2	1	1	1	...	1
2	2	2	1	1	...	1

.
.
.

2	2	2			...	2

with a total of $k-2=\lg n-1$.

To count the possible number of control states a bitonic split can be in, we note that the switch s_1 is always in mode 2. If the split occurs to the first 3 loops, i.e., total size 4, then the setting of the switches can be either

2	3	1	1	...	1

or

2	4	1	1	...	1

depending on the type required.

By the same reasoning, we have all the control states for bitonic splits of various sizes as follows:

2	3	1	1			...	1
2	4	1	1			...	1
2	2	3	1	1		...	1
2	2	4	1	1		...	1

.
.
.

2	2	2	2	...	2	3
2	2	2	2	...	2	4

with a total of $2(k-2) = 2 \lg n - 2$.

Finally, the total number of control states is

$$C_4(n) = 3 + \lg n - 1 + 2\lg n - 2$$

$$= 3 \lg n.$$

3.6.7. Summary We summarize our results as follows. Note that Models 3.6.3a and 3.6.3b are instances of Model 3.6.3 where parameter h is given values $\sqrt{n}$ and $\sqrt{n/\lg n}$.

For applications where sorting time is not critical, Model 3.6.1 is obviously the best choice, because of its small number of switches and control states and the simplicity of its control scheme. Model 3.6.2 seems to require too many switches to be of any practical use, unless n is small. It is interesting to see how Batcher's bitonic sorting scheme can be adapted in a restricted memory system such as the bubble memory (Model 3.6.3 and 3.6.4); and how the choice of the number of switches and control states can affect the sorting time. Model 3.6.3b is especially interesting since it can sort in linear time without requiring $O(n)$ number of switches.

Little is known about the relationship among the three parameters (i.e., sorting time, number of switches and number of control states) for an optimal bubble structure designed for sorting. For a linear array of loops, it is obvious that $O(n)$ number of steps is necessary. Also, from the information theoretic argument, we know that n lg n comparisons are necessary in sorting. Therefore, n lg n is also a lower bound for the product

(number of steps to sort) × (number of switches).

Table 3.6.3

Summary of results

Model	Number of Steps to Sort	Number of Switches	Number of Control States
3.6.1	n^2-n	1	3
3.6.2	$\dfrac{n}{2}$	$n-1$	2
3.6.3a	$(h = \sqrt{n})$: $\dfrac{1}{2}n \lg n + O(n)$	$2\sqrt{n} - 1$	$\dfrac{1}{8}\lg^2 n + \dfrac{5}{4}\lg n + 1$
3.6.3b	$(h = \sqrt{n/\lg n})$: $\dfrac{7}{2}n + O(n \lg \lg n/\lg n)$	$2\sqrt{n \lg n} - 1$	$\dfrac{1}{8}\lg^2 n + O(\lg n \lg \lg n)$
3.6.4	$n \lg^2 n + 2n \lg n$	$\lg n$	$3 \lg n$

In this respect, Model 3.6.4 comes closest to this bound. This lower bound, however, is probably too loose, since we do not take into consideration the restrictions imposed by the bubble memory.

3.7 Searching algorithms in different models of bubble memories

3.7.1. Introduction The last two sections studied the problems of permutation and sorting in various models to compare their performance in terms of time, number of switches and number of control states. In this final section, we use the same approach to the problem of maintaining data files, in magnetic bubble memory systems. We shall propose a specific structure for magnetic bubble memories in which records can be stored in the form of a tree. We would like to carry out the operations usually associated with a data tree namely, searching for a record, inserting a new record into the tree, and deleting a record from the tree. Such a structure can be used as a major part of a data base machine. Since the magnetic bubble memory is intrinsically a very restricted memory, such operations would be more difficult to carry out than in a conventional random access memory. We would also like, on the other hand, to access the records in a sequential order and to maintain high storage utilization.

In the first part of this section (Subsection 3.7.3), a model for the bubble memory structured in the form of a tree is presented, and a special 3-input, 3-output switch is introduced. With a special ordering scheme for the memory loops, and a set of independently controlled switches, we show that searching a record in an n-record file takes time $\lg^2 n/(2 \lg \lg n) + O(\lg n)$; insertion and deletion of a record takes additional time $\lg n + O(1)$. Moreover, records can very easily be output in sequential order, and since the tree is always in balanced form, storage can be fully utilized. The only drawbacks for such a scheme are the complexity of the control mechanism and the slightly inferior search time.

In the second part of this section, (Subsection 3.7.4), another ordering scheme for the memory loops is presented. With only two control operations for the switches, we show how searching, insertion and deletion of records of the tree (without balancing) can be done. Although in the worst case space would be very poorly utilized, such a scheme can be useful in applications where deletions and insertions are infrequent. In such cases, records can be reorganized into a balanced tree form from time to time and a $5/2 \lg n + O(1)$ search time can then be achieved.

3.7.2 Physical organization and properties

A. Physical model

The memory consists of k levels of loops. The levels are numbered 0, 1, 2, ..., k-1 respectively and level i has 2^i loops. All the loops are of the same size, i.e., have the same number of bits. Furthermore, we assume that each loop occupies the same physical area.

The loops can fit into a rectangle of size $h \times w$ as follows (see Figure 3.7.1): level 0 has only 1 loop of dimension $h \times w/(2^k - 1)$; level i has 2^i loops, each of dimension $h/2^i \times w2^i/(2^k - 1)$.

There are 2^i switches connecting loops at level i to loops at level i+1. Each loop at level i is connected to two loops at level i+1, as shown in Figure 3.7.1. The function of the switch will be specified in the next subsection. In our model, we require that the bubbles circulate only in one direction, say, the clockwise direction.

B. The switch

The switches are located at the places where three loops meet, i.e., they are switches with 3 inputs and 3 outputs (see Figure 3.7.2).

Each switch has 4 modes of operation: mode 1 (detached): $I_1 \rightarrow O_1$, $I_2 \rightarrow O_2$, $I_3 \rightarrow O_3$; mode 2 (left connected): $I_1 \rightarrow O_2$, $I_2 \rightarrow O_1$, $I_3 \rightarrow O_3$; mode 3 (right connected): $I_1 \rightarrow O_3$, $I_3 \rightarrow O_1$, $I_2 \rightarrow O_2$; mode 4 (connected): $I_1 \rightarrow O_3$, $I_3 \rightarrow O_2$, $I_2 \rightarrow O_1$;

Figure 3.7.2 shows the four ways the loops can be connected under these four modes of operation. It should be pointed out that such a switch can be implemented by means of 2-input, 2-output switches and delay elements. The 2-input, 2-output switch has two modes of operation, as depicted in Figure 3.7.3(a). Such a switch can be implemented by bubble technology and was discussed in Sections

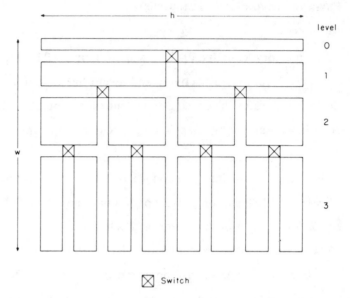

Figure 3.7.1

3.2 and 3.5. In Figure 3.7.3(b), the implementation of our 3-input, 3-output switch is shown, where D is a delay element. The delay elements are used to make the bubbles in each loop come out in phase.

C. Storage of data

Since each loop is connected to two switches to simplify the storage scheme of data within the loops, we further require that the two portions of any loop between the two switches be of equal length.

In addition, there is another loop adjacent to the loop at level 0. This loop is used as input/output buffer only, and is not used for the storage of data. This buffer loop is connected to the loop at level 0 by a 2-input, 2-output switch on one side and to a read-write-compare unit on another. Thus, any I/O or comparison can only be performed here. Its use will become clear when insertion and deletion are considered.

From now on, we shall assume that each loop contains a record. Schematically, our memory structure can be represented by the graph in Figure 3.7.4, where the nodes of the graph represent the loops. The nodes in the graph form an obvious binary tree, namely, the node at level 0 is the root, the two nodes at level 1 are its descendants, and so on. To avoid confusion, we shall sometimes call a single record loop a basic loop, and a collection of connected basic loops a macro loop.

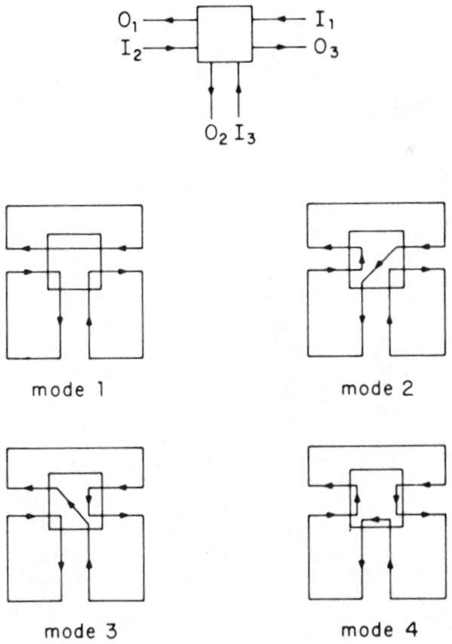

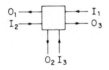

mode 1

mode 2

mode 3

mode 4

Figure 3.7.2

mode 1

mode 2

(a)

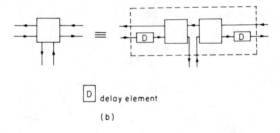

$\boxed{D}$ delay element

(b)

Figure 3.7.3

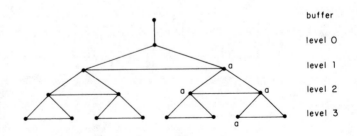

buffer

level 0

level 1

level 2

level 3

Figure 3.7.4

There are some interesting properties about this memory structure. By setting all the switches to "connected" mode, the whole memory can be made to form a macro loop. In fact, if we define an imbedded tree as a subset of nodes which also forms a tree (for example, the nodes marked "a" in Figure 3.7.4), then by appropriate setting of the switches, any imbedded tree can be made to form a loop. Furthermore, any path from the root to a leaf (which is also an imbedded tree) not only forms a loop, but also forms a structure equivalent to a uniform ladder (see Subsection 3.5.7). We define a step as the time needed to simultaneously shift all the basic loops in the memory in clockwise direction for a complete revolution. If the switches are set appropriately, this is exactly the time required to move a record from one place to the other. Later on, we shall also use the phrase "rotating the memory for a step or half a step" with the obvious meaning.

3.7.3. First model – multiple independent control

A. Allocation of records

We shall assign an ordering to the loops in our memory structure and then store the records in consistence with this ordering. To assign an ordering, we shall take advantage of the underlying tree structure of the loops. For convenience, we shall use the terminology of trees to describe our memory structure and shall refer to each loop as a node. Therefore, according to the conventional way of ordering nodes in a binary search tree, the nodes in the left subtree precede the root, which in turn precedes the nodes in the right subtree. Searching will be efficient, but insertion and deletion will not be. Furthermore, since the memory is not always full, it is desirable to keep the records in a balanced tree form after insertion and deletion, so that higher storage utilization and better performance can be achieved. However, the usual tree balancing scheme will not work here since, while it is a simple matter to change pointers in a random access memory, a whole subtree will have to be moved physically in our memory structure. We now give a recursive definition of a way to traverse the tree. The order of the traversal will be used as the ordering of the loops in the tree - hence, the ordering of the memory loops.

Traversal algorithm:

    (1) If root is empty, return.

    (2) Visit the root.

    (3) Traverse the left subtree of the left descendant.

    (4) Traverse the right subtree of the left descendant.

    (5) Visit the left descendant.

    (6) Traverse the left subtree of the right descendant.

    (7) Traverse the right subtree of the right descendant.

    (8) Visit the right descendant.

Such a traversal can also be described by the following two coroutines:

```
procedure T1 (node);
        begin if node ≠ nil then
              begin visit (node);
                     T2 (left (node));
                     T2 (right (node));
              end;
        end;
procedure T2 (node);
        begin if node ≠ nil then
              begin T1 (left (node));
```

            T1 (right (node));
            visit (node);

    end;

  end;

Figure 3.7.5 is an example of such a traversal of a tree of 26 nodes.

There are some interesting properties about such an ordering of the nodes in the tree.

(1) All the nodes in the left subtree are less than those in the right subtree.

(2) The root of a subtree is the smallest if it is on an even level, the largest if it is on an odd level.

(3) Two nodes that are labeled consecutively are, at most, two edges apart in the representative graph of the memory structure.

B. Movement of records in the memory structure

As before, assume each loop contains a record. Further, assume the records are all distinct and have an ordering among them.

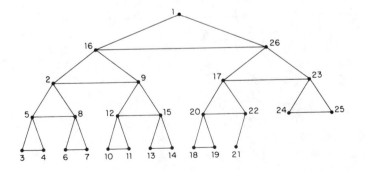

Figure 3.7.5

The records are stored in consistence with the ordering of the loops, as described in A. We shall call the record located at loop i record i. Suppose each record has a head and a tail and the heads are at the odd-leveled switches (see Figure 3.7.6). Recall that a subset of nodes in the tree is called an imbedded tree if it forms a tree itself. For example, the records 16, 9, 12, 15 and 13 reside in an imbedded tree. We have the following property about the records in any imbedded tree:

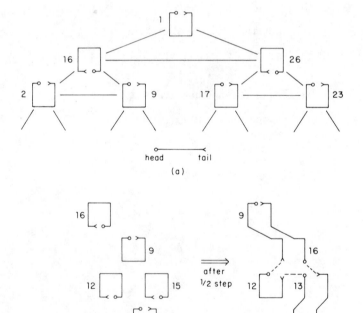

Figure 3.7.6

(1) By properly setting the switches, the records in an imbedded tree can form a loop with all the records in order.

To achieve this, we have first to isolate the records in the imbedded tree from the rest of the tree by setting the appropriate switches to "detached" mode. From now on, we shall be concerned only with the switches relevant to the imbedded tree.

Next, set the odd-leveled switches to "connected" mode. This should be interpreted as "left connected," "right connected," or "connected," depending on the actual imbedded tree. The even-leveled switches are set to "detached" mode. Rotate the memory for half a step. At the end, we have a loop consisting of all the records in the imbedded tree, and all records are in order. Figure 3.7.6(b) shows the loop formed by the records in the imbedded tree.

(2) We shall be concerned mostly with a special kind of imbedded tree consisting of two parts: a path from the root to a node at level i and an imbedded tree rooted at this node, say, of size q (including the root). See the illustration in Figure 3.7.7.

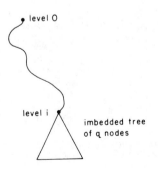

Figure 3.7.7

As described in (1), in half a step, the records in the imbedded tree form a macro loop with records in order. If we now set all the relevant switches to "connected" mode, i.e., for both the odd- and even-leveled switches, in (i+q) steps this loop completes a full revolution since there are (i+q) records in the loop. Finally, we set the odd-leveled switches to "detached" mode and the even-leveled switches to "connected" mode. In half a step, we will return to the original state of the memory, as in Figure 3.7.6(a). This total process takes (i+q+1) steps. In other words, in (i+q+1) steps, the records in the imbedded tree form an ordered macro loop and cycle through the root of the tree and back to the original position. This process is very important to our tree searching, insertion and deletion schemes, which will be described later.

(3) If we refer to the cyclic permutation

$$\begin{pmatrix} 1 & 2 & 3 \dots n-1 & n \\ n & 1 & 2 \dots n-2 & n-1 \end{pmatrix}$$

of all the records in the tree as moving the records one position forward (i.e., record 1 is to be moved to the current position occupied by record n, record 2 to that of record 1, etc.), then to move m positions forward will take (m+1) steps. To see this, we have only to regard the whole tree as an imbedded tree and to apply the method described above.

However, it is interesting to note that moving the records backward can also be done efficiently.

(4) If we refer to the cyclic permutation

$$\begin{pmatrix} 1 & 2 & 3 & ... & n-1 & n \\ 2 & 3 & 4 & ... & n & 1 \end{pmatrix}$$

of all the records in the tree as moving the records one position backward, then to move m positions backward will take $(3m+1)$ steps. (Note that to achieve a large backward shift, one may simply shift forward.)

First consider the case when $m=1$. Set the switches at even levels to "connected" mode and switches at odd levels to "detached" mode and rotate the memory for two steps. Next, set the switches at even levels to "detached" mode and switches at odd levels to "connected" mode and rotate the memory for two steps. Figure 3.7.8 shows the results as the rotations are applied to the records in the tree of Figure 3.7.5. Note that in Figure 3.7.8(b), the switch connecting records 20 and 21 is set to "left connected" mode first, followed by "detached" mode, instead of two consecutive "connected" modes. Thus, a total of four steps is needed to move the records one position backward.

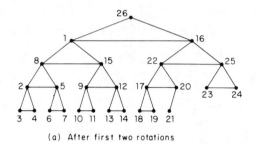

(a) After first two rotations

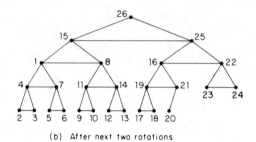

(b) After next two rotations

Figure 3.7.8

For general m, if we apply this method m times, the total number of steps will be 4m. However, we can overlap the last half step of the first two rotations with the first half of the next two rotations (see Figure 3.7.9) to achieve the same result. The total number of steps is thus (3m + 1/2). Finally, we set all the switches to "detached" mode and rotate the memory for half a step so that all the records are in the correct orientation. Thus, the total process takes (3m+1) steps.

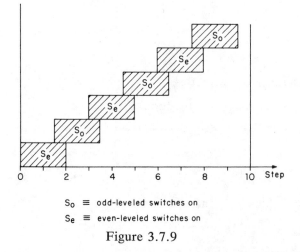

$S_o \equiv$ odd-leveled switches on

$S_e \equiv$ even-leveled switches on

Figure 3.7.9

(5) All the n records in the tree can be output in sorted order through the buffer loop in $(n+2)$ steps. To see this, we move all the $(n+1)$ loops forward (including the buffer loop) by $(n+1)$ positions. The records in the tree would pass the buffer loop one by one, in sorted order.

(6) As mentioned in Subsection 3.7.2-C, any path from the root to a leaf is equivalent to a uniform ladder. As such, we can perform any desired permutation of the records on the path in at most $(x+1)/2$ steps, where x is the number of records on the path (see Subsection 3.5.7).

C. Searching

We are now ready to describe algorithms for searching, inserting and deleting records in such a memory structure. Before and after each of these operations, we require that the records in the tree be kept in order and in a balanced tree form. More specifically, we require that the records be kept in the order described in A of this subsection (Figure 3.7.5) and that all records in the leaves of the tree be at level h or (h-1), with all those at level h positioned as far left as possible. Figure 3.7.5 is an example.

Because of properties (1) and (2) of the ordering of the nodes in the tree (A of this subsection), to search for record k, one can extend the binary search strategy for ordinary binary trees to the present case. The resulting algorithm consists of two parts. The first part can be described as follows. Suppose we are at the root of a subtree. If this root is at an even (odd) level, then a comparison of k with the left (right) descendant (instead of the root) will determine whether the search should continue on the left or the right subtree. Specifically, we have the following procedure:

procedure search (root, given__record);
    (comment: search for a record which equals given__record in a tree rooted at root);
  begin if root=nil **then** return;
      if level (root)=even **then** t ← left (root)
                  else t ← right (root);
      if t=given__record **then** report__found
      else if t< given__record
          then search (right (root), given__record)
          else search (left (root), given__record);
  end;

However, this procedure may have skipped the record to be searched. For example, if we want to search for record 2 in Figure 3.7.5, by this procedure, we shall compare records 16, 9, 5 and 4 without finding record 2. Therefore, the second part of the search procedure is to perform a binary search on the set of skipped records. Fortunately, the number of records in this set is at most $\frac{1}{2}$lg n, where n is the number of records in the tree and lg n is taken, for simplicity, to be the longest path length. Thus, for the worst case, the search time for the present search procedure is lg n + O(lg lg n).

This algorithm can be adapted to our memory structure such that the two parts need not be performed separately.

In our memory structure, we have only one read-write-compare unit, which is located at the buffer loop. Thus, records must be physically moved to the unit before they can be compared. Afterwards, the records must be moved back to their original positions. To compare a record at level i, we form a big loop consisting of the record together with all the records on the path from the node of this record to the root and the contents of the buffer node. Thus, the total number of records in the loop is (i+2). By the method described in B of this subsection, cycling all the records through the buffer node exactly once takes a total of (i+3) steps. For the worst case, the first part of the previous search algorithm has to compare records at levels 1, 2, 3, ..., lg n. Thus, the worst-case number of steps is

$$4 + 5 + ... + (\lg n + 3) = \frac{1}{2}\lg^2 n + O(\lg n).$$

Note that the second part of the search algorithm can actually be executed while the first part is in operation. This is because the "skipped" records are always on the path of some of the records to be compared and can therefore be read without extra cost. For example, consider searching for record 2 in Figure 3.7.5. After comparing with records 16 and 9, we have to compare record 5, while skipping record 2. But to compare record 5, we have to form a loop containing the buffer contents and records 1, 2, 5 and 16, in that order, and rotate the loop for one complete revolution. Thus, we can compare record 2 in the process.

We can further improve search time by bringing q records together to the buffer, instead of only one record at a time.

Suppose the next record to be compared is at level i (Figure 3.7.7); consider the records in a triangle of q nodes rooted at this record. This triangle is a special case of an imbedded tree. (It is chosen only for the ease of later calculation.) Thus, the method in B of this subsection applies here. Since we include the buffer loop, the total number of steps to cycle all the records through the loop is (i+q+2). Let us call this process an iteration. Then each iteration enables us to choose one out of the $\frac{1}{2}$ (q+1) subtrees hanging at the end of the triangle, and brings us lg (q+1)−1 levels down the tree, since all subtrees are of height lg (q+1)−1 levels.

Let h be the number of levels of the tree, i.e., $2^{h+1} - 1 = n$ (assuming the tree is full), and let $t = h/(\lg(q + 1) - 1)$. Then the number of search steps is

$$\leq \sum_{j=0}^{t-1} \left\{ j[\lg(q + 1) - 1] + q + 2 \right\}$$

$$= \frac{1}{2} t(t - 1) \{ \lg(q + 1) - 1 \} + t(q + 2)$$

$$\leq \frac{\frac{1}{2} h^2 + 2h + hq}{\lg(q + 1) - 1} + \frac{h}{2} + q + 2.$$

To find an optimal value of q such that the expression is

minimized, we set the derivative of the expression to zero:

$$\frac{1}{2}h^2 + 2h + hq = (\ln 2)(q + 1)[\lg(q + 1) - 1]$$

$$\cdot[h + \lg(q + 1) - 1].$$

Neglecting low order terms in h, we have

$$q = \frac{h}{2(\ln 2)\lg h}.$$

Thus, the previous upper bound becomes

$$(\ln 2)(q + 1)h + (\ln 2)(q + 1)[\lg(q + 1) - 1] + \frac{h}{2} + q + 2$$

$$= \frac{1}{2}\frac{h^2}{\lg h} + O(h)$$

$$\doteq \frac{1}{2}\frac{\lg^2 n}{\lg \lg n}.$$

In conclusion, for the worst case, the number of search steps is approximately

$$\frac{1}{2}\frac{\lg^2 n}{\lg \lg n}.$$

D. Insertion

We shall next present an algorithm for inserting a record into the file, so that the records in the file will again be in order and the file in balanced tree form. Assume the record to be inserted is p, initially located in the buffer node. By the previous searching algorithm, we find out where p belongs, say, $x < p < y$. Next, to hold

one extra record, a new node (loop) has to be added to the tree. By
our definition of a balanced tree, this node must be the rightmost one
at the bottom level of the tree. For ease of description, we assume
this new node has a record b, which agrees with the traversal ordering
of the nodes described before, say, $i<b<j$. Therefore, the tree
insertion problem reduces to placing a record p from the buffer node
to its destination node in the tree, and putting record b to the buffer
node while keeping the tree balanced and records in order. We have
two cases,

$$(p \ 1 \ 2...i \ b \ j...x \ y...n)$$

and

$$(p \ 1 \ 2...x \ y...i \ b \ j...n).$$

The corresponding final configurations are

$$(b \ 1 \ 2...i \ j...x \ p \ y...n)$$

and

$$(b \ 1 \ 2...x \ p \ y...i \ j...n)$$

respectively.

Case 1:

Initial configuration:

$$(p \ 1 \ 2...i \ b \ j...x \ y...n).$$

Final configuration:

$$(b \ 1 \ 2...i \ j...x \ p \ y...n).$$

Conceptually, an obvious algorithm is cyclically to shift the
records (b j...x) forward once and then replace b by p to obtain
(j...x p). Fortunately, a similar strategy can be adapted to our
memory structure.

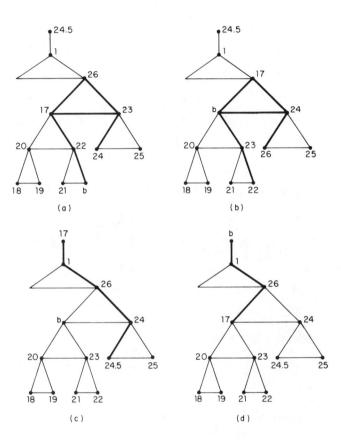

Figure 3.7.10

Insertion algorithm:

(1) Pick the smallest imbedded tree that includes the records b,j,...,x. This is the subtree that includes the shortest path from b to x, and x is located in the previous search step while b is assumed known beforehand. Isolate them from the rest of the tree and shift the records forward for one position. For example, in the tree of Figure 3.7.5, suppose the record 24.5 is to be inserted (Figure 3.7.10(a)).

Then the smallest imbedded tree will consist of records 17, b, 22, 23, 24 and 26. Note that $21<b<22$. After shifting the records forward for one position, we have the configuration in Figure 3.7.10(b).

(2) Consider the path from the buffer node to the destination node of record p. Let the set of records on this path be S, with records arranged in ascending order of levels. Let the set of records on the same path in the final configuration, i.e., after the insertion is complete, be T, with records arranged in ascending order of levels. By the method mentioned in B of this subsection, permute S, so that the number of records appearing on the same places as in T is the largest. In our example, S = {24.5,1,17,24,26} (Figure 3.7.10(b)) and T = {b,1,26,24,24.5} (Figure 3.7.10(d)). Therefore, we permute the former to {17,1,26,24,24.5} because it has four records in the same places as {b,1,26,24,24.5}. This is shown in Figure 3.7.10(c).

As a result of this step, the record p is in its destination node, while b is somewhere in the tree.

(3) Consider the path from the buffer node to the node with record b. Permute it to the final configuration. In our example, the path is {17,1,26,b} (Figure 3.7.10(c)). After permutation, we have {b,1,26,17} (Figure 3.7.10(d)).

The whole tree is now in the correct order and insertion is complete.

To estimate the number of steps required, we see that (1) takes 2 steps; (2) and (3) each take at most $(\lg n+1)/2$ steps. Thus, the total is $\lg n+3$ steps. The steps can actually be reduced since (2) and (3) can be partially overlapped.

Case 2:

Initial configuration:

(p 1 2...x y...i b j...n).

Final configuration:

(b 1 2...x p y...i j...n).

The algorithm for insertion is similar, except that we shift the records in the smallest imbedded tree containing (y...ib) backward for one position instead of forward. Since this operation can be done in four steps, the whole procedure takes lg $n+5$ steps.

E. Deletion

The algorithm for the deletion of a record from the tree is similar to the previous insertion algorithm. As usual, we require the records to be in a balanced tree form after deletion. Assume p is the record to be deleted and $x<p<y$. After deletion, a node will become empty. To keep the records in a balanced tree form, we require that this node be the rightmost one on the bottom level of the tree. If the order of this node in the final tree is between i and j, we assume the buffer node contains a record b such that $i<b<j$. The deletion problem now becomes bringing p to the buffer node, and putting b to the empty node while keeping the tree balanced and records in order. (See Figure 3.7.11.)

Again we have two cases.

Case 1.

Initial configuration:

(b 1 2...x p y...i j ...n).

Final configuration:

(p 1 2...x y...i b j...n).

Case 2.

Initial configuration:

(b 1 2...i j...x p y...n).

Final configuration:

(p 1 2...i b j...x y...n).

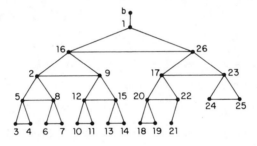

(a) Before deletion

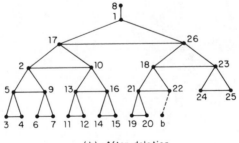

(b) After deletion

Figure 3.7.11

But they are exactly the two cases in insertion if we interchange b and p. Therefore, the previous procedure applies here with deletion time lg $n+3$ in Case 1 and lg $n+5$ in Case 2.

3.7.4 Second model – two independent controls

A. Memory structure with simpler controls

The memory structure described so far requires that it be possible to set each switch independently, a feature that may not be practical. In this subsection, we shall demonstrate that with a new ordering of the loops of the memory structure, searching, insertion and deletion in a tree can be implemented with only two control states for the switches.

In general, a switch has four modes of operation. Thus, x switches enable a total of 4^x possible states. In our proposed memory structure, only two of these states are needed.

Before proposing our memory structure and the ordering of loops, let us consider the conventional binary search of n nodes. The search process can be described by the following procedure:

```
procedure search (p);
    (comment: search a tree rooted at p for given__record);
        begin while p ≠ nil do
            if given__record = p then
                begin report__found;
                return
            else if given__record > p then p←right (p)
                else p← left (p);
            report__not__found;
```

end;

A node at level i>0 in the tree can be reached from the root by a sequence of steps

$$x_1 x_2 ... x_k ... x_i,$$

where x_k can be L or R, representing the left or right branch taken at that step. If a leaf is reached before a match is found, then the search fails.

Figure 3.7.12 shows a completely balanced binary search tree of 31 nodes. To search for record 14, the search steps can be described by the sequence (LRR), while for a record 18.5 the sequence is (RLLR).

In order to simulate the search algorithm for a binary search tree on a bubble memory, three conditions must be satisfied:

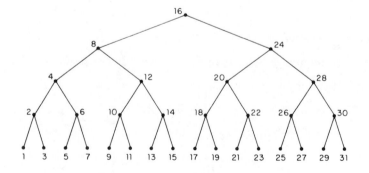

Figure 3.7.12

(1) For each of the sequences $(x_1x_2...x_i)$ describing a search operation, there must be a corresponding sequence of operations in the bubble memory.

(2) If a node p in the search tree can be reached by the sequence $(x_1x_2...x_i)$, the corresponding sequence of operations in the bubble memory should cause record p to be brought to a read-write-compare unit.

(3) If the sequence $(x_1x_2...x_i)$, corresponds to a sequence of operations $(y_1y_2...y_j)$ in the bubble memory, then the sequence $(x_1x_2...x_ix_{i+1})$ should correspond to the sequence of operations $(y_1y_2...y_j...y_k)$.

To illustrate the necessity of condition (3), in Figure 3.7.12, to search records 2 and 3, we have the search sequences LLL and LLLR respectively. The first three L's correspond to comparisons with 16, 8 and 4 in both cases. During these comparisons, we cannot distinguish between 2 and 3. Thus, in the corresponding sequences of operations in the bubble memory, they should correspond to exactly the same operations.

We shall propose a scheme for implementing such a binary search algorithm in bubble memory. It follows a tree-structured memory proposed by Kluge [33]. Although this structure was originally intended for tree traversal, with suitable relabeling of nodes, it can be adapted to tree searching.

In this scheme, there are two tree-structured bubble memories and a single-record memory that stores the root of the search tree. There are three read-write-compare units: one at each root of the tree-structured memories and the other at the single-record memory. Let M denote the single-record memory; T_1 and T_2 respectively, the tree-structured memories.

There are two allowable operations in this structure. Operation A performs a cyclic shift of the records for one step in the clockwise direction with the following setting of the switches in the two tree-structured memories: the even-leveled switches in T_1 are set to "connected" mode, odd-leveled switches in T_1 to "detached" mode, while the even-leveled switches in T_2 are set to "detached" mode, the odd-leveled switches in T_2 to "connected" mode. Operation B is the same as A except that the modes "connected" and "detached" are interchanged. Figure 3.7.13 shows such a memory structure for 31 nodes, with the solid and dashed lines indicating the record movements associated with operations A and B, respectively. The numbers at the nodes are the records. They are placed in such a way that the search can be performed easily. This specific allocation scheme is discussed next.

B. Allocation of records

For ease of description, we consider only the tree in Figure 3.7.12. Generalization to larger trees is obvious. We first label the edges of the tree in Figure 3.7.12 with symbols A^{-1}, A, B^{-1}, B from left

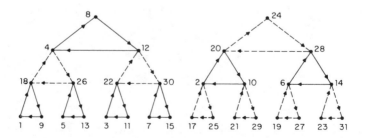

Figure 3.7.13

to right and level by level, starting with the second level down. Each edge will have one of these four symbols. The general labeling rule is: if the current edge has symbol A or A^{-1}, then the two edges connected to it in the next level will have B^{-1},B. Conversely, if the current edge has symbol B or B^{-1}, then the two edges below will have A^{-1},A. The result is shown in Figure 3.7.14.

Now we see that each node of the tree corresponds to exactly one sequence of edge symbols if we trace the path up from this node to the root. For example, the node 29 corresponds to $B^{-1}AB$ and 6 to BA^{-1}.

Now replace A^{-1},B^{-1} by AA, BB respectively (because physically AAA=BBB=identity) in each sequence and call the final sequence the *node sequence* of the node. These sequences define the locations of the records in the memory in the following way:

For the records which are the root of the tree and the roots of the two subtrees T_1,T_2 in Figure 3.7.12 (i.e., records 16, 8, 24), place them in the tree memory exactly the same way, namely, at the root of the tree and the roots of the two subtrees (Figure 3.7.13).

For any other record, say x, find out the node sequence of node x in the tree of Figure 3.7.14 and scan it from left to right. If the first symbol is A (B), then put record x at the root of the left (right) subtree of Figure 3.7.13, and apply operation A (B). In general, whenever symbol A (B) is encountered in our scan, apply operation A (B) to the memory. The final location where record x lands is its memory location. For example, record 29 has node sequence $B^{-1}AB = BBAB$. Since the leftmost symbol is B, we put it at the root of the right subtree, i.e., the location labeled 24 in Figure 3.7.13. Then apply the sequence of operations BBAB one by one (from left to right). Its final location is as shown in Figure 3.7.13.

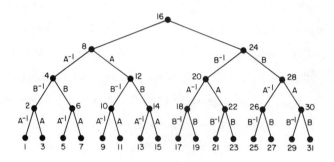

Figure 3.7.14

Note that the above scheme not only is used to determine the memory locations of record, but also can be physically carried out. In other words, we can use this scheme to input into the tree memory one by one a given set of records, and no conflict will result.

C. Search sequence

Given a tree memory with records allocated by the scheme in B, searching for a record in that memory now becomes easy. All we have to do is to invoke the inverse of the node sequence. We shall discuss this in detail next.

Define a *complementary sequence* of a node sequence as a sequence of symbols A and B such that the composition of the node sequence followed by the complementary sequence yields the identity by means of the equalities AAA=BBB=identity. Thus, the complementary sequence of ABB is BAA since ABBBAA=identity.

The complementary sequence of the node sequence of each record defines uniquely the search sequence for this record in our tree memory. For example, the search sequence for record 29 is BBAAB since its node sequence is BBAB. Obviously, if we apply the operations specified by the search sequence (from left to right) to the memory, the corresponding record will move up the tree and ends up at the root of either the left subtree or the right subtree. The following table shows the original L/R sequence of some nodes in the tree of Figure 3.7.12 and their node sequences for the tree memory of Figure 3.7.13 and the corresponding complementary sequences.

Node	Original sequence	Node sequence	Search sequence
6	LLR	BAA	ABB
5	LLRL	AABAA	ABBA
7	LLRR	ABAA	ABBAA
29	RRRL	BBAB	BBAAB

In general, any original L/R sequence $(x_1 x_2...x_i)$ can be directly translated into a search sequence of A, B's according to the following rule:

(1)   Suppose $x_1 = L$. For $2 \leq k \leq i$,

if $x_k = L$, then x_k is substituted by A for k even and by B for k odd;

if $x_k = R$, then x_k is substituted by AA for k even and by BB for k odd.

(2)   Suppose $x_1 = R$. The substitution rule is the same as in (1) except that A and B are interchanged.

Note that how the records are allocated in our tree memory is extremely important. For example, if we allocate records as in Figure 3.7.12, then there is no way for us to translate the original L/R sequence to the correct search sequence. For example, the original sequences for 6 and 5 are LLR and LLRL respectively. On the other hand, their search sequences must be BBA and ABBA respectively since these are the only operation sequences which can bring 6 and 5 to the root of T_1. However, condition (3) of Subsection 3.7.4-A is not satisfied and the search cannot be performed in the bubble memory. On the other hand, it is easy to check that our scheme and its accompanying translation rule indeed satisfy all three conditions.

D. Searching

The remaining question is: given a record to be searched, how can we determine its search sequence directly without knowing which record it is?

The following search algorithm will do exactly that. Informally, if the record to be searched is u, then we have the following:

(1)   Compare u with M.

(2)   If the result is L, then compare u with the root of T_1; otherwise, with that of T_2. Two outcomes are possible, namely, L and R. We can now translate the sequence into operation sequence, e.g., LL will be translated into A and LR into AA. Then apply these operations to the memory.

(3)   If the last operation in the sequence is A, then compare u with the root of T_1; otherwise, with that of T_2. The process is then repeated.

Formally, we have the following procedure:

procedure search (level);

(comment: search for a record u in bubble memory);

(comment: upon initial entry to this procedure, level has value 0, value__read equals M);

var state, value__read;

(comment: these are global variables);

procedure move (x, direction)

(comment: apply operation A or B x times, and read a record from T_1 or T_2 direction indicates whether the traversal is upward or downward);

begin if (level=even) **and** (state=left) **or**

(level=odd) **and** (state=right)

then begin for i ← 1 **to** x **do** A;

(comment: apply A x times);

if (direction=down) **then** value__read ← T_1;

(comment: read T_1);

else value__read ← T_2;

end;

else begin for i ← 1 **to** x **do** B;

if (direction=down) **then** value__read ← T_2;

else value__read ← T_1;

end;

end;

begin

(comment: beginning of search);

if value__read=nil **then** report__not__found;

else if level=0 **then**

if u=value__read **then** report__found;

else if u<value__read **then**

begin state ← left;

value__read ← T_1;

```
                                    search (level+1);
                           end;
                 else begin state ← right;
                                    value__read ← T₂;
                                    search (level+1);
                           end;
        else begin level ← level+1;
                 if u=value__read then report__found;
                 else if u<value__read then
                           begin move (1,down);
                                    (comment:  apply operation corresponding to L);
                                    search (level);
                                    move (2,up);
                                    (comment:   apply complementary operations to
                                    move back to parent node);
                           end;
                 else begin move (2,down);
                                    (comment:  apply operations corresponding to R);
                                    search (level);
                                    move (1,up);
                                    (comment:   apply complementary operation to move
                                    back to parent node);
                           end;
                 end;
        end;
```

For example, if $u=6$, we compare 6 and 16 and L is the
outcome (Figure 3.7.13). After comparing 6 with 8, we have another
L. LL gets translated into A. Application of this operation to the

memory brings 4 to 8 and 6 to 28. Then comparing 6 with 4 yields outcome R, which can be translated into BB. After application of BB, 6 is at the root of T_2, and we compare 6 with it, resulting in a successful search.

Notice that the file must be brought back to its original configuration after each search. Therefore, complementary operations should be applied at the end of the search.

For a very skewed tree, the search time can be bad and storage poorly utilized. To improve performance and to better utilize the storage, the file could be reorganized by unloading the records in sequential order and then loading them back into the memory in a balanced tree form. For a balanced tree of n records, the worst-case search time occurs when searching records at the leaves of the tree. Specifically, the worst-case search time occurs at the search sequence (RR...R) with $(\lg (n+1)-1)$ R's, which corresponds to the operation sequence BBAABB...BB, or BBAABB...AA, with a total of 2 $(\lg(n+1)-2)$ operations. In this case, the total cycle time (search time plus the time to bring the file back to its initial configuration), which is the number of search operations plus the number of complementary operations, is equal to $3(\lg (n+1)-2)$.

Since a record must be completely read and compared before the next operation can be determined, search operations cannot be overlapped. But since the complementary operations are known beforehand, they can be overlapped and a saving of $\frac{1}{2}(\lg(n + 1) - 2)$ results. Thus, $\frac{5}{2}\lg(n + 1) - 5$ operations will suffice.

E. Unloading, loading, insertion and deletion of records

Unloading records from the bubble memory in sequential order corresponds to traversing the binary search tree in in-order (some authors use the term postorder):

procedure in-order (p);

(comment: traverse a tree rooted at p in in-order);

      begin if p=nil **then** return;

          in-order (left(p));

          visit(p);

          in-order (right(p));

      end;

To simulate such a traversal in bubble memory, the substitution rule for searching can be used. In addition, complementary operations are used when returning from the subtrees to the parent nodes.

We have the following formal procedure:

procedure traverse (level);

      (comment: unload the records in sequential order);

      (comment: upon initial entry to this procedure, level has value

      0, value__read equals M);

var state, value__read;

      (comment: these are global variables);

      procedure move (x, direction);

      (comment: same as in **procedure** search);

begin if value__read=nil **then** return;

      if level=0 **then**

          begin state $\leftarrow$ left;

             value__read $\leftarrow T_1$;

```
        traverse (level+1);

        (comment: traverse left subtree);

        output (M);

        state ← right;

        value__read ← T₂;

        traverse (level+1);

        (comment:  traverse right subtree);

    end;

else begin level ← level+1;

    move(1,down)

    (comment: apply operation corresponding to L);

    traverse (level);

    move(2, up);

    (comment: apply complementary operations to move back
    to parent node);

    output (value__read);

    move(2, down);

    (comment: apply operations corresponding to R);

    traverse (level);

    move (1, up);

    (comment:  apply complementary operation to move back
    to parent node);

    end;

end;
```

To load an ordered file of records into the bubble memory in a balanced tree form, the corresponding balanced binary search tree must be traversed. When the record reaches a read-write-compare unit, a write operation is performed instead of a read operation. The procedure is similar to the unload operation, and is omitted here.

To count the number of steps to unload or load a tree of n records, we notice that each edge in the binary search tree is traversed exactly twice, once down and once up. Since it takes three operations to traverse an edge twice, and since there are $(n-1)$ edges in the binary search tree, a total of $3(n-1)$ operations is needed. This can be improved if operations are overlapped. To insert a new record, we do a search for it. When the search fails, a nil record would be brought to one of the read-write-compare unit. To insert the record into the tree, the nil record could be replaced by the record to be inserted. When the tree is brought back to its initial configurations, the new records becomes a new leaf.

To delete a record, we have to search for the record p which just precedes it in the ordering, delete it, and then replace the record to be deleted with p. For example, in Figure 3.7.12, in order to delete 12 we search for 12, then follow a sequence of LR...R until we reach a leaf in the tree, which is 11, the record just preceding 12 in the ordering. In our case, the sequence to reach 11 is (AABAA). We then read 11 into the buffer loop and replace it by a nil record. We then apply the complementary sequence ABBA. After the first A, record 10 will be at the root of the subtree. After the next BB, 12 will be at the root. At this moment, we can replace 12 with 11. Continuing with the remaining operations in the complementary sequence will bring the tree back to the correct configuration.

3.7.5. Summary In this section, we propose a magnetic bubble memory structure for storing records in the form of a binary tree for efficient retrieval and updating operations. Two memory schemes that can perform these operations efficiently are proposed. In the first scheme, trees are maintained in balanced form after each operation, but it requires that it be possible to set all switches independently. In the second scheme, only two control states of the switches are needed, but the tree cannot be easily maintained in balanced form. The second scheme is very attractive, especially for applications where updating operations are infrequent, because of its superior search time and simple control algorithms.

It remains to be investigated whether any other memory models with a moderate number of control states can perform the retrieval and updating operations and still keep the data tree in some kind of balanced form.

3.8. Appendix 3.1.   Proof of relation (3.4.18)

Recall that $a_1 = 1 + \dfrac{2}{\sqrt{5}}$, $b_1 = \dfrac{1 + \sqrt{5}}{2}$,

$a_2 = 1 - \dfrac{2}{\sqrt{5}}$, $b_2 = \dfrac{1 - \sqrt{5}}{2}$ and $H_n = a_1 b_1^n + a_2 b_2^n - 1$.   Thus,   the

recurrence relation for F_n can be written as

$$F_n = F_{n-1} + F_{n-2} + a_1 b_1^n + a_2 b_2^n - 1. \tag{A3.1.1}$$

The general solution to the recurrence relation

$$F_n = F_{n-1} + F_{n-2} \tag{A3.1.2}$$

is

$$F(n) = c_1 b_1^n + c_2 b_2^n,$$

where c_1, c_2 are to be determined by the initial conditions on F_n. The
recurrence relations

$$F_n = F_{n-1} + F_{n-2} + a_1 b_1^n \tag{A3.1.3}$$

$$F_n = F_{n-1} + F_{n-2} + a_2 b_2^n \tag{A3.1.4}$$

$$F_n = F_{n-1} + F_{n-2} - 1 \tag{A3.1.5}$$

have particular solutions:

$$A(n) = \frac{a_1 b_1^2}{2 + b_1} n b_1^n$$

$$B(n) = \frac{a_2 b_2^2}{2 + b_2} n b_2^n$$

$$C(n) = 1.$$

(Note that these solutions may not satisfy the initial conditions on F_n.)
Finally, (A3.1.1) has the general solution

$$F_n = F(n) + A(n) + B(n) + C(n)$$

$$= c_1 b_1^n + c_2 b_2^n + d_1 n b_1^n + d_2 n b_2^n + 1, \qquad (A3.1.6)$$

where

$$d_1 = \frac{a_1 b_1^2}{2 + b_1} \text{ and } d_2 = \frac{a_2 + b_2^2}{2 + b_2}.$$

To determine the coefficients c_1, c_2, we use the initial conditions
$F_0 = 1$ and $F_1 = 3$:

$$\begin{cases} c_1 + c_2 + 1 = F_0 = 1 \\ \\ c_1 b_1 + c_2 b_2 + \dfrac{a_1 b_1^3}{2 + b_1} + \dfrac{a_2 b_2^3}{2 + b_2} + 1 = F_1 = 3. \end{cases}$$

So

$$c_1 \left(2 - \frac{a_1 b_1^3}{2 + b_1} - \frac{a_2 b_2^3}{2 + b_2} \right) / (b_1 - b_2) = -c_2$$

$$= -0.0894.$$

We therefore have (3.4.18).

Appendix 3.2.   Proof of relation (3.4.19a)

Note that $b_1 b_2 = -1$ and $a_1 a_2 = \dfrac{1}{5}$. By substituting the
solutions for H_n and F_n to (3.4.17), and grouping together terms with

the same function in n, we have

$$T_n = T_{n-1} + T_{n-2} + \alpha_1 b_1^n + \alpha_2 b_2^n + \beta(-1)^n$$

$$+ \gamma_1 b_1^{2n} + \gamma_2 b_2^{2n} + \delta_1 n b_1^{2n} + \delta_2 n b_2^{2n}$$

$$+ \epsilon n(-1)^n + 1, \tag{A3.2.1}$$

where

$$\alpha_1 = a_1 - \frac{a_1}{b_1} - 2\frac{a_1}{b_1^2}$$

$$\alpha_2 = a_2 - \frac{a_2}{b_2} - 2\frac{a_2}{b_2^2}$$

$$\beta = -\frac{1}{5b_2} - \frac{1}{5b_1} + \frac{a_2 c_1}{b_1^3} + \frac{a_1 c_2}{b_2^3} - \frac{3a_2 d_1}{b_1^3} - \frac{3a_1 d_2}{b_2^3} + \frac{a_2 c_1}{b_1^4}$$

$$+ \frac{a_1 c_2}{b_2^4} - \frac{4a_2 d_1}{b_1^4} + \frac{a_2 d_1}{b_1^2} - \frac{4a_1 d_2}{b_2^4} + \frac{a_1 d_2}{b_2^2}$$

$$\gamma_1 = \frac{a_1^2}{b_1^4} + \frac{a_1^2}{b_1^1} - \frac{a_1^2}{b_1^5} + \frac{a_1 c_1}{b_1^3} - \frac{3a_1 d_1}{b_1^3} + \frac{3a_1 d_1}{b_1^4}$$

$$- \frac{a_1 c_1}{b_1^6} - \frac{4a_1 d_1}{b_1^4} + \frac{4a_1 d_1}{b_1^6}$$

$$\gamma_2 = \frac{a_2^2}{b_2^4} + \frac{a_2^2}{b_2^2} - \frac{a_2^2}{b_2^5} + \frac{a_2 c_2}{b_2^3} - \frac{3a_2 d_2}{b_2^3} + \frac{3a_2 d_2}{b_2^4}$$

$$- \frac{a_2 c_2}{b_2^6} - \frac{4a_2 d_2}{b_2^4} + \frac{4a_2 d_2}{b_2^6}$$

$$\delta_1 = \frac{a_1 d_1}{b_1^3} - \frac{a_1 d_1}{b_1^6}$$

$$\delta_2 = \frac{a_2 d_2}{b_2^3} - \frac{a_2 d_2}{b_2^6}$$

$$\epsilon = \frac{a_2 d_1}{b_1^3} + \frac{a_2 d_1}{b_1^2} + \frac{a_1 d_2}{b_2^3} + \frac{a_1 d_2}{b_2^2} + \frac{a_2 d_1}{b_1^4} - \frac{a_2 d_1}{b_2^2}$$

$$+ \frac{a_1 d_2}{b_2^4} - \frac{a_2 d_2}{b_1^2}$$

Relation (A3.2.1) has a solution of the form

$$T_n = c_1 b_1^n + c_2 b_2^n + \frac{\alpha_1 b_1^2}{2 + b_1} n b_1^n + \frac{\alpha_2 b_2^2}{2 + b_2} n b_2^n +$$

$$\frac{\gamma_1 b_1^4}{b_1^4 - b_1^2 - 1} b_1^{2n} + \frac{\gamma_2 b_2^4}{b_2^4 - b_2^2 - 1} b_2^{2n} + \frac{\delta_1 b_1^4}{b_1^4 - b_1^2 - 1} n b_1^{2n}$$

$$-\frac{b_1^4(b_1^2+2)\delta_1}{(b_1^4-b_1^2-1)^2}b_1^{2n} + \frac{\delta_2 b_2^4}{b_2^4-b_2^2-1}nb_2^{2n} - \frac{b_2^4(b_2^2+2)\delta_2}{(b_2^4-b_2^2-1)^2}b_2^{2n}$$

$$+ \beta(-1)^n + \epsilon n(-1)^n + \epsilon - 1, \tag{A3.2.2}$$

where c_1 and c_2 are to be determined by the initial conditions. For simplicity, we rewrite (A3.2.2) as follows:

$$T_n = c_1 b_1^n + c_2 b_2^n + A_1 nb_1^n + A_2 nb_2^n + B_1 b_1^{2n} + B_2 b_2^{2n}$$

$$+ D_1 nb_1^{2n} - E_1 b_1^{2n} + D_2 nb_2^{2n} - E_2 b_2^{2n} + \beta(-1)^n$$

$$+ \epsilon n(-1)^n + \epsilon - 1,$$

where $A_1, A_2, B_1, B_2, D_1, E_1, D_2, E_2$ stand for the corresponding coefficients. To determine c_1 and c_2, we have

$$T_0 = 0 = c_1 + c_2 + B_1 + B_2 - E_1 - E_2 + \beta + \epsilon - 1$$

$$T_1 = 1 = c_1 b_1 + c_2 b_2 + A_1 b_1 + A_2 b_2 + B_1 b_1^2$$

$$+ B_2 b_2^2 + D_1 b_1^2 - E_1 b_1^2 + D_2 b_2^2 - E_2 b_2^2 - \beta - 1.$$

$$c_2 = E_1 + E_2 - B_1 - B_2 - \beta - \epsilon + 1 - c_1$$

$$c_1 = -\frac{1}{(b_1 - b_2)}(b_2 E_1 + b_2 E_2 - b_2 B_1 - b_2 B_2 - b_2 \beta - b_2 \epsilon$$

$$+ b_2 + A_1 b_1 + A_2 b_2 + B_1 b_1^2 + B_2 b_2^2 + D_1 b_1^2 - E_1 b_1^2$$

$$+ D_2 b_2^2 - E_2 b_2^2 - \beta - 2).$$

We list the numerical values below:

$$\alpha_1 = -0.7236068 \qquad\qquad A_1 = -0.5236068$$

$$\alpha_2 = -0.2763932 \qquad\qquad A_2 = -0.0763932$$

$$\beta = -0.1600001 \qquad\qquad B_1 = -0.2094426$$

$$\gamma_1 = -0.0988854 \qquad\qquad B_2 = -0.0305573$$

$$\gamma_2 = 0.2588855 \qquad\qquad D_1 = 0.991935$$

$$\delta_1 = 0.4683282 \qquad\qquad E_1 = 1.4155419$$

$$\delta_2 = -0.0683282 \qquad\qquad D_2 = 0.008065$$

$$\varepsilon = 0.2 \qquad\qquad E_2 = -0.0155418$$

$$c_1 = 2.6416408$$

$$c_2 = -0.0416407$$

So the solution is

$$T_n = 1.3944272 a_1 b_1^n - 0.2763932 n a_1 b_1^n - 0.4527864 a_1^2 b_1^{2n}$$

$$+ 0.2763932 n a_1 b_1^{2n} - 0.1600001 (-1)^n + 0.2n(-1)^n - 1,$$

which is (3.4.19a).

3.9. References

[1]   Antonini, B., Bacchi, M. and Bongiovanni, G., "A bubble string comparator for information processing," IEEE Trans. Magn., vol. MAG-15, July 1979, 1183-1184.

[2]   Batcher, K. E., "Sorting networks and their applications," in Proc. AFIPS Spring Joint Comput. Conf., 1968, vol. 32, 307-314.

[3]   Beausoleil, W. F., Brown, D. T. and Phelps, B. E., "Magnetic bubble memory organization," IBM J. Res. Develop. **16** (1972), 587-591.

[4]   Bender, E. A., "Central and local limit theorems applied to asymptotic enumeration," J. Combinatorial Theory **15** (1973), 91-111.

[5]   Bobeck, A. H., Bonyhard, P. I. and Geusic, J. E., "Magnetic bubbles - an emerging new memory technology," Proc. of the IEEE **63** (1975), 1176-1195.

[6]   Bobeck, A. H., Blank, S. L., Butherus, A. D., Ciak, F. J. and Strauss, W., "Current-access magnetic bubble circuits," Bell Syst. Tech. J. **58** (1979), 1453-1540.

[7]   Bongiovanni, G., and Luccio, F., "Permutation of data blocks in a bubble memory," Commun. ACM **22** (1979), 21-25.

[8]   Bongiovanni, G., and Luccio, F., "Maintaining sorted files in a
        magnetic bubble memory," IEEE Trans. Comput., vol. C-29
        (1980), 855-863.

[9]   Bongionvanni, G., and Wong, C. K., "A number representation
        converter for magnetic bubble string comparators," IBM J.
        Res. Devel. **25** (1981), 83-87.

[10]   Bongiovanni, G., and Wong, C. K., "Tree search in
        major/minor loop magnetic bubble memories," IEEE Trans.
        Comput., vol. C-30 (1981), 537-545.

[11]   Bonyahrd, P. I., Danylchuk, I., Kish, D. E. and Smith, J. L.,
        "Applications of bubble devices," IEEE Trans. Magn., vol.
        MAG-6 (1970), 447-451.

[12]   Bonyhard, P. I., Geusic, J. E., Bobeck, A. H., Chen, Y. S.,
        Michaelis, P. C. and Smith, J. L., "Magnetic bubble memory
        chip design," IEEE Trans. Magn., vol. MAG-10 (1973),
        285-289.

[13]   Bonyhard, P. I., and Nelson, T. J., "Dynamic data relocation in
        bubble memories," Bell System Tech. J. **52** (1973), 307-317.

[14]   Carlitz, L., and Scoville, R., "Some permutation problems," J.
        Combinatorial Theory, Ser. A **22** (1977), 129-145.

[15]   Chandra, A. K., and Wong, C. K., "The movement and
        permutation of columns in magnetic bubble lattice files," IEEE
        Trans. Comput., vol. C-27 (1979), 8-15.

[16]   Chang, H., *Magnetic Bubble Technology: Integrated-Circuit Magnetics for Digital Storage and Processing,* IEEE Press, New York, 1975.

[17]   Chang, H., and Pungaliya, P., "A magnetic-bubble sort/search chip incorporating automatically-balanced binary search tree," IBM Res. Rep., 1979.

[18]   Chen, T. C., Eswaran, K. P., Lum, V. Y. and Tung, C., "Simplified odd-even sort using multiple shift-register loops," Int. J. Comput. Inform. Sci. **7** (1978), 295-314.

[19]   Chen, T. C., Lum, V. Y. and Tung, C., "The rebound sorter: An efficient sort engine for large files," in Proc. 4th Int. Conf. Very Large Data Bases, 1978, 312-318.

[20]   Chen, T. C., and Chang, H., "Magnetic Bubble Memory and Logic," in *Advances in Computers,* Academic Press, Inc., New York, 1978.

[21]   Chen, T. C., and Tung, C. "Storage management operations in linked uniform shift register loops," IBM J. Res. Develop. **20** (1976), 123-131.

[22]   Chen, T. C., Tung, C., Lum, V. Y. and Eswaren, K. P., "Efficient sorting using uniform bubble ladders," in Proc. Int. Conf. on Magnetic Bubbles, Eindhoven, The Netherlands, Sept. 13-15, 1976.

[23]   Chin, F. Y., and Fok, K. S., "Fast sorting algorithms on uniform ladders (multiple shift-register loops)," IEEE Trans. Comput., vol. C-29 (1980), 618-631.

[24]   Chung, K. M., Luccio, F. and Wong, C. K., "A new permutation algorithm for bubble memories," Information Processing Lett. **10** (4,5) (1980), 226-230.

[25]   Chung, K. M., Luccio, F. and Wong, C. K., "Minimum number of steps for permutation in a bubble memory," Information Processing Lett. **11** (2), (1980), 81-83.

[26]   Chung, K. M., Luccio, F. and Wong, C. K., "Magnetic bubble memory structures for efficient sorting and searching," in *Information Processing, 80,* S. H. Lavington, Ed., North-Holland, Amsterdam, 1980, 439-444.

[27]   Chung, K. M., Luccio, F. and Wong, C. K., "On the complexity of permuting data in magnetic bubble memory systems," IBM J. Res. Develop. **24** (1980), 75-84.

[28]   Chung, K. M., Luccio, F. and Wong, C. K., "On the complexity of sorting in magnetic bubble memory systems," IEEE Trans. Comput., vol. C-29 (1980), 553-562.

[29]   Chung, K. M., Luccio, F. and Wong, C. K., "A tree storage scheme for magnetic bubble memories," IEEE Trans. Comput., vol. C-29 (1980), 864-874.

[30]   Foster, C. C., "A generalization of AVL trees," Commun. ACM, **16** (1973), 513-517.

[31]   Hirschberg, D. S., "An insertion technique for one-sided height-balanced trees," Commun. ACM **19** (1976), 471-473.

[32]   Huddleston, C. S., "O(log N) insertion and deletion in one-sided height-balanced trees," Dep. Comput. Sci., Univ. of Washington, Seattle, Tech. Rep. 78-04-03, Apr. 1978.

[33]   Kluge, W. E., "Traversing binary tree structures with shift-register memories," IEEE Trans. Comput., vol. C-26 (1977), 1112-1122.

[34]   Kluge, W. E., "Data file management in shift-register memories," ACM Trans. Database Syst. **3** (1978), 159-177.

[35]   Knuth, D. E., *The Art of Computer Programming,* Vol. III, Addison-Wesley, Reading, Ma., 1973.

[36]   Kosaraju, R. S., "Insertions and deletions in one-sided height-balanced trees," Commun. ACM **21** (1978), 226-227.

[37]   Kung, H. T., and Leiserson, C. E., "Systolic arrays for VLSI," Carnegie-Mellon Univ., Pittsburgh, Pa., Tech. Rep. CMU-CS-79-103, Apr. 1978; also appears in Mead and Conway, *Introduction to VLSI Systems,* Addison-Wesley, Reading, Ma., 1980.

[38]   Lee, D. T., Chang, H. and Wong, C. K., "An on-chip compare/steer bubble sorter," IEEE Trans. Comput., vol. C-30 (1981), 396-404.

[39]   Leiserson, C. E., "Systolic priority queue," Carnegie-Mellon
        Univ., Pittsburgh, Pa., Tech. Rep. CMU-CS-79-115, Apr.
        1979.

[40]   Luccio, F., and Pagli, L., "On the height of height-balanced
        trees," IEEE Trans. Comput., vol. C-25 (1976), 87-90.

[41]   Luccio, F., and Pagli, L. "Rebalancing height-balanced trees,"
        IEEE Trans. Comput., vol. C-27 (1978), 386-396.

[42]   Ottmann, T., Six, H. W. and Wood, D., "Right brother trees,"
        Commun. ACM **21** (1978), 769-776.

[43]   Ottmann, T., Six, H. W. and Wood, D., "One-sided
        k-height-balanced trees," Computing **22** (1979), 283-290.

[44]   Ottmann, T., and Wood, D., "Deletion in one-sided
        height-balanced search trees," Int. J. Comput. Math. **6** (1978),
        265-271.

[45]   Raiha, K.-J., "An O(log n) insertion algorithm for one-sided
        height-balanced binary search trees," Dep. Comput. Sci., Univ.
        of Helsinki, Helsinki, Finland, Rep. A-1977-9.

[46]   Reingold, E., Nievergelt, J. and Deo, N., *Combinatorial
        Algorithms,* Prentice-Hall, Englewood Cliffs, N.J., 1977.

[47]   Sandfort, R., and Burke, E., "Logic functions for magnetic
        bubble devices," IEEE Trans. Magn., vol. MAG-7 (1971),
        358-360.

[48]   Tung, C., Chen, T. C. and Chang, H., "A bubble ladder structure for information processing," IEEE Trans. Magn., vol. MAG-11 (1975), 1163-1165.

[49]   Voegeli, O., Calhoun, B. A., Rosier, L. L. and Slonczewski, J. C., "The use of bubble lattices for information storage," in Proc. 20th Ann. Conf. on Magnetism and Magnetic Material, San Francisco, Ca., Dec. 3-6, 1974.

[50]   Wong, C. K., and Coppersmith, D., "The generation of permutations in magnetic bubble memories," IEEE Trans. Comput., vol. C-25 (1976), 254-262.

[51]   Wong, C. K., and Yue, P. C., "The anticipatory control of a cyclically permutable memory," IEEE Trans. Comput., vol. C-22 (1973), 481-488.

[52]   Wong, C. K., and Yue, P. C., "Data organization in magnetic bubble lattice files," IBM J. Res. Develop. **20** (1976), 576-581.

[53]   Zweben, S. H., "An optimal insertion method for one-sided height-balanced trees," Dep. Comput. Inform. Sci., Ohio State Univ., Columbus, Oh., Oct. 1977.

[54]   Zweben, S. H., and McDonald, M. A., "An optimal method for deletion in one-sided height-balanced trees," Commun. ACM **21** (1978), 441-445.

INDEX